FUN WITH THE FAMILY™

in PENNSYLVANIA

HUNDREDS OF IDEAS
FOR DAY TRIPS WITH THE KIDS

THIRD EDITION

By EMILY PAULSEN

and

FAITH PAULSEN

The Globe Pequot Press

Guilford, Connecticut

D0916393

Fun with the Family is a trademark of The Globe Pequot Press.

Cover and text design by Nancy Freeborn
Cover photograph by Julie Bidwell
Clothing on cover provided courtesy of North Cove Outfitters, Old Saybrook, Connecticut
Maps by M.A. Dubé

Library of Congress Cataloging-in-Publication Data
Paulsen, Emily.
    Fun with the family in Pennsylvania : hundreds of ideas for day trips with the kids / by Emily Paulsen and Faith Paulsen. — 3rd ed.
        p.   cm. — (Fun with the family series)
    Includes indexes.
    ISBN 0-7627-0620-1
    1. Pennsylvania—Guidebooks. 2. Family recreation—Pennsylvania—Guide-books. I. Paulsen, Faith. II. Title. III. Series.

F147.3.P38   2000
917.4804'43—dc21   00-021364

Manufactured in the United States of America
Third Edition/First Printing

To our parents, who taught us the love of travel
and the joy of discovery.

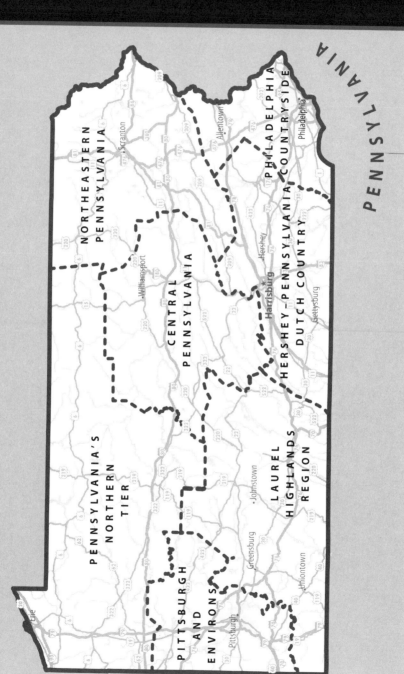

PENNSYLVANIA

NORTHEASTERN PENNSYLVANIA

PHILADELPHIA

PHILADELPHIA COUNTRYSIDE

HERSHEY-PENNSYLVANIA DUTCH COUNTRY

PENNSYLVANIA'S NORTHERN TIER

CENTRAL PENNSYLVANIA

LAUREL HIGHLANDS REGION

PITTSBURGH AND ENVIRONS

Scranton

Allentown

Philadelphia

Williamsport

Hershey

Harrisburg

Gettysburg

Johnstown

Greensburg

Uniontown

Pittsburgh

Erie

Contents

Acknowledgments

Our names may be on the cover, but there are a lot of people who have helped make this book possible. We'd like to thank all the people at the tourist boards and sites who took extra time to answer our questions and point us in the right direction. Thanks to Tami Sheard who helped with research and telephone calls. We'd also like to thank our husbands, Martin Livezey and Bart Sacks, and Faith's children, Judah, Seth, and Gideon Paulsen-Sacks, and Emily's son Eli Livezey, for their enthusiasm and support.

Introduction

When we first visited Pennsylvania on a family vacation in 1969, neither of us realized that someday we would each adopt the state as our home, and we certainly never dreamed we would write a book about it. As children then, we saw the Liberty Bell and the Franklin Institute with our parents and our brother, Bruce. Now we take our own children to these places and many more.

Between us, we have four children, three dogs, and four cats. Our homes are in two different regions of Pennsylvania. Together and separately, we've enjoyed many family adventures here. But until we began to write it all down, we never fully appreciated the richness of this state.

Of course, everyone knows there's history here. Not just the Revolutionary War, but the French and Indian War, the War of 1812, Pontiac's Rebellion, the Whiskey Rebellion, and the Civil War all left their marks. Historic landmarks and living history sites can be found in every corner of the state.

Whether you're looking for a place to hike, bike, camp, ski, horseback ride, or just take a Sunday afternoon drive, Pennsylvania has a park for you. We've tried to cover the highlights of the state park system in this book, but to devote the space each deserves, we'd have to write another book on the subject. If you want more information about Pennsylvania state parks, call their special toll-free number: (800) 63-PARKS.

Pennsylvania has nine major caves open to the public, including the only water-filled cave in the country. Many of the caves offer educational programs on such topics as geology, bats, and Native American history—all geared especially for children.

In 1969, when we walked through the beating heart at the Franklin Institute, it was exciting because it was our first experience with hands-on, interactive science education. Today, the newly expanded Franklin Institute Science Museum joins a host of other "user-friendly" science centers, including the Carnegie Science Center, Williamsport's Children's Discovery Workshop, Erie's expERIEnce Children's Museum, and Harrisburg's up-and-coming Discovery Science Museum, to name just a few. Some of the best family adventures can be adventures in learning.

Many parents are afraid to take kids to art museums, but we've found that our children respond well to art museums as long as they experience them in small doses. Sometimes we visit the gift shop first, pick up a few postcards, then see who can find the pictured artworks in the galleries. Pennsylvania has some first-rate art museums, large and small, from the Philadelphia Museum of Art to the Carnegie Museum of Art.

No matter what the season, whether you like your adventures indoors or outdoors, Pennsylvania is a wonderful destination for families. We're certainly enjoying what the state has to offer, and we hope you will too.

Please note that some sections of Pennsylvania have "ten-digit dialing." In these areas it is necessary to dial the area code before dialing any telephone number, even if you're only calling next door. This is true in the 610 and 215 area codes.

> The prices and rates listed in this guidebook were confirmed at press time. We recommend, however, that you call establishments to obtain current information before traveling.

Attractions Key

The following is a key to the icons found throughout the text.

 Swimming

 Animal Viewing

 Boating / Boat Tour

 Food

 Historic Site

 Lodging

 Hiking / Walking

 Camping

 Fishing

 Museums

 Biking

 Performing Arts

 Amusement Park

 Sports/Athletic

 Horseback Riding

 Picnicking

 Skiing/Winter Sports

 Playground

 Park

 Shopping

Help Us Keep This Guide Up to Date

Every effort has been made by the authors and editors to make this guide as accurate and useful as possible. However, many changes can occur after a guide is published—establishments close, phone numbers change, hiking trails are rerouted, facilities come under new management, etc.

We would love to hear from you concerning your experiences with this guide and how you feel it could be made better and be kept up to date. While we may not be able to respond to all comments and suggestions, we'll take them to heart and we'll make certain to share them with the author. Please send your comments and suggestions to the following address:

The Globe Pequot Press
Reader Response/Editorial Department
P.O. Box 480
Guilford, CT 06437

Or you may e-mail us at: editorial@globe-pequot.com

Thanks for your input, and happy travels!

Philadelphia

Big things are happening in Philadelphia. The City of Brotherly Love has long been a popular family destination, chock-full of great things to do and see together—and it's about to get even better. Between 2000 and 2002, the Liberty Bell is moving to a new home, a new visitor center will provide a gateway to the entire region, a new National Constitution Center is opening, and Disney is coming.

Condé Nast Traveler magazine has rated Philly "America's Friendliest City" and one of the two "most honest" cities. FBI statistics name Philadelphia as the safest of the nation's twelve largest cities.

Over one and one-half million visitors see the Liberty Bell each year. In 2000, the Bell will be moved to its new home, a "Bell Chamber" from which the Bell will be visible all the time as it is today. The Chamber is part of a new Liberty Bell Complex, near Sixth and Chest-

Faith & Emily's
Favorite Philadelphia Attractions

1. Franklin Institute Science Center
2. Academy of Natural Sciences
3. Please Touch Museum
4. Independence Hall
5. Liberty Bell
6. Betsy Ross House
7. Philadelphia Zoo
8. Insectarium
9. Elfreth's Alley
10. Smith Playground
11. Lights of Liberty

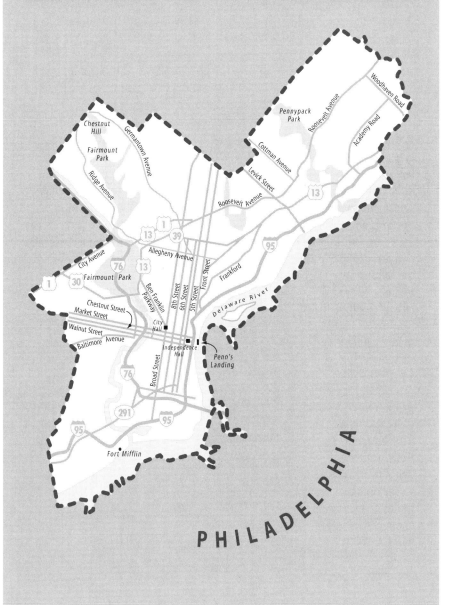

Chestnut
Hill

Fairmount
Park

Germantown Avenue

Ridge Avenue

Pennypack
Park

Roosevelt Avenue

Woodhaven Road

Cottman Avenue

Academy Road

Levick Street

Roosevelt Avenue

13

1

13

39

City Avenue

Allegheny Avenue

76

13

Front Street

5th Street

Frankford

95

1

30

Fairmount Park

Ben Franklin Parkway

8th Street

6th Street

Delaware River

Chestnut Street

Market Street

Walnut Street

Baltimore Avenue

City
Hall

Independence
Hall

Penn's
Landing

76

Broad Street

291

95

95

Fort Mifflin

PHILADELPHIA

nut across from Congress Hall, to include an exhibit hall and sheltered queuing area. According to a new master plan, the Bell will be linked with a brand-new visitor center, the National Constitution Center, and Independence Hall.

By early 2000, thanks to a donation of over $1 million from the Pew Charitable Trust, the West Wing of Independence Hall will feature a new exhibit of historical documents older than anything in the National Archives in Washington D.C. This exhibit will also highlight the original Syng inkstand used for the signing of the Declaration of Independence.

DisneyQuest is coming to Philadelphia in the summer of 2000, with a five-story, 80,000 square-foot indoor interactive theme park to be located at the corner of Eighth and Market Streets. You'll be able to shoot the rapids on a "Virtual Jungle Cruise," help Hercules battle Hades in "Hercules in the Underworld," or fly on a magic carpet on "Aladdin's Magic Carpet Ride."

Sometime in 2001 the new (as-yet-unnamed) visitor center will open at Sixth and Market Streets. Both of the old visitor centers (Third and Chestnut Streets, and Sixteenth and JFK Boulevard) will be replaced by the new center, which will serve as a gateway both to Philadelphia and to the region. On the same block as the visitor center will be improved parking, an outdoor cafe, and special events space.

Faith & Emily's
Favorite Events in Philadelphia

- **Welcome America! Celebration** (July), (800) 770–3403; www.americasbirthday.com.
- **Mummer's Day Parade** (January 1, summer version in June), (215) 336–3050.
- **Summer Concerts at Penn's Landing** (June through August), (held in an alternate location from 1999 to 2001), (215) 923–8181.
- **Philadelphia International Children's Festival** (last week of May), (215) 898–6791 or 898–6683.
- **Philadelphia Flower Show** (late February through early March), (215) 988–8839; www.philaflowershow.com.
- **Daily News Presents "Yo! Philadelphia"** (Labor Day weekend), (215) 636–1666.
- **Philadelphia Orchestra Concerts at Mann Music Center** (outdoor summer series), 52nd and Parkside Avenue, (215) 893–1995 or (215) 893–1999; www.manncenter.org.

By September 17, 2002 (Constitution Day), the new National Constitution Center will be open on Independence Mall between Arch and Race Streets. The new center will be the first-ever museum honoring and explaining our Constitution. Its website is already up and running at www.constitutioncenter.org. The site offers a Kids Corner with lots of useful information for school projects, including a place to order a pocket copy of the Constitution.

Check out www.libertynet.org/phila-visitor for more details about these new attractions. This excellent website also includes "Family Friendly Philadelphia Online." But even before the new additions arrive, don't put off your trip to Philly. There's plenty to see right now.

If you're visiting Philly for several days, we recommend the new CityPass, which gets you into six of Philly's favorite attractions for one price and with no ticket lines. You can save about 50 percent off the combined box office prices for: the Philadelphia Museum of Art; The Franklin Institute; the Philadelphia Zoo; The Academy of Natural Sciences; Independence Seaport Museum; and in New Jersey, the New Jersey State Aquarium and Camden Children's Garden. Tickets are valid for nine days from first date of use. Admission to all six sites is $27.50 for adults, $23.75 for seniors 65 and over, and $20.00 for youths ages 3 to 11. You can purchase CityPass at any participating attraction, the visitor centers, or in advance at www.citypass.net.

Philadelphia is a great walking city. Most attractions are an easy jaunt from hotels and from each other. And when the feet get sore or the kids get cranky, you can always hop on the purple PHLASH bus, which stops at most of the major tourist spots downtown. To get to some of the attractions in the outskirts of the city, a car can be handy, but the one-way streets in Center City and cost of parking can be frustrating. Public transportation or walking is your best bet.

Sometimes when traveling with small children, or just to get the lay of the land, an organized tour is a good idea. There are lots of companies offering tours of Philadelphia, on everything from a reproduction of an old-time trolley or a horse and buggy to a streamlined coach. Here are some companies to

Amazing Philadelphia Facts

"Most Honest" City According to FBI statistics, Philadelphia is the safest of the nation's twelve largest cities. It is also one of the cleanest, and according to *Conde Nast Traveler*, America's "Most Honest" City.

contact: American Trolley Tours/Choo-Choo Trolley, (215) 333–2119; '76 Carriage Co., (215) 923–8517 (tours begin at Independence National Park); Gray Line Tours, (800) 577–7745/(215) 569–3666; Liberty Belle Charters, Inc., (215) 629–1131 (cruises leave from Penn's Landing); Old Town Trolley, (215) 928–8687; Philadelphia Trolley Works, (215) 923–TOUR; PHLASH bus, (215) 4–PHLASH; Society Hill Carriage Co., (215) 627–6128 (tours depart from Independence Hall).

Historic Philadelphia

When most people think of Philadelphia, they think of its place in United States history. You'll hear the word *first* a lot while touring this historic city. In fact, the area that makes up Independence National Historic Park (from Second to Sixth Street along Walnut Street) is called "America's most historic square mile." Here, you'll meander the streets walked by Benjamin Franklin, Thomas Jefferson, Betsy Ross, George Washington, Dolley Madison, John Adams . . . the list goes on and on.

INDEPENDENCE NATIONAL HISTORIC PARK (all ages)

www.nps.gov/inde

    Forty-five acres in Center City, comprising more than forty different historic buildings, make up Independence National Historic Park, including the Liberty Bell Pavilion, Independence Hall, Congress Hall, Old City Hall, Second Bank of the United States, Carpenters' Hall, New Hall Military Museum (formerly the Army-Navy Museum and Marine Corp Museum), Franklin Court, Christ Church, Bishop White House, Todd House, and Declaration House.

INDEPENDENCE HALL NATIONAL HISTORIC PARK VISITOR CENTER (all ages)

Third and Chestnut Streets; (215) 597–8974; www.libertynet.org/~inhp. Most park buildings are open 9:00 A.M. to 5:00 P.M. daily. These hours are subject to some change and in summer some buildings are open into the evening. Admission Free.

    Be forewarned: Sometime in 2001 this Center will be replaced by the new visitor center at Sixth and Market Streets.

    Although most people just head right for the Liberty Bell or Independence Hall, it's a good idea to start your visit to the city with a stop 2 blocks east at the Visitor Center. Here you can see *Independence,* a twenty-eight-minute award-winning film directed by John Huston, and take a look at some of the special exhibits. A special brochure detailing handicapped-accessibility information is available. There is a parking garage on Second Street between Walnut and Chestnut. There's also a very good bookstore and gift shop that has some great hard-to-find regional books.

Here also you can sign up for a variety of special walking tours. Tour themes change seasonally.

Most buildings within the park are **Free** and open to the public, but a guide is required to tour some, and for others, such as the Todd House and the Bishop White House, tickets are required. There is a $2.00 admission fee for persons aged 16 and older to enter The Second Bank of the United States, as well as for the House Tour that includes the Bishop White and Todd Houses. The urban park rangers of the National Park Service obviously love their jobs, and they'll make history come alive with their stories of colonial Philadelphia.

Also making history come alive are the Town Criers and other actors in period costumes that help transport visitors back in time. A special-events list distributed by the Town Criers gives a schedule of presentations, such as Ben Franklin's Greatest Hits and the Echoes of Liberty Parade. Families are encouraged not only to watch these events, but also to participate. Most events take place on weekends, with daily performances in summer. For more information call (800) 76–HISTORY or (215) 629–5801.

SECOND BANK OF THE UNITED STATES AND CARPENTER'S HALL (ages 10 and up)

Second Bank is located on Chestnut Street between Fourth and Fifth Streets; (215) 925–0167; open daily 9:00 A.M. to 5:00 P.M. Admission $2.00 for 16 and older. Carpenters' Hall is open Tuesday through Sunday 10:00 A.M. to 4:00 P.M.; closed Tuesday in January and February. Admission is **Free***. Carpenters' Hall information, (215) 925–0167.*

The Second Bank of the United States and Carpenters' Hall, where the First Continental Congress met in 1774, are worth noting. Perhaps with kids you'd like to see the exterior only. Today Carpenters' Hall displays early carpenter's tools and chairs. The Second Bank houses the park's portrait gallery, featuring portraits of many Revolutionary War heroes. For information, call the visitor center at (215) 597–8974.

NEW HALL MILITARY MUSEUM (ages 6 and up)

Carpenter's Court between Third and Fourth Streets on the south side of Chestnut Street; call the Visitor Center (215–597–8974) for information. Open daily 10:00 A.M. to 2:00 P.M., but hours may change seasonally. Admission is **Free**.

The Army-Navy Museum and Marine Corps Museum have recently been combined to form the New Hall Military Museum. This museum offers a treasure trove for military buffs. On display are uniforms, dioramas, weapons, ship models, battle flags, and other memorabilia of the U.S. armed forces, going back to the Revolution. Museum features a gun deck preserved from an eighteenth-century naval ship, as well as interactive displays such as one that allows visitors to control a ship's sails and rudder, and an honor roll of Marines who gave their lives in battle.

BISHOP WHITE HOUSE and TODD HOUSE (ages 8 and up)

Walnut Street between Third and Fourth Streets; (215) 597–8974. The Todd House and Bishop White House are open daily from 9:00 A.M. to 4:30 P.M. Tickets are $2.00 for adults over 16 and may be purchased at the Independence National Historic Park Visitor Center.

The Bishop White House and Todd House present an interesting opportunity to compare and contrast two different early American lifestyles.

Bishop White was the first Episcopal bishop of Pennsylvania and chaplain of the Continental Congress and of the new United States Senate, and this elegant home was built for him and his family in 1786. Children will enjoy the boys' and girls' bedrooms, where initials were carved into the wood more than 200 years ago.

The Todd House, on the other hand, represents a middle-class Quaker home from the same period. Although well-to-do, this family lived more simply. After the death of John Todd, Dolley Todd married James Madison and became one of the most famous United States First Ladies.

INDEPENDENCE HALL (ages 6 and up)

Chestnut Street between Fifth and Sixth Streets; (215) 597–8974. Open by tour only. Admission is **Free**.

It goes without saying that Independence Hall is a must-see for all ages. This building was originally known as the Pennsylvania State House, but in 1824 when General Lafayette returned to Philadelphia, he called it "the hall of independence," and the name stuck. The Declaration of Independence was adopted here, and the United States Constitution was written here. The Assembly Room has been restored to look exactly as it did in 1776, and although most of the furnishings are reproductions, you can see the original inkwell in which the signers dipped their quills before putting their names to the Declaration of Independence.

Between 1790 and 1800, when Philadelphia was the capital of the United States, the Congress met in Congress Hall next door. On the other side of Independence Hall is Old City Hall, where the U.S. Supreme Court met from 1791 to 1800. Unlike many historic buildings, Old City Hall is handicapped-accessible.

 LIBERTY BELL (all ages)

Independence Mall, on Market Street between Fifth and Sixth Streets; (215) 597–8974. The Liberty Bell Pavilion is open from 9:00 A.M. to 5:00 P.M., with extended hours in summer. Admission is Free. *Handicapped-accessible.*

The Liberty Bell is currently located in the park across the street from Independence Hall. Young and old will want to see and touch this emblem of freedom and democracy for people all over the world. In 2000, the Bell will move to a new Liberty Bell complex near Sixth and Chestnut Streets. The new complex will include a Bell Chamber, exhibits concerning the Bell, and a queuing area.

Contrary to popular belief, the Liberty Bell's famous crack was not the result of overzealous ringing on July 4, 1776. Instead, the one-ton bell has been plagued by cracks ever since it was originally cast. It was recast twice, and then cracked again when the bell was rung for thirty-six hours at the death of John Marshall, Chief Justice of the Supreme Court, in 1835. Repaired once more, its final crack occurred in 1846 on George Washington's birthday.

Amazing Philadelphia Facts

Philadelphia is the largest city in Pennsylvania, the second largest on the East Coast (New York is first, but you knew that), and the fifth largest city in the United States.

DECLARATION HOUSE (GRAFF HOUSE) (ages 8 and up)

Seventh and Market Streets; (215) 597–8974. Declaration House is open daily 9:00 A.M. to 1:00 P.M. Hours may change seasonally, so call ahead for information. Admission is Free. *Handicapped-accessible.*

A couple of blocks away from the Liberty Bell is Declaration House (or Graff House), also part of the National Historic Park. In 1776 the Virginia delegate (Thomas Jefferson) to the Second Continental Congress rented rooms in this building, and it was in these rooms that he wrote a little document called the Declaration of Independence. School-age kids will be especially interested to see the exact place where the Declaration of Independence was penned.

On the same block, but not part of the park, are two unusual museums: the Atwater Kent Museum and the Balch Institute of Ethnic Studies.

 ATWATER KENT MUSEUM (ages 6 and up)

15 South Seventh Street; (215) 922–3031; www.philadelphia.org. Open daily except Tuesday 10:00 A.M. to 4:00 P.M. Closed on major holidays. Admission is $3.00 for adults, $1.50 for children 3 to 12. Handicapped-accessible.

The Atwater Kent Museum tells the history of Philadelphia, a city whose story parallels that of our nation as a whole. Children under 12 enjoy the low-tech, hands-on approach. Special family programs include hat making or a visit from the "candy man," as well as exhibitions such as the annual Toys of Holidays Past, Trains and Trolleys, and Children Turning the Centuries.

 BALCH INSTITUTE OF ETHNIC STUDIES (ages 6 and up)

18 South Seventh Street; call (215) 925–8090 for information. Both the museum and library are open Tuesday through Saturday from 10:00 A.M. to 4:00 P.M. Admission is $3.00 for adults; $1.50 for children, students, AAA members, and seniors.

The first floor of the Balch Institute of Ethnic Studies is a museum of memorabilia illustrating the history of the many ethnic groups that immigrated to Philadelphia. Kids can use a computer to key in their ethnic background and print out a listing of Philadelphia sites related to that ethnic group. The second floor of the institute is an extensive genealogical research library.

Walking Tour of Independence National Historic Park

Area There's no way a family can see all the sites in this neighborhood in one day, but here's a walking tour that will give you an idea where things are. Some of these destinations are not within easy walking distance for young children, but older ones should do fine.

Park your car at the parking garage on Second Street between Walnut and Chestnut. Although most people head right for the Liberty Bell or Independence Hall, it's a good idea to start your visit with a stop 2 blocks east at the Visitor Center, located at Third and Chestnut Streets. If you wish to see Todd House or the Bishop White House, this is where you get your tickets.

If you take the footpath across Third Street from the Visitor Center exit on your way toward Independence Hall, you'll pass on the left the Second Bank of the United States and Carpenters' Hall, where the first Continental Congress met in 1774.

Across Fourth Street from the Second Bank, you may wish to stop at the New Hall Military Museum.

Todd House is on the same block as the New Hall Military Museum, and the Bishop White House is across the street.

Independence Hall is located on Chestnut Street between Fifth and Sixth Streets. You may have to wait on line for a tour, especially in summer. Exiting Independence Hall, cross Chestnut Street to Independence Mall, where you'll pass Old City Hall. The modern glass structure on the mall is the Liberty Bell Pavilion. Although you can see the bell from the outside, it's well worth going inside to hear what the guides have to say.

Walking east on Arch Street, you'll pass the Free Quaker Meeting House Museum and the Christ Church Burial Ground (at Fifth and Arch), where many Colonial and Revolutionary War heroes are buried. For good luck toss a penny on Benjamin Franklin's grave.

Cross Sixth Street (Independence Mall West), and go down Market to the corner of Market and Seventh to see Declaration House. On the same block, but not part of the National Historic Park, are the Atwater Kent Museum and Balch Institute of Ethnic Studies. North on Seventh Street is the African-American Museum.

Just 2 blocks away, on Arch between Second and Third Streets, is the Betsy Ross House, administered independently. From here walk down Arch Street toward Second Street, turn left on Second and then make a right down the little street called Elfreth's Alley. Take your time enjoying this lovely spot. Fireman's Hall is right around the corner. You're only a couple of blocks from City Tavern if you'd like a break right now.

Walking on Second Street back toward the Visitor Center, stop in at Christ Church, between Arch and Market Streets. Benjamin Franklin is buried in the churchyard here. From Christ Church walk toward Market Street, turn left, and go 2 blocks to Franklin Court. You are now 1 block away from where you parked.

LIGHTS OF LIBERTY (all ages)

Shows depart from PECO Energy Liberty Center, Sixth and Chestnut Streets, and take place throughout Independence National Historic Park. Nightly, dusk to 11:15 P.M., up to six shows per hour, May through October. Additional shows may be added during holiday seasons. Pricing to be determined. Purchase tickets at the PECO Energy Liberty Center, or reserve in advance by calling (215) LIBERTY or (877) GO–2–1776.

Lights of Liberty has been dazzling visitors since June of 1999. The world's first walking sound and light show uses the latest technology to immerse you in the Revolution as it happened and where it happened. Walking along these historic streets, you'll see five-story projections on historic buildings. Wireless headsets equipped with 3-D sound complete the illusion. Headsets are available in a children's version, as well as several different languages. Since each person gets an individual headset, everyone can choose the version that's most appropriate.

U.S. MINT (ages 8 and up)

Fifth and Arch Streets; (215) 597–7350. January through April, open 9:00 A.M. to 4:30 P.M. Monday through Friday; May through June, open Monday through Saturday; July and August, open Monday through Sunday; September through December, open Monday through Friday. Closed major holidays. Admission is Free.

The U.S. Mint is the world's largest coinage operation. Visitors can take a self-guided audiovisual tour and watch money in the making from a glass-enclosed gallery.

AFRICAN-AMERICAN MUSEUM (all ages)

701 Arch Street; call (215) 574–0380 for more information. The museum is open Tuesday through Saturday 10:00 A.M. to 5:00 P.M. and Sunday noon to 5:00 P.M. Admission is $4.00 for adults, $2.00 for children.

11

The African-American Museum is a leading museum of African-American culture. The former Afro-American Historical and Cultural Museum has recently changed its name and its image. Under a new director, this museum shows exciting promise.

Amazing Philadelphia Facts

Philadelphia is America's number one city for African-American tourism.

BETSY ROSS HOUSE (ages 6 and up)

239 Arch Street; (215) 627–5343; www.libertynet.org/iha/BETSY. Open Tuesday through Sunday 10:00 A.M. to 5:00 P.M. Suggested donation: $1.00 for adults, 25 cents for children.

Just 2 blocks away from the U.S. Mint, on Arch between Second and Third Streets, is the Betsy Ross House. Yes, Betsy Ross really lived here at 239 Arch Street. And yes, she really did sew flags for the Continental Congress, although nobody is certain how active a role she played in the design of the American flag. Her house, which was recently reopened after renovation, is an excellent example of a colonial artisan's home. Greeters are in colonial garb, and tours are self-guided, with kid-friendly signs. Call ahead, and they'll fax you a "house hunt" sheet for children.

ELFRETH'S ALLEY (all ages)

Between Arch and Race Streets on Second Street in Old City; (215) 574–0560. Mantua Maker's House Museum and Windsor Chairmaker's House are open Tuesday through Saturday 10:00 A.M. to 4:00 P.M. and Sunday noon to 4:00 P.M. Admission is $2.00 per person, $5.00 per family.

To get an idea of what Philadelphia may have looked like in the 1700s, take a walk down Elfreth's Alley, the oldest residential street in America. Families still inhabit this cobblestone alley tucked between Arch and Race Streets on Second Street in Old City. Walking down this charming street, you can imagine what life must have been like when these thirty houses were built between 1728 and 1836, when carpenters and other artisans lived here.

Number 126, the 1762 Mantua Maker's House Museum, and Number 124, the Windsor Chairmaker's House, are open to the public. (A mantua was a type of gown made by the house's first residents, a pair of seamstresses.) A costumed guide will show you around. Other houses are open during special Open House events. On weekends in summer there are demonstrations of traditional crafts, such as basket weaving, broom making, needlework, and candle dipping. During the first weekend of June, the Elfreth's Alley Association hosts Fete Days, when many of the houses and gardens are opened to the public, and colonial crafts are demonstrated. The garden and Windsor Chairmaker's House are handicapped-accessible. People still live in these houses, so remind your children to use their manners.

 ## MUM PUPPET THEATRE (all ages)

115 Arch Street; (215) 925–8686; e-mail: mum@libertynet.org. Productions run from October through April. Admission varies with productions.

The remarkable Mum Puppet Theatre has built a reputation for fun and innovative puppet performances. Some productions are aimed at younger children, others are more sophisticated. Call ahead for specifics.

 ## FIREMAN'S HALL (all ages)

147 North Second Street; (215) 923–1438). Open Tuesday through Saturday 9:00 A.M. to 5:00 P.M. Admission is **Free**.

Just about every family has somebody who wants to be a fire fighter when he or she grows up. Fireman's Hall will fascinate that somebody. Ever since Benjamin Franklin founded the city's first fire department in 1736, Philadelphia has had fire equipment and fire fighters. You'll see old-fashioned leather buckets, hand pumpers, three fire wagons that date from 1730, a spider hose reel from 1804, fire helmets from around the world, and the scorched helmets of fire fighters who died in the line of duty. Aspiring fire fighters can try out the re-created living quarters of real fire fighters or take the helm of a fireboat. Fireman's Hall is in the historic district, half a block from Elfreth's Alley.

Amazing Philadelphia Facts

Fairmount Park is the nation's largest landscaped city park.

CHRIST CHURCH (ages 8 and up)

Second Street between Arch and Market Streets; call (215) 922–1695 to check winter hours and for group reservations. The church is open to the public from 9:00 A.M. to 5:00 P.M. Monday through Saturday and from 1:00 to 5:00 P.M. on Sunday.

At Christ Church you can find the pews occupied by George Washington, Benjamin Franklin, Betsy Ross, and other characters out of your history books. Kids will be interested to learn that this is also the birthplace of a character from a children's book: Amos, the mouse who befriended Ben Franklin in the classic *Ben and Me.* "The Nation's Church" is now celebrating 300 years as an active Episcopal parish, with Sunday morning services at 9:00 and 11:00 and Communion services on Wednesday at noon. All are welcome to attend.

FRANKLIN COURT (ages 6 and up)

Market Street between Third and Fourth Streets; for information call (215) 597–8974.

Benjamin Franklin's home no longer stands at this site, but you can still see its foundation, as well as several other houses that Franklin owned. This area has been transformed into Franklin Court, an interactive learning experience aimed at school-age kids that's like meeting the great man himself.

Kids can listen to the voices of such notable historic figures as John Adams, Ralph Waldo Emerson, Thomas Jefferson, Harry S. Truman, Mark Twain, Lord Byron, and General Lafayette, all offering their opinions of Franklin. A series of dioramas illustrates Franklin's career, and the movie *Portrait of a Family* tells about his family life.

To enter Franklin Court enter the archway between Market and Chestnut, in the middle of the block between Third and Fourth Streets. You can also use the walkway on Orianna Street from Chestnut Street.

"BEN FRANKLIN" (all ages)

For details contact "Ben Franklin" at P.O. Box 40178, Philadelphia 19106, call (215) 238–0871, or fax (215) 238–9102. **Free.**

When Franklin returned to Philadelphia from Paris in 1785, he used to sit under the mulberry tree at Franklin Court—and there you can find him still, daily Memorial Day through Labor Day, 10:00 A.M. to noon. An especially wonderful treat for young children, "Ben Franklin" himself invites kids to gather around and listen to stories of his life.

CITY TAVERN (ages 6 and up)

138 South Second Street. Call (215) 413–1443.

Now that you're completely steeped in history, why not eat a historic meal? Don't make the mistake of assuming City Tavern is just a restaurant on a colonial theme. Dining here gives a real feeling of the past. This historic gathering place, now part of the Independence National Historic Park, was opened in 1774. Paul Revere came here in May of that year to announce that the Port of Boston was closed. General Washington set up headquarters here, and Benedict Arnold slept here. John Adams called it "the most genteel tavern in America."

The building was rebuilt in 1975 to look exactly as it did in colonial times. The tavern serves Thomas Jefferson Ale, brewed exclusively by the Dock Street Brewing Company, along with colonial specialties such as turkey-thigh stew and beef and pork pie. More tame entrees are also available, but this is not the place to bring picky eaters.

City Tavern is in the heart of the Historic District, a short walk from Elfreth's Alley.

ALSO IN THE HISTORIC DISTRICT

Other sites within the Historic District include **Congregation Mikveh Israel** and the **National Museum of American Jewish History,** at 44 North Fourth Street, which tells the story of the American-Jewish experience. Open daily except Saturday and Jewish holidays. Admission: $2.50 for adults, $1.75 for children. Call (215) 923–3811 for more information.

The Waterfront/Penn's Landing

New things are happening all over Philadelphia, and the site that once hosted William Penn's arrival in 1682 bustles with new activity—including construction. A new Hyatt Regency hotel is under construction, as well as a state-of-the-art amphitheater with new festival space encompassing the area from Walnut to Market Streets along Columbus Boulevard.

Construction of the new amphitheater will run from fall 1999 until fall 2001. During that time, the summer concert series and events such as the annual Memorial Day concert and July 4th fireworks will be held at an alternate location to be announced. For more information, call (215) 923-8181.

INDEPENDENCE SEAPORT MUSEUM (all ages)

211 Columbus Boulevard at Walnut Street; (215) 925–5439. Museum hours are 10:00 A.M. to 5:00 P.M. daily. Admission is charged.

Start your visit to Penn's Landing with the Independence Seaport Museum, which uses exciting family-oriented interactive exhibits to tell the story of four centuries of maritime history. The collection of nautical artifacts and ship models that were formerly housed in the old Philadelphia Maritime Museum have been incorporated into a panorama and are enlivened at every turn by audiovisuals and multimedia computers. Kids can try out an immigrant's steerage bunk or a rowing machine, or learn about the history of underwater exploration. Great for any folks with a taste for the nautical.

In exhibits like Home Port Philadelphia, children can chart a course for Penn's Landing and navigate underneath the three-story replica of the Benjamin Franklin Bridge. Protecting the Nation features the bridge of the guided-missile destroyer USS *Lawrence,* most recently used in the Persian Gulf Conflict. Divers of the Deep explores the development of diving technologies such as helmets and scuba gear.

The Independence Seaport Museum also includes Historic Ship Zone, where you can see two real vessels: the *Olympia* and the *Becuna* (319 Delaware Avenue, at Spruce Street; 215-922-1898). Step aboard the *Olympia,* flagship of Admiral Dewey's Asiatic fleet, and see the bronze impressions of the admiral's feet in the exact spot where he stood in 1898 and said, "You may fire when you are ready, Gridley." Then take the kids aboard the *Becuna,* a guppy-class submarine from World War II, where sixty-six men shared the tight living quarters.

If you purchase a RiverPass, it includes round-trip fare on the Riverbus ferry from Penn's Landing to Camden, New Jersey, plus admission to both the New Jersey State Aquarium and the Independence Seaport Museum. The Aquarium is worth a visit, especially if you have school-age kids. They can even pet a shark (a small, harmless one, of course). A new Children's Garden is adjacent to the Aquarium.

DAVE & BUSTER'S (ages 6 and up before 10:00 P.M.)

Pier 19 North, 325 North Columbus Boulevard, (formerly Delaware Avenue). Call (215) 413–1951 for additional details. Open to children 11:00 A.M. to 10:00 P.M.

Older children or young adults will probably enjoy Dave & Buster's. This unusual attraction bills itself as a family entertainment center with something for everyone. New attractions include Virtual World and Eye-work, a turbo-ride theater.

Parents should be aware, however, that not all activities are appropriate for all ages. For example, many of the video games have violent content. There are also bars here. Dave & Buster's has taken over all 70,000 square feet of Pier 19 on the Philadelphia waterfront and filled it with skee-ball, hoop toss, video games, a variety of bars and restaurants for different tastes, music, and virtual-reality games. You can even play golf on a virtual golf course. There are billiards, shuffleboard, and an outdoor deck with a view of the Ben Franklin Bridge.

All games are activated by a "power card." The only additional charges are for food, beverages, billiards, and the turbo-ride. No one under 21 is permitted unless accompanied by a parent. Clean and neat clothing required; no tank tops. No more than three children to one guardian over 25 years of age.

Parkway Attractions

Philadelphia has a tradition of excellence in museums. On Benjamin Franklin Parkway, sometimes called "Philadelphia's Champs-Elysées," there's something for everyone—from toddlers to teenagers. We've found that for most of the museums on the Parkway, it's best to beat the crowd by arriving in the morning right when the museum opens.

 ### ACADEMY OF NATURAL SCIENCES (all ages)
Nineteenth Street and Ben Franklin Parkway. Call (215) 299–1000 for more information. Open Monday through Friday 10:00 A.M. to 4:30 P.M., weekends and selected holidays 10:00 A.M. to 5:00 P.M. Admission: adults and children over 13, $6.50; seniors, $5.00; children 3 to 12, $5.50; under 3, Free. *Handicapped-accessible.*

In March of 1998 the "Dinosaur Museum" introduced its all-new $4.2-million Dinosaur Hall, with a simulated dig site and lots of spectacular skeletons. Near the lower entrance, on the same level with the cafeteria, is a robotic dinosaur not to be missed. It roars! (Very little children may be frightened.)

You really should not miss the butterfly exhibit, which can only be described as "magical." On the third floor Outside In is a hands-on exhibit for children 12 and under. Kids can touch mice, snakes, "legless lizards" (skinks), frogs, turtles, and enormous cockroaches from Madagascar. Enthusiastic and well-informed volunteers are available to answer questions.

Make sure you check the schedule when you arrive at the academy, because there are live animal shows and films at regular intervals. Wheelchair-accessible. Family memberships are available.

FRANKLIN INSTITUTE (ages 5 and up)

Twentieth Street and Benjamin Franklin Parkway; (215) 448–1200; www.fi.edu. The Science Center is open daily 9:30 A.M. to 5:00 P.M. The Futures Center and Omniverse Theater are open Monday through Wednesday 9:30 A.M. to 5:00 P.M., Thursday through Saturday 9:30 A.M. to 9:00 P.M., and Sunday 9:30 A.M. to 6:00 P.M. Call for prices and Omni and planetarium show times. Admission starts at $8.50 for children 4 to 11, $9.50 for adults.

If you visited the Franklin Institute as a child, as we did in 1969, you'll probably remember walking through the model of the human heart, following the path that the blood vessels take, hearing the sound of the heartbeat. Or maybe for you the highlight was climbing up on the real 1926 Baldwin locomotive or sitting in the cockpit of an airplane. If you have fond memories of these exhibits, don't worry—they're still here, still delighting children. But today there's a lot more, too.

The Franklin Institute was founded in 1824, and exhibits such as the heart pioneered the idea of hands-on museum displays. The museum has continued its tradition of forward-looking exhibits with The Futures Center, added in 1992, examining science and technology of the twenty-first century. Older children and teenagers will enjoy playing with computers and other interac-

*S*eeing Independence National Historic Park with Limited Time

If you have only time for a half-day visit, use your time wisely. Don't miss these highlights:

- Visitor Center
- Independence Hall and Congress Hall
- Liberty Bell Pavilion
- Franklin Court

If you have a little more time, we recommend these sites:

- Declaration House
- Bishop White House
- Todd House

tive displays that teach about astronomy, medicine, botany, biology, and other sciences. Little ones will find many buttons to push.

Be sure to also check out the Science Center, which includes exhibits about flight, optical illusions, and the Fels Planetarium.

The Tuttleman Omniverse Theater showcases very special movie experiences on its huge screen, giving a 179-degree field of view. Check to see what movie is currently playing, but the short feature *Philadelphia Symphony,* which usually precedes the main show, presents an excellent introduction to Philly.

The gift shops offer an unusual assortment of educational and sci-entifically oriented toys, books, posters, and so forth.

 ## PLEASE TOUCH MUSEUM (ages 2 to 8)

210 North Twenty-first Street. For details, call (215) 963–0666. Hours are 9:00 A.M. to 4:30 P.M. daily, 9:00 A.M. to 6:00 P.M. from July 1 to Labor Day. Admission is $6.50 for ages 1 and over; children under 1 are Free*; seniors $5.00. In late 2001, the museum is expected to move to a new location on Penn's Landing.*

The Franklin Institute may be best for older kids, but the Please Touch Museum, is designed especially for children 8 and under. Your child can visit again and again, always discovering something new.

Sendak at Please Touch Museum presents an ingenious landscape of settings and characters from the beloved books of Maurice Sendak, including *Where the Wild Things Are* and *In the Night Kitchen.* Kids can climb onto Max's 10-foot by 6-foot bed as the walls actually turn into a jungle filled with "Wild Things."

There are seven other major exhibit areas. In Supermarket Science, kids push kid-sized shopping carts through a fully-stocked supermarket complete with cash registers. Studio PTM is a child-sized TV studio in which kids can create sound effects and see themselves on TV. Children can board the cab of a real SEPTA bus or sit in the driver's seat of a miniature trolley. There is even a special area for the youngest visitors, ages 3 and under.

Recently recognized by *USA Today* as one of the top children's muse-ums in the country, the Please Touch Museum is also one of the first museums to cater to small children.

Adult supervision is required, and the museum specifies that no more than three children can accompany one adult. The signs posted give helpful suggestions to parents. Wheelchair-accessible. Strollers not permitted on gallery floor. Membership available.

A Paulsen Family Adventure It was obvious from the moment we entered the main floor of the Please Touch Museum for the first time, with three-year-old Judah and infant Seth, that this was a pretty stimulating place.

The large open space had been divided into different environments to attract young visitors. There were children building with blocks, playing with puppets, trying on costumes, petting a rabbit, and climbing in and out of the cab of a SEPTA bus. The voices of play surrounded us.

We looked down and Judah was missing. We checked all the exciting places that we thought he'd gravitate toward. No Judah.

We finally found him in the reading corner curled up with a book.

SCIENCE PARK PRESENTED BY FIRST UNION BANK (all ages)

Twenty-first Street, between Winter and Race Streets. Admission through Please Touch Museum or Franklin Institute. Open May through October only.

Recently, the Franklin Institute teamed up with the Please Touch Museum to build the Science Park presented by First Union, a 38,000-square-foot playground with a purpose (adjacent to both museums). Kids can climb around on thirty high-tech learning and play structures including a maze and three-dimensional optical illusions. There's a Sky Bike, Miniature Golf, and a Radar Detector. Admission is 𝐅𝐫𝐞𝐞 with admission to either museum.

FREE LIBRARY OF PHILADELPHIA (all ages)

Nineteenth and Vine Streets. Call (215) 686–5322 for hours. Admission is 𝐅𝐫𝐞𝐞.

The Free Library of Philadelphia stands across Logan Square from the Franklin Institute and the Academy of Natural Sciences and down the Parkway from the Art Museum and Rodin Museum. It houses more than six million books, magazines, newspapers, and other printed items and frequently hosts special events and exhibits. The library is open daily in winter, closed Sunday in summer. On Sunday there are tours of its remarkable rare books department.

RODIN MUSEUM (ages 6 and up)

Twenty-second Street and Benjamin Franklin Parkway; (215) 684–7788. Open Tuesday through Sunday 10:00 A.M. to 5:00 P.M. Voluntary donations are requested. Guided tours are given on the first and third Saturday of the month at 1:00 P.M.

Everybody knows Rodin's *Thinker*. You can see this popular sculpture at the Rodin Museum, along with the most complete collection of Auguste Rodin's work outside Paris. This museum is administered by the Philadelphia Museum of Art, down the parkway.

PHILADELPHIA MUSEUM OF ART (ages 6 and up)

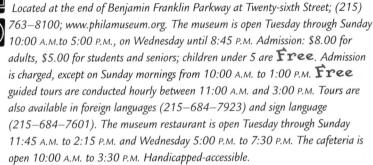

Located at the end of Benjamin Franklin Parkway at Twenty-sixth Street; (215) 763–8100; www.philamuseum.org. The museum is open Tuesday through Sunday 10:00 A.M. to 5:00 P.M., on Wednesday until 8:45 P.M. Admission: $8.00 for adults, $5.00 for students and seniors; children under 5 are Free. *Admission is charged, except on Sunday mornings from 10:00 A.M. to 1:00 P.M.* Free *guided tours are conducted hourly between 11:00 A.M. and 3:00 P.M. Tours are also available in foreign languages (215–684–7923) and sign language (215–684–7601). The museum restaurant is open Tuesday through Sunday 11:45 A.M. to 2:15 P.M. and Wednesday 5:00 P.M. to 7:30 P.M. The cafeteria is open 10:00 A.M. to 3:30 P.M. Handicapped-accessible.*

At the far end of the parkway, on the other side of Eakins Oval, are some steps that many people will recognize. Who can forget that memorable scene from *Rocky* when the boxer runs up all these steps? But the collection inside the Philadelphia Museum of Art is even more memorable—with a permanent collection of some 300,000 works, including one of the largest and most important collections of European art in the United States. The art museum takes a somewhat unusual approach, juxtaposing the painting, sculpture, furniture, ceramics, textiles, and architectural elements from the same period to convey a sense of that time. The museum is also known for its outstanding collection of rural Pennsylvania crafts and works by Thomas Eakins. We know a 7-year-old boy who could spend all day in the Arms and Armor collection.

The Art Museum's neoclassical facade stands at the end of Benjamin Franklin Parkway at Twenty-sixth Street, within walking distance (unless your children's legs are very short) of the Franklin Institute, Free Library of Philadelphia, Please Touch Museum, Logan Circle, and other parkway sites.

"Something every Sunday" is how the museum describes its family activities. Different programs are offered, usually on a walk-in basis, for families with children ages 3 to 13. Most of the programs take place on Sunday at 11:30 A.M. or 1:30 P.M. so that you can take advantage of the Sunday-morning Free admission. Programs range from storytelling to hands-on art activities, with titles like Tales and Treasures, Try a Technique, and Gallery Games. Children especially like the Japanese teahouse,

Chinese palace hall, and the thirteenth century French cloister. Many of these programs are 𝐅𝐫𝐞𝐞, and the rest are $2.00 for children of members, $3.00 for children of nonmembers. Accompanying adults are 𝐅𝐫𝐞𝐞. Every day of the week you can pick up a family-oriented, self-guided tour brochure at the West Information Desk. The museum's automated information line is (215) 684–7500. For information about family activities and children's art classes, call (215) 684–7605. Handicapped-accessible, with changing tables in the rest rooms.

EASTERN STATE PENITENTIARY (ages 5 and up)

Fairmount Avenue at Twenty-second Street, 5 blocks from the Philadelphia Museum of Art and the Parkway; (215) 236–3300; www.easternstate.com. Open 10:00 A.M. to 5:00 P.M. on selected days May through October: in May, Saturday and Sunday; in June, July, and August, Wednesday through Sunday; in September and October, Saturday and Sunday. Guided tours are available every hour from 10:00 A.M. to 4:00 P.M. Children under 5 are not admitted. Admission: adults $7.00, students and seniors $5.00, children ages 5 to 17 $3.00.

When Charles Dickens visited the United States in 1842, there were two sights he didn't want to miss: Niagara Falls and the Eastern State Penitentiary. It has been called the most influential prison in the world, because its design was grounded on the nineteenth century's most modern ideas about civic responsibility and criminal behavior. Instead of using physical punishment, this prison was designed to encourage solitude and penitence.

A nationally broadcast special on the History Channel and a full-page spread in the *New York Times* have focused on the prison, and the number of visitors has tripled in recent years.

Al Capone did time here, as did the "gentleman bandit" Willie Sutton. An operating prison for more than 140 years, until 1971, the building has recently been reopened as the Eastern State Penitentiary Prison Society makes plans for its future. At present there are special art exhibits here, and sometimes dramatic productions.

The building has been made safe for tours but has otherwise been left "as is." Visitors must wear hard hats and stay with tour groups. Most people won't have to be reminded; the decaying plaster, dampness, and remnants of prison life make this a pretty eerie place—great for teenagers! The Halloween Ghost Tours are very popular; call (215) 763–NITE. The gift shop offers T-shirts, posters, and books on a prison theme.

Fairmount Park

At 8,700 acres Philadelphia's Fairmount Park is one of the world's largest city parks and an amazing source of activities. The park includes: Andorra Natural Area, Bartram's Gardens, Boathouse Row, Japanese House and Garden, Smith Playground and Playhouse, and the Philadelphia Zoo. Of lesser interest to families with children are the following sites: Historic Fairmount Waterworks, Horticultural Center, Memorial Hall, Ryerss Library and Museum, and the ten colonial mansions of Fairmount Park. Although the Philadelphia Museum of Art is technically part of Fairmount Park as well, we have included it in our discussion of "Parkway Attractions."

The Fairmount Park Information Center is located at Memorial Hall, North Concourse Drive near Forty-second Street and Parkside Avenue; (215) 685–0000 (yes, those zeroes are correct). For a guided tour of the mansions, please contact Mansions of Fairmount Park, Park House Guides Office, Philadelphia Museum of Art, or call (215) 684–7926. There are also trolleys that circulate around the park, stopping at all the historic mansions so that you may tour the houses self-guided. For information about these trolleys, please call (215) 925–TOUR.

Amazing Philadelphia Facts

More Revolutionary War battles were fought within a 50-mile radius of Philadelphia than in all the New England states combined. It was also the capital during the Revolution, except for nine months when it was occupied by the British. It then served as the nation's capital from 1790 to 1800.

ANDORRA NATURAL AREA (all ages)

Between Ridge and Germantown Pikes on Northwestern Avenue; (215) 685–9285. The park is open daily dawn to dusk. The Visitor Center is usually open on weekends noon to 4:00 P.M. **Free**; *some educational programs have fees.*

Andorra Natural Area offers many wonderful programs for children including nature trails, exhibits, and special events. Most activities begin at Treehouse Visitor Center, a 100-year-old home where you can explore a touch table and other exhibits. Even when the Visitor Center is closed, there are maps, activity sheets, program calendars, and other information available.

Two annual festivals emphasize hands-on participation. In October you can pick apples and make them into apple butter at the Harvest Festival, and in February you can tap a tree at the Maple Sugar Festival.

 ### BARTRAM'S HISTORIC GARDEN (gardens: all ages; house: ages 8 and up)

Fifty-fourth Street and Lindbergh Boulevard; (215) 729–5281; www.libertynet. org/bartram. The garden is open daily from dawn to dusk; admission is Free*. The home is open Tuesday through Sunday noon to 4:00 P.M. There is a charge for the house tour: adults $3.00, children under 12 $2.00.*

The oldest surviving botanical garden in the country includes the pre-Revolutionary home of botanist John Bartram, as well as forty-four acres of gardens.

 ### BOATHOUSE ROW (all ages)

A lovely place for a stroll along the Schuylkill River, Boathouse Row consists of twelve nineteenth-century buildings where Philadelphia's rowing clubs keep their boats. The outline of each boathouse is trimmed with lights, to create a luminous view of the boathouses from across the river at night.

 ### JAPANESE HOUSE AND GARDEN (ages 5 and up)

Near the Horticultural Center, at Belmont and Montgomery Avenues; (215) 878–5097. Open May 1 through October, Tuesday through Sunday 10:00 A.M. to 4:00 P.M. Admission is $2.50 for adults, $2.00 for students and seniors.

The Japanese House and Garden offers many events that your family might enjoy, including a Japanese tea ceremony presented in the Japanese House. At the annual Children's Festival, held in May, kids can learn about origami, kimonos, Japanese crafts, dolls, and armor. They can also see a traditional tea ceremony, hear traditional music and stories, and try Japanese food. This event is modeled after the Japanese celebrations of Boys' Day and Girls' Day. At the Summer Festival in June, kids can participate in the beautiful custom of launching lantern boats.

SMITH PLAYGROUND AND PLAYHOUSE (ages 2 to 10)

Kelly Drive; (215) 765–4325. Enter the park at the statue of Ulysses S. Grant on Kelly Drive and follow the signs to the playground. Open year-round when the park is open. Admission is **Free**.

If you haven't heard about Smith Playground and Playhouse, you're in for a treat. This attraction in Fairmount Park hosts an average of 1,000 children daily during the summer and celebrated its one-hundredth birthday in 1999. On one recent weekend, an 86-year-old woman and three generations of her family all slid down the Giant Slide (built in 1908) together, all reliving their own childhood memories.

Inside the playhouse there are three floors of activities for preschoolers. The new train on the first floor was donated by the group Boyz II Men, whose members played here as children. The foam-block room has recently been expanded, and a reading room with books and cozy corners has been added. Little kids climb into the kid-sized cars and "drive" on kid-sized roads, with delightful details like traffic lights and parking meters.

The house is partially handicapped-accessible. There are rest rooms in the house, and a concession stand is open seasonally. There is also plenty of **Free** parking.

A Paulsen Family Adventure Typical first-time parents, we doted on everything Judah did. At the Smith Playground, we coaxed our three-year-old up the ladder to the slide. Every rung was greeted with cheers. We applauded him as he cautiously shuffled across the catwalk and slid down the slide.

We were so busy encouraging Judah we didn't pay any attention to seven-month-old Seth, who crawled up the ladder and across the catwalk and slid down the slide all by himself!

THE PHILADELPHIA ZOO (all ages)

3400 West Girard Avenue; (215) 243–1100; www.primatereserve.philly.com. Open daily 9:30 A.M. to 5:00 P.M. Admission: adults, $8.50; seniors and children ages 2 to 11, $6.00; members and children under 2, **Free**.

The Philadelphia Zoo has some exciting new additions. In June 1998 the newly renovated Reptile House opened, featuring a replica of an

Everglades thunderstorm and Indiana Jones Temple of Doom, with not one, but two, king cobras.

In July 1999 the new Primate Reserve opened. Philadelphians' love for their zoo was dramatized by the outpouring of support following the December 24, 1995, fire that destroyed the old World of Primates exhibit and killed twenty-three beloved animals. Chaka, a silverback gorilla whose parents died in the fire, has come home to reside with five other great apes in the new Primate Reserve.

A new annual feature is not to be missed. From April to October, weather permitting, the rainbow lorikeets exhibit is open. Even bigger kids are wide-eyed with wonder when these colorful birds drink nectar from the children's hands.

The zoo offers a treat for all ages—a chance to meet more than 1,800 animals housed in naturalistic settings, all surrounded by beautiful trees and plantings. Other highlights include the white lions, warthogs, and capybaras—the works.

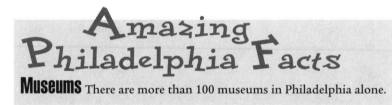

Amazing Philadelphia Facts

Museums There are more than 100 museums in Philadelphia alone.

The Rest of Center City

Former Philadelphia mayor Edward G. Rendell realized the importance of tourism to his city. One of his first actions upon taking office was to start renovating the amazing City Hall (at the intersection of Broad and Market Streets, the dead center of William Penn's original plan for the city) and open it for **Free** tours.

CITY HALL (observation deck, all ages; tour, ages 8 and up)
Broad and Market Streets; (215) 686–2840. Tours available daily at 12:30 P.M. Tours are **Free***, but donations are welcome. The observation deck is open daily 9:30 A.M. to 4:15 P.M.*

See the courtroom where the film *Philadelphia* was made and the 548-foot-tall tower that is topped by a statue of William Penn. When the Phillies became the National League champions in 1994, maintenance workers placed a baseball cap on Penn's head. The observation deck (at William Penn's feet) affords a spectacular view of the city.

DISNEYQUEST

Eighth and Market Streets; hours to be announced; admission fees to be announced.
Disney's indoor interactive theme park is coming to Philly. With a grand opening planned for the summer of 2000, DisneyQuest is billed as "a breakthrough concept in family entertainment." It will be a five-story, 80,000 square-foot interactive theme park using high-tech concepts like virtual reality. Our kids are eagerly anticipating the "Virtual Jungle Cruise," "Cyber-Space Mountain," "Hercules in the Underworld," and "Aladdin's Magic Carpet Ride."

PHILADELPHIA VISITORS CENTER (all ages)

Sixteenth Street and JFK; (215) 636–1666 or (800) 537–7676; www.gophila.com.
While you're in the neighborhood, drop by the Philadelphia Visitors Center. For information about **Free** historical musical theater productions, costumed town criers, *The Liberty Tale,* and *Under the Mulberry Tree,* call Historic Philadelphia, Inc. at (215) 629–5801 or the Greater Philadelphia Tourism Marketing Organization at (888) GO–PHILA.

This Visitors Center, which represents the entire city, will be combined with the Independence National Historic Park Visitors Center in the new location at Sixth and Market Streets sometime in 2001.

CLAES OLDENBURG'S CLOTHESPIN (all ages)

Located in Centre Square Plaza at Fifteenth and Walnut Streets.
Either you love it or you hate it. Either way, Claes Oldenburg's public sculpture of a giant clothespin is one you're not likely to forget.

ROBERT INDIANA'S PHILADELPHIA LOVE (all ages)

Located at Kennedy Plaza, Fifteenth Street and JFK.
This public sculpture became famous in the 1960s and 1970s. It has been newly cleaned and looks better than ever.

ACADEMY OF FINE ARTS (ages 8 and up)

118 North Broad Street at Cherry; (215) 972–7600. The museum is open Monday through Saturday 10:00 A.M. to 5:00 P.M. and on Sunday 11:00 A.M. to 5:00 P.M.; closed New Year's Day, Thanksgiving, and Christmas. Admission is $5.95 for *adults, $3.95 for children under 12, $4.95 for seniors and students with ID, and* Free *to members and children under 5.*

Walking up Broad Street near Cherry, 1 block from City Hall and the Convention Center, you can't miss the graceful front staircase of the Academy of Fine Arts, home of the nation's first art museum, the Museum of American Art of Pennsylvania, and its first art school, the Academy School. The building, with its Gothic arches and lacy ironwork, is a masterpiece of High Victorian Gothic architecture. The museum collection includes works by Benjamin West, Charles Willson Peale (one of the academy's founders), Thomas Eakins (who served as the academy's director during the 1880s), Mary Cassatt, Winslow Homer, Horace Pippin, Andrew Wyeth, Alexander Calder, Louise Nevelson, and many others.

You can make your visit more lively with Family Inform, an audio-guide system. Look around the galleries to find numbers that you key into the audio machine's keypad, and you can hear messages about the works of art.

Avenue of the Arts Broad Street south of City Hall has recently been renamed the Avenue of the Arts. Already home to the Academy of Music, the Merriam Theater, and the University of the Arts, several new theaters are planned for the street.

ACADEMY OF MUSIC (ages 10 and up)

Broad and Locust Streets; call (215) 893–1935 for information or to make reservations.

That spectacular opera house seen in the movie *The Age of Innocence* is Philadelphia's own Academy of Music. You can see the landmark if you attend a concert by the Philadelphia Orchestra or a performance by the Opera Company of Philadelphia. But by reservation only, you can take a one-hour afternoon tour of this beloved building on Broad and Locust Streets, including a peek backstage and into the artists' dressing rooms.

READING TERMINAL MARKET (all ages)

Twelfth and Arch Streets; (215) 922–2317. Open Monday through Saturday, 8:00 A.M. to 6:00 P.M. year-round.

If you're hungry and you don't know what to eat, or if you're planning a picnic, stop by the Reading Terminal Market, where farmers and merchants from around the Philadelphia area (many of them Amish) sell very fresh produce, cheese, fish, meats, baked goods, and much more. There are hundreds of stalls to browse through, so each member of the family is sure to find something delicious.

While you're at the market, head across the street and up the stairs to the old **Reading Terminal,** which has recently been converted as part of the Pennsylvania Convention Center. This cavernous hall was at one time the main train station in downtown Philadelphia.

 ### CHINATOWN (all ages)
Between Arch and Vine Streets, Eleventh to Eighth Streets. For information about Chinatown call (215) 922–2156.

One block east of the Reading Terminal and you're in the heart of Philadelphia's Chinatown. Stop here for authentic Chinese cuisine and products.

 ### EDGAR ALLAN POE NATIONAL MEMORIAL (ages 10 and up)
Seventh and Spring Garden Streets; (215) 597–8780; nps.gov/edal/. Open November through May, Wednesday through Sunday 9:00 A.M. to 5:00 P.M.; June through October, daily 9:00 A.M. to 5:00 P.M. Closed Thanksgiving, Christmas, and New Year's Day. Admission is Free.

A couple of long blocks north of Chinatown is the house where Edgar Allan Poe lived with his wife and mother-in-law in 1843–1844. There is a brief slide presentation about the author's life.

 ### ROSENBACH MUSEUM AND LIBRARY (ages 10 and up)
2010 Delancey Place, on Rittenhouse Square; (215–732–1600); www.libertynet. org/~rosenb1. Open Tuesday through Sunday 11:00 A.M. to 4:00 P.M. (last tour, 2:45 P.M.). Closed Monday, national holidays, and the period from August 1 to the second Tuesday after Labor Day. Admission is $5.00; seniors and students (including children) $3.00.

To get a feeling for a traditional, stately Philadelphia neighborhood, stroll around the blocks surrounding Rittenhouse Square. On Rittenhouse Square, the Rosenbach Museum and Library houses an astounding collection of rare books, manuscripts, antique furniture, silver, porcelain, and works of art in the beautiful home of the Rosenbach brothers, who lived here from 1948 until their deaths in 1952 and 1953. This wonderful museum is more suited to older children and literary folks, although occasionally there are special exhibits of illustrated books that may appeal to youngsters.

Among the more than 30,000 rare books and 300,000 manuscripts are letters penned by George Washington, Thomas Jefferson, Benjamin

Franklin, and Abraham Lincoln. You may also see Lewis Carroll's own copy of *Alice's Adventures in Wonderland,* the manuscript for James Joyce's *Ulysses,* and the notes for Bram Stoker's *Dracula.* The museum also owns more than 3,000 original drawings by Maurice Sendak, noted author of classic children's books.

For information about handicapped-accessibility, call (215) 732–1600, ext. 25 or e-mail to maw-rml@libertynet.org.

 CIVIL WAR LIBRARY AND MUSEUM (ages 10 and up)

1805 Pine Street; (215) 735–8196. Open Tuesday through Saturday 11:00 A.M. to 4:30 P.M. Admission: $5.00 for adults, $4.00 for seniors, $3.00 for students with ID.

A couple of blocks away from the Rosenbach Museum, the Civil War Library and Museum houses artifacts from that tumultuous era in our history.

North Philadelphia

Philadelphia is home to a huge number of colleges and universities. Besides adding to the rich cultural diversity of the city, these institutions offer some unusual museums.

 TEMPLE UNIVERSITY DENTAL MUSEUM (ages 8 and up)

Broad Street and Allegheny Avenue; (215) 707–2816. Open by appointment only.

The Temple University Dental Museum has an unusual collection of dental memorabilia going back to the 1700s. Its best-known piece is the first dental chair in the United States, dating from the 1790s. New in spring of 1998, you can visit a Victorian dental office.

 WAGNER FREE INSTITUTE OF SCIENCE (ages 8 and up)

1700 West Montgomery Avenue; (215) 763–6529; e-mail: dashiell@ llpptn.pall.org. Open Tuesday through Friday 9:00 A.M. to 4:00 P.M. for self-guided tours. Occasional Saturday openings; call for schedule. Admission is Free.

The Wagner Free Institute of Science presents an unusual opportunity to visit a science museum that looks pretty much the way it did in about 1890. This is a great place for amateur naturalists and paleontologists.

Amateur scientist William Wagner founded the institute in 1855 to provide free science education to all, regardless of race, gender, or financial resources. He used his personal collections to illustrate the lectures, and these objects now form the core of the museum's exhibits, which were given their present arrangement after Wagner's death in 1885.

More than 100,000 specimens, including fossils, minerals, shells, mounted animals, skeletons, and insects, are displayed in the Victorian cherrywood cases. (Very young children may have difficulty seeing into some of the cases.) All children under 18 must be accompanied by an adult.

SHOE MUSEUM (ages 10 and up)

Eighth and Race Streets, at the Temple University School of Podiatric Medicine. **Free** *tours must be arranged in advance by calling (215) 625–5243.*

A unique diversion, the Shoe Museum at the Temple University School of Podiatric Medicine displays footwear belonging to celebrities such as Ringo Starr, Julius Erving, Lucille Ball, Mamie Eisenhower, and Ronald and Nancy Reagan. There are also shoes from around the world, tiny chinese shoes for bound feet, huge shoes for circus giants, tap shoes, ballet slippers, and many more.

UNIVERSITY OF PENNSYLVANIA MUSEUM (ages 8 and up)

Thirty-third and Spruce Streets; (215) 898–4000; www.upenn.edu/museum. The University Museum is open Tuesday through Saturday 10:00 A.M. to 4:30 P.M. and Sunday 1:00 to 5:00 P.M. It is closed Sunday in summer. Admission is $5.00 for adults, $2.50 for students and children; children under 6 are **Free**. *For information on Family Fun Days, call (215) 898–4890. For children's workshops call (215) 898–4015.*

The University Museum is a treasure trove for your budding archaeologist or anyone interested in sphinxes, mummies, African sculpture, or ancient Mayan, Greek, or Polynesian culture. The three floors of this museum are crammed with a wealth of artifacts unearthed by the University Museum's own world-renowned archaeological and ethnographic expeditions.

Kids will be awe-struck by the genuine Sphinx of Ramesses II, weighing in at thirteen tons of solid granite. They will be mystified, and perhaps a little unnerved, by the real mummies. The huge crystal ball is a favorite with our kids. Other ongoing exhibits include Raven's Journey: World of Alaska's Native People.

The annual Chinese New Year celebration and the Celebration of African Cultures, both popular family events, are held on Saturdays in January and February. Please note that while the large marble halls keep pretty cool, the building is not air-conditioned. The Cafe, which has recently been upgraded, offers a kid-friendly menu, especially on weekends. The Pyramid Gift Shop has educational and inexpensive items for children. Handicapped-accessible, with diapering facilities in some bathrooms. The website includes a nice artifact game.

 MUTTER MUSEUM AND COLLEGE GALLERY OF THE COLLEGE OF PHYSICIANS OF PHILADELPHIA (ages 10 and up)

19 South Twenty-second Street, between Chestnut and Market Streets; (215) 563–3737; www.collphyphil.org. The Mutter Museum and College Gallery are open Tuesday through Saturday 10:00 A.M. to 4:00 P.M. Admission to the Mutter Museum and College Gallery is $8.00 for adults, $4.00 for seniors, students, and children 6 to 18.

For years the College of Physicians of Philadelphia (not an educational institution but the nation's oldest private medical society) has maintained the Mutter Museum of medical anomalies. Begun as a teaching collection for medical students in a time when students had little access to clinical situations, it has become known for its wall of more than one hundred skulls, the tumor removed from President Cleveland's jaw, and the preserved body of an eighteenth-century woman.

The college's exhibits, however, are now moving into the twenty-first century by taking on some of the hottest issues in current medicine. The new College Gallery features temporary exhibits that examine important issues. For example, a recent exhibit studied the dilemma posed "When the President is the Patient." The new C. Everett Koop Community Medical Information Center (CHIC) is a **Free** library on health, with books, CD-ROM, Internet access, and videos.

ALSO IN THE AREA

Also on the Penn campus, kids might enjoy a look at **College Hall,** one of two Philadelphia structures reputed to be a model for the Addams Family house. (Charles Addams went to Penn and was well acquainted with this building. The other candidate is the Ebeneezer Maxwell Mansion in Chestnut Hill.) There are also some interesting sculptures on this campus, such as Claes Oldenburg's oversized button and the statue of Benjamin Franklin.

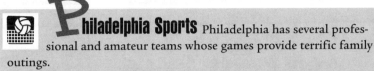

hiladelphia Sports Philadelphia has several profes- sional and amateur teams whose games provide terrific family outings.

The Eagles and the Phillies play at Veterans Stadium (Phillies: 215-463-1000; Eagles: 215-463-5500).

The First Union Complex now includes the new First Union Center, home to the Philadelphia Flyers (NHL), Sixers (NBA), and Wings (MILL); and the First Union Spectrum, home of the Phantoms (AHL) and Kixx (NPSL). The box office at (215) 339-7600 serves both.

Veterans Stadium and the First Union Complex are located across the street from each other in South Philadelphia, at Broad Street and Pattison Avenue.

South Philadelphia

South Philadelphia is home to many of the city's ethnic neighborhoods, as well as the world's largest outdoor market, the Italian Market.

ITALIAN MARKET (all ages)

Ninth Street, between Warton and Christian Streets; (215) 922–5557.

The Italian Market is a great place to find unusual cheeses, fresh fruits and vegetables, homemade pasta, exotic spices, and unusual kitchen wares.

MUMMER MUSEUM (ages 8 and up)

1100 South Second Street; (215) 336–3050; www.voicenet.com/%7egbanks/ mummers.html. Open Tuesday through Saturday from 9:30 A.M. to 4:30 P.M., and Sunday from noon to 4:30 P.M. It is closed on Monday, and on Sunday in July and August. Admission is $2.50 for adults, $2.00 for children and seniors; guided tours are available by reservation.

No Philadelphian can hear the tune of "Golden Slippers" without picturing the sequined costumes, the feathers, and, of course, the dis- tinctive strut of the Mummers. But non-Philadelphians may need a word of explanation.

A phenomenon unique to Philadelphia, Mummery is centered around the annual Philadelphia New Year's Day Parade, when the string bands, fancy brigades, and clowns strut up Broad Street. The Mummers Museum surrounds you with the spangles, the colors, the history, and the music of the Mummers. You can see videos of past parades, learn how the costumes are made, and practice your "Mummers' Strut." In nice weather, the string bands appear for concerts on selected Tuesday evenings at 8:00 P.M.

FORT MIFFLIN ON THE DELAWARE (ages 8 and up)

Fort Mifflin Road; call (215) 492–1881; www. spiritof76.com. Open April through November, Wednesday through Sunday, 10:00 A.M. to 4:00 P.M. During the off-season prebooked tours may be available. Admission is $5.00 for adults, $3.50 for seniors, $2.00 for children 12 and younger, Free *for children under 2.*

Fort Mifflin played a strategic role in the Revolutionary War. In 1777, 250 British warships sailed up the Delaware River with needed supplies for British troops occupying Philadelphia. For seven weeks the little fort held back the mightiest navy in the world. Although it was almost completely destroyed in the process, Fort Mifflin never surrendered.

On Sunday afternoons, in addition to tours, there are militia-guard drills. A blacksmith also demonstrates how weapons were made in this period.

Manayunk and Chestnut Hill

Although located within Philadelphia's city limits, the Manayunk and Chestnut Hill sections feel more like small towns than urban neighborhoods. Manayunk, one of the country's oldest villages, has a reputation as an artists' community. Main Street in Manayunk is lined with art galleries, boutiques, and unusual shops. Chestnut Hill has a different atmosphere, with its beautiful old homes and elegant shops. Both offer wonderful restaurants (see the Where to Eat section of this chapter).

 ### EBENEEZER MAXWELL MANSION (ages 8 and up)

Greene and Tulpehocken Streets, Chestnut Hill; (215) 438–1861. Open Friday through Sunday 1:00 to 4:00 P.M.

Rumor has it that the Ebeneezer Maxwell Mansion is the model for the Addams Family house, as depicted by Philadelphia's own Charles

Addams. It is unclear how much the cartoonist Charles Addams was influenced by the Victorian buildings he saw, but it is known that he was familiar with both College Hall (on the Penn campus) and the Ebeneezer Maxwell Mansion, and both may have shaped the architecture of the Addams Family house. This eighteen-room Victorian mansion in the Chestnut Hill section was built in 1859. Young children will love the children's bedroom, filled with games and toys of the period. The gadgets are also wonderful, including an apple corer and a sausage stuffer. The gardens include a grape arbor and a small lake. At Christmas there's a Dickensian Christmas celebration and in fall a ghost walk.

MORRIS ARBORETUM (all ages)

Germantown Pike at 100 Northwestern Avenue, Chestnut Hill; (215) 247–5777. Open Monday through Friday 10:00 A.M. to 4 P.M., Saturday and Sunday from November through March 10:00 A.M. to 4:00 P.M., and April to October 10:00 A.M. to 5:00 P.M. Guided tours are given Saturday and Sunday at 1:00 P.M. Admission: adults $6.00, students $4.00, and seniors $5.00; children under 6 Free.

The Morris Arboretum, the botanical garden of the University of Pennsylvania, is filled with exotic plants and picturesque vistas. The arboretum fills ninety-two acres in Chestnut Hill, including Japanese gardens, rose gardens, the only Victorian fernery in the United States, and a charming pond complete with swans.

A Paulsen Family Adventure On a beautiful summer day some years ago, we took six-year-old Judah, three-year-old Seth, and a friend, Patrick, to the Morris Aboretum. In the Rose Garden, I arranged the boys beside a fountain for a photo. When I snapped the picture, all three boys were smiling. But by the time I put my camera down and looked up, the only part of Seth I could see was his legs. He'd fallen head-first into the water. I pulled Seth up, expecting him to be frightened, but he grinned and said "I go scuba diving!"

Northeast Philadelphia

 ### INSECTARIUM (all ages)

8046 Frankford Avenue in Northeast Philadelphia; (215) 335–9500. The Insectarium is open 10:00 A.M. to 4:00 P.M., Monday through Saturday. Admission is $4.00 per person. It is Free *for anyone younger than 2 with a paying adult.*

Named "Philly's Best Kid's Attraction, Odd" in 1997, the Insectarium has recently been featured in *Life* magazine. Steve's Bug-Off Exterminating Co. has assembled the Insectarium, a collection of live insects in naturalized settings, mounted specimens, and interactive displays. This one-of-a-kind museum is designed to teach the importance of insects as part of the diversity of nature—but mostly it's a lot of fun. You won't be able to forget the "cockroach kitchen," the "glow-in-the-dark" scorpion, the live termite tunnel, or the tarantulas (no matter how hard you try).

 ### JOHN HEINZ NATIONAL WILDLIFE REFUGE (all ages)

Eighty-sixth Street and Lindbergh Boulevard, in the Tinicum section; call (215) 365–3118 for information. Entrance to both park and federal environmental education center are Free.

As of June 2000, the John Heinz National Wildlife Refuge features a large new federal environmental center, approximately 18,000 square feet, with many exhibits about the refuge and marsh, as well as the Fish and Wildlife Service, which administers the site. The center also includes a library and resource center with Internet access, classrooms, meeting rooms, and a gift shop. The refuge is alive with butterflies, geese, pheasants, woodcocks, egrets, muskrats, turtles, foxes, deer, and wildflowers galore. This is a great place to hike, bike, or canoe (bring your own canoe), and don't forget your binoculars to enhance the view from the Observation Tower.

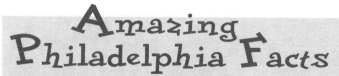

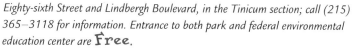
The Benjamin Franklin Parkway has been called "Philadelphia's Champs-Elysées."

Amazing Philadelphia Facts

Philadelphia is known for its distinctive foods, including cheese steaks, scrapple, snapper soup, and soft pretzels with mustard.

Where to Eat

IN PHILADELPHIA

Philadelphia Fish & Co. Restaurant, *207 Chestnut Street; (215) 625–8605.*

Pizzaria Uno, *509–511 South Second Street; (215) 592–0400.* Located in South Street area. High chairs, booster seats, children's coloring menu with crayons.

Reading Terminal Market, *Twelfth and Arch Streets; (215) 922–2317.*

Italian Market, *Ninth Street between Christian and Dickinson; (215) 922–5557.*

Katmandu, *417 North Columbus Boulevard; (215) 629–7400.* High chairs, booster seats, children's menu. Great view of the Ben Franklin Bridge.

Magnolia Cafe, *1602 Locust Street; (215) 546–4180.* Cajun/Creole food. Booster seats, children's menu.

Marabella, *1700 Benjamin Franklin Parkway; (215) 981–5555.* Italian food. High chairs and booster seats, children's menu, crayons, and balloons.

Mulberry Market, *236 Arch Street; (215) 592–8022.* Deli-style food, sandwiches, hoagies. Across the street from the Betsy Ross House.

City Tavern, *138 South Second Street, (215) 413–1443.* Children's menu, booster seats. In the heart of the historic district.

IN MANAYUNK

Le Bus, *4266 Main Street; (215) 487–2663.* Children's menu, high chairs, casual atmosphere.

Sonoma, *4411 Main Street; (215) 483–9400.* "Italifornia" food. High chairs, booster seats; babies and toddlers welcome.

Where to Stay

IN PHILADELPHIA

Best Western Center City Hotel, *501 North Twenty-second Street; (215) 568–8300 or (800) 528–1234.* Convenient to major museums and other attractions. Restaurant, outdoor pool.

Holiday Inn–Center City, *1800 Market Street; (215) 561–7500 or (800) HOLIDAY.*

Holiday Inn–Express Midtown, *Thirteenth and Walnut; (215) 735–9300 or (800) 5–MIDTOWN.*

Holiday Inn–Independence Mall,
(Historic Area), 400 Arch Street; (215)
923–8660 or (800) HOLIDAY. Seasonal
outdoor rooftop pool.

For More Information

Philadelphia Convention and
Visitors Bureau, *(800) 537–7676*
or (215) 636–1666; www.
libertynet.org/phila-visitor.

Philadelphia Countryside

Imagine a rainbow of giant crayons and giant glass walls you're not only allowed but *supposed* to color on! The Crayola Factory is the perfect place to let your imagination run wild. And that's just one of the exciting things happening in the Philadelphia Countryside.

Sesame Place's Vapor Trail, its first-ever roller coaster, is designed to include all members of the family. Dorney Park has Steel Force, the tallest, longest, and fastest steel roller coaster on the East Coast. Norristown's Elmwood Park Zoo has expanded and improved, with its new aviary, bayou, and grasslands exhibits.

A 3-day Revolutionary War Driving Tour begins with the Battle of Brandywine in September 1777, the tour traces the Continental Army's struggles against the British through the Paoli Massacre, the Battle of Germantown, Whitemarsh Encampment, and the Battle of Old Gulph Road to Valley Forge. It

Faith & Emily's
Favorite Philadelphia Countryside Attractions

1. Sesame Place
2. Crayola Factory
3. Colonial Pennsylvania Plantation
4. Childventure Museum
5. Valley Forge National Park
6. Mercer Museum
7. Dorney Park and Wildwater Kingdom
8. Tubing at Point Pleasant
9. Elmwood Park Zoo

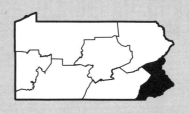

Nazareth

Delaware
River

Easton

Schnecksville
Bethlehem

Claussville
Allentown
Hellertown

Breinigsville

Alburtis
Pipersville

Point Pleasant

New
Hope

Hilltown
Lahaska
Washington
Doylestown
Crossing

Schwenksville
Chalfont

Skippack
Morrisville

Elverson
Worcester
Churchville
Langhorne

Fort Washington
Glenside

Phoenixville
Audubon

Valley Forge
Norristown

Chester
Springs
Merion

Paoli

Philadelphia

Media

Chadds Ford
Swarthmore

Delaware
River

PHILADELPHIA COUNTRYSIDE

includes a narrative of the events, along with driving instructions to eleven historic sites in Montgomery, Chester, Delaware, and Berks counties, and in Philadelphia. For information, call the Valley Forge Convention and Visitors Bureau at (610) 834–1550 or (888) VISIT-VF.

The area surrounding Philadelphia offers many other opportunities for family adventure. Living-history sites such as Hopewell Furnace, Colonial Pennsylvania Plantation, and Peter Wentz Farmstead bring kids face-to-face with the past. The Barnes Foundation's collection of Impressionist art is dazzling, and its building has been recently restored. The streets of New Hope teem with art galleries, craft shops, and restaurants. Historic parks such as the Brandywine Battlefield, Washington Crossing, and Valley Forge offer a great combination of history and outdoor fun, all in the beautiful Pennsylvania countryside.

Faith & Emily's
Favorite Philadelphia Countryside Events

- **Philadelphia Folk Festival** (weekend before Labor Day); (215) 242–0150, (215) 247–1300, or (800) 556–FOLK; www.folkfest.org.

- **Scarecrow Festival Weekend at Peddler's Village**; (215) 794–4000.

- **Great Allentown Fair** (starts on the Tuesday before Labor Day); (610) 435–7469; www.allentownfairpa.org.

- **Mercer Museum FolkFest** (May); (215) 345–0210.

- **Pennsylvania Fair, Bensalem** (May); (215) 633–0404 or (215) 639–9000; www.pennsylvaniafair.com

- **Musikfest, Bethlehem**; (August); (610) 861–0678; www.musikfest.org

- **Great Pumpkin Carve and Show in Chadds Ford** (October); (610) 338–7376; www.voicenet.com/ncfhs/

- **Devon Horse Show** (ten days surrounding Memorial Day weekend); (610) 964–0550.

- **Time of Thanksgiving**, Lenni Lenape Museum (autumn); (610) 797–2121.

- **Longwood Gardens Christmas Display** (November to January 1); (610) 388–6741.

The following websites introduce you to this area:

- Bucks County: www.bctc.org/

- Valley Forge: www.valleyforge.org/

- Chester County: www.brandywinevalley.com/

- Delaware County: www.delcocub.org/

- Montgomery County: www.montcopa.org

Brandywine Valley

For a trip that includes historic homes and battlefields, art, gardens, and a mushroom museum, all within easy distance of one another, contact the Chester County Tourist Bureau (800–228–9933). You may wish to make a weekend visit to the towns of Kennett Square and Chadds Ford. The website for the Chadds Ford Historical Society can be found at www.voicenet. com/~cfhs/.

The fields, mills, and farms of rural Pennsylvania have found their way into the art of Chadds Ford's most famous artist, Andrew Wyeth. Here you're surrounded by Wyeth's landscapes and his art. You can visit the historic Brandywine Battlefield, eat lunch in a historic inn, shop, and take a walk along the Brandywine River.

 ### LONGWOOD GARDENS (all ages)

Route 1 in Kennett Square; (610) 388–1000; www.longwoodgardens.org. The outdoor gardens and Conservatory open at 9:00 and 10:00 A.M., respectively, every day of the year. Both close at 5:00 P.M. from November through March and at 6:00 P.M. from April through October, although both are frequently open later for special events and holiday displays. Call ahead for a complete schedule. Admission is $12.00 for adults ($8.00 on Tuesday), $6.00 for youths ages 10 to 20, $2.00 for children ages 6 to 12, and Free *under age 6.*

Longwood Gardens is a place to enjoy the variety of nature, both indoors and out. In a four-acre conservatory, Longwood's visitors can see orchids, roses, bonsai, exotic jungle plants, and waterfalls, even on the coldest winter days. And on warmer days, you can tour the outside gardens and the fountains. No matter what the weather, don't miss the annual holiday topiary display.

The Children's Garden includes a maze of hedges, stone cottage, topiary rabbits, and fountains designed to splash in. Please note that starting in January 2001 this garden will be closed for renovations.

The Kids Corner Clubhouse opened in 1997 with a sunflower house, A–Z garden, weather station, root-view box, and a scarecrow. Check the schedule for special children's events in the Kids Corner Clubhouse. The Terrace Restaurant includes both a cafeteria and a sit-down dining room. Reservations are recommended for the dining room.

PHILLIPS MUSHROOM PLACE (ages 6 and up)

Route 1, 909 East Baltimore Pike, Kennett Square; (610) 388–6082. Open daily 10:00 A.M. to 6:00 P.M. Closed Christmas, New Year's Day, Easter, and Thanksgiving. Admission: adults, $1.25; seniors, 75 cents; children 7 to 12, 50 cents; children 6 and under, Free.

Kennett Square is called the Mushroom Capital of the World. More mushrooms are grown here than in any other area. One-half mile south of Longwood Gardens, Phillips Mushroom Place is a replica of a mushroom farm. The museum tells how the ancient Egyptians believed that the mushroom would make them immortal and how

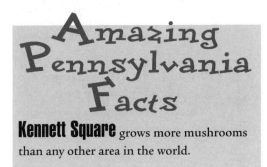

Amazing Pennsylvania Facts

Kennett Square grows more mushrooms than any other area in the world.

the Romans reserved mushrooms for the exclusive use of royalty. A variety of fresh and jarred mushrooms is available in the gift shop.

BRANDYWINE RIVER MUSEUM (ages 6 and up)

Route 1; (610) 388–2700; www.brandywinemuseum.org. Open daily 9:30 A.M. to 4:30 P.M. Admission is $5.00 for adults, $2.50 for senior citizens, students with ID, and children 6 to 12; Free *for children under 6.*

Andrew Wyeth came from a family of distinguished artists. The Brandywine River Museum, in a converted gristmill on Route 1 in Chadds Ford, has the world's largest collection of Andrew Wyeth's work, as well as that of his father, N. C. Wyeth, his son, Jamie Wyeth, and other family members.

Children especially go for Jamie Wyeth's painting *Portrait of Pig* and the life-sized animal sculptures along the riverbank. Many visitors will recognize the illustrations of N. C. Wyeth for such swashbuckling classics as *Treasure Island* and *Kidnapped*. Works by other artists from the

Brandywine region hang near still life paintings, landscapes, and an unparalleled collection of American illustration.

Surrounding the museum are stands of wildflowers, trees, and shrubs indigenous to the Greater Brandywine Valley. •

JOHN CHADS HOUSE (ages 8 and up)

Route 100; (610) 388–7376. Open during summer, Saturday and Sunday from noon to 5:00 P.M. Admission is $3.00 for adults, $1.00 for children. Combination ticket to both John Chads House and Barns-Brinton House is $5.00 for adults and $1.50 for children.

Often you can watch bread being baked in the beehive oven. On the weekend after Labor Day, the Chadds-Ford Historical Society, which administers both John Chads House and Barns-Brinton House, hosts the annual Chadds Ford Days. The event features pony rides, music, Brandywine Valley art, games, and crafts. People often come for the sausage sandwich.

CHADDS FORD VILLAGE (ages 6 and up)

Route 1; (610) 388–7361. **Free***.*

Chadds Ford Village is a charming place to browse in craft shops or to enjoy a meal at the Chadds Ford Inn, which has been serving travelers since 1736.

BARNS-BRINTON HOUSE (ages 8 and up)

Route 1; (610) 388–7376. Same hours and admission fees as the John Chads House.

At the Barns-Brinton House, guides in period costume demonstrate colonial crafts and give tours of this eighteenth-century home and tavern. Just past the herb garden, you'll find the Chaddsford Winery.

BRANDYWINE BATTLEFIELD (ages 8 and up)

Route 1; (610) 459–3342; libertynet.org/iha/brandywine. The battlefield park grounds are open, **Free***, year-round Tuesday through Saturday 9:00 A.M. to 5:00 P.M. and Sunday noon to 5:00 P.M. The Visitor Center is open Tuesday through Saturday 9:00 A.M. to 5:00 P.M. and Sunday noon to 5:00 P.M. Closed Monday. Admission for house tour only: adults, $3.50; youth (ages 1 to 16), $1.50; seniors and AAA members, $2.50. A family rate of $8.50 is available.*

After retreating at the Battle of Brandywine, George Washington's troops moved on to camp at Valley Forge. At the Brandywine Battlefield you can tour the house where Washington set up his headquarters. The Visitor Center offers an audiovisual introduction to the park, along with maps for a self-guided driving tour that includes twenty-eight historic points of interest. A reenactment of the battle is held every September. There is a museum shop, and picnic areas are available.

Elverson

 ### HOPEWELL FURNACE (ages 8 and up)
Located at 2 Mark Bird Lane; (610) 582–8773, TDD 582–2093; nps.gov/hofu/. Open daily 9:00 A.M. to 5:00 P.M., except Martin Luther King Jr. Day, Presidents Day, Veterans Day, Thanksgiving, Christmas, and New Year's Day. Entrance fee is $4.00 per person. For living-history events an additional fee of $1.00 per person is charged. Annual passes, family passes, and senior passes are available.

Watch a real blacksmith hammer a shape from white-hot iron. Visit a cast house where iron weapons were made for the Continental Army. Learn how colonists prepared food and clothing. Hopewell Furnace National Historic Site gives you a chance to see what life was like in a colonial iron-making town. As you take your self-guided walking tour, taped messages give you a first-hand feeling for the experiences of the people who lived and worked here. Although open year-round, the site is most active in summer, when authentically costumed artisans demonstrate their crafts. Mother's Day is sheep-shearing day. Generally, handicapped-accessible.

ALSO IN THE AREA
Nearby, **French Creek State Park** offers outdoor family adventures such as hiking, fishing, swimming, and camping, as well as winter sports. You may wish to have lunch or do some shopping in **Victorian St. Peter's Village.**

Chester Springs

Where nature brought forth yellow water with medicinal properties, man has brought forth *The Blob*. Some would say Chester Springs' attractions have run "from the sublime to the ridiculous."

HISTORIC YELLOW SPRINGS (ages 8 and up)

Art School Road; (610) 827–7414. Open for self-guided tours, Monday through Friday 9:00 A.M. to 4:00 P.M., weekends by reservation. Closed major holidays. A donation is suggested.

For centuries, starting with indigenous peoples and, later, colonial settlers, presidents, and entertainers, people have come to Yellow Springs in hopes of finding a cure for their illnesses. In 1722 there was a health spa here. From 1916 to 1952 the Pennsylvania Academy of Fine Arts ran a landscape school on these beautiful grounds. And later still, Valley Forge Films made movies here, including the 1958 Steve McQueen classic *The Blob* and *4-D Man*.

At present this site is operated as Historic Yellow Springs, Inc. Visitors may take a self-guided tour of the grounds and eighteenth- and nineteenth-century buildings, but it's most fun to come during a special event such as art shows, classes, and workshops or to attend annual events such as the Frolicks.

Valley Forge

 ### VALLEY FORGE NATIONAL HISTORIC PARK (all ages)

 Visitor Center at State Route 23 and North Gulph Road; (610) 783–1077; www.valleyforge.org. Park buildings are open daily except Christmas from 9:00 A.M. until 5:00 P.M. Admission is $2.00 for historic buildings only. Park grounds are open to the public **Free**.

The nice thing about Valley Forge National Historic Park is its mixture of history and outdoor fun.

After viewing the eighteen-minute introductory film and exhibits at the Visitor Center, you can get information about touring the park. The Visitor Center also displays various exhibits and artifacts that help you get more out of your visit.

There are so many different ways to enjoy Valley Forge that you can choose the one that's just right for your family. From April to October tour buses take a regular route, allowing visitors to get off when a particular site sparks their interest and then catch the next bus. A map allows families to take a self-guided driving tour accompanied by a narrated audiotape, if desired.

Six miles of trails are available for visitors who prefer to see the park by bike, on foot, or on horseback. There are fields perfect for kite flying and three different picnic areas. The first encampment site on the auto tour, just past the Visitor Center, has some great hills for sledding.

No matter how you go, your kids will not want to miss the re-created encampment where Washington's troops spent the winter of 1777–78. And it may be sexist to say so, but boys are especially inter-ested in the Artillery Park, reconstructed fortifications, and the Grand Parade Grounds, where the troops trained for battle. General Washing-ton set up his temporary headquarters in Isaac Potts' House (also known as Washington's Headquarters), now restored to look as it did during that famous winter. Costumed interpreters appear at the Muh-lenberg Brigade on Saturdays and Sundays from June through August, 10:00 A.M. to 4:00 P.M.

The **Washington Memorial Chapel,** on park grounds but privately operated, commemorates the Revolutionary War and the armed forces. Also privately operated, the **Valley Forge Historical Society Museum** on Route 23 (610-783-0535) exhibits a collection of Revolutionary War memorabilia.

The self-guided driving tour is open all year from 6:00 A.M. to 10:00 P.M. Accessibility for the disabled is available in most areas of the park by inquiring at the Visitor Center Information Desk. The park hosts special events on Washington's Birthday, the anniversary of the march into Valley Forge (December 19), and the anniversary of the march out (June 19).

ALSO IN THE AREA

For another kind of family adventure in the Valley Forge area, contact **United States Hot Air Balloon Company,** P.O. Box 490, Hopewell Road, St. Peters 10470; (800) 76-FLY US.

The nation's second largest shopping mall, the **Plaza and Court of King of Prussia,** is only minutes from Valley Forge Park, on Route 202.

Amazing Pennsylvania Facts

Valley Forge Battered by defeats throughout the fall of 1777, General George Washington and his troops retreated to Valley Forge for the win-ter. By February 1778 he had lost nearly half his men to death, disease, and desertion.

Audubon

Although John James Audubon lived at Mill Grove for only three years, it was his first home in America (he arrived here in 1804), and the perfect place to inspire his career as a painter of birds.

MILL GROVE (house, ages 6 and up; grounds, all ages)

Audubon and Pawlings Roads; (610) 666–5593. Open Tuesday through Saturday 10:00 A.M. to 4:00 P.M.; Sunday 1:00 P.M. to 4:00 P.M.; **Free**.

One hundred and seventy acres of greenery and 180 species of birds surround the house, built in 1762. This is a lovely spot to stroll in the woods or enjoy a peaceful view of Perkiomen Creek. Inside the home you may tour eleven rooms filled with Audubon's collection of paintings, stuffed birds, and birds' eggs. The museum also owns a complete set of Audubon's greatest work, *The Birds of America,* with each bird painted in actual size.

Paoli

What is it about the Philadelphia area that seems to breed unforgettable characters? Doylestown has Henry Mercer, Merion has Albert Barnes, and Paoli has Wharton Esherick.

WHARTON ESHERICK STUDIO (ages 8 and up)

Horseshoe Trail Road. For directions and reservations, call (610) 644–5822. Reservations are required for one-hour tours of Esherick's home and studio. Tours are available March through December, Saturday 10:00 A.M. to 5:00 P.M. and Sunday 1:00 to 5:00 P.M. Admission is $6.00 for adults, $3.00 for children under 12.

Wharton Esherick started out as a painter, but after moving in 1913 to a stone farmhouse near Paoli, he became fascinated with wood. The Wharton Esherick Studio reflects this fascination. Everywhere you look, you discover some whimsical wooden object: wooden sculptures, wooden picture frames, wooden furniture.

Esherick was also entranced by what is now called "found objects." The handrail of his astounding double-spiral staircase is a real mastodon tusk! The artist created chairs out of hammer handles or wagon wheels.

Phoenixville

WATER WORLD (all ages)

On Route 724 in Phoenixville; (610) 935–1290. Open May through September. Hours vary seasonally. Admission on weekdays is $6.25 per person, on weekends $6.75 per person, after 5:00 P.M. $4.00. Access to water slides is $5.00 for one slide, $9.00 for both. Monday and Friday are "Slide Days" with discounted prices.

Water World is a relaxing place to cool off on a sticky summer day, with two water slides, a rope swing, a large pool, and a wading pool for the little ones. There is a small snack bar and picnicking facilities.

Norristown

ELMWOOD PARK ZOO (all ages)

Harding Boulevard, in Elmwood Park; (610) 277–DUCK. Open daily 10:00 A.M. to 4:00 P.M. Admission: adults, $3.50; children 3 to 12, $2.00; seniors, $2.00. Pony rides $2.00.

Exciting things have been happening at Elmwood Park Zoo, always a favorite for younger children. Enter the aviary, and you are surrounded by a naturalistic wetland environment filled with waterfowl, beaver, and two fun-loving river otters. The murky bayou houses alligators, snakes, and snapping turtles. The bison and elk grasslands opened

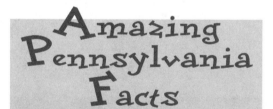

Amazing Pennsylvania Facts

William Penn Although he founded Pennsylvania, William Penn lived here for only a total of four years.

in 1997, and in 2000, the new bear exhibit will debut. In all there are more than 200 animals representing forty species including jaguars, cougars, timber wolves, and a peregrine falcon.

The youngest children still love feeding the ducks in the duck lake and petting the sheep and goats in the Petting Barn (open seasonally). There is also a snack shop, a gift shop, and pony rides. Handicapped-accessible, with diapering facilities in the rest rooms.

Media

Media is the home of Ridley Creek State Park, where you can see the Colonial Pennsylvania Plantation.

COLONIAL PENNSYLVANIA PLANTATION (ages 6 and up)

Located in Ridley Creek State Park; (610) 566–1725. Open weekends, April to November, 10:00 A.M. to 5:00 P.M. Usually closed for rain.

On an eighteenth-century farm, animals were left to graze freely, not penned up as they are today. In the root cellar the farmer's family stored carrots, onions, and potatoes; in the springhouse, flowing water cooled milk and eggs. The clothing was made by hand, spun of natural fibers. All these details are meticulously re-created at Colonial Pennsylvania Plantation.

This is actually a working farm where 120 acres of crops are grown, using methods that date back more than 200 years. Here you can observe the staff demonstrating cooking, spinning, weaving, sheep shearing, planting, and harvesting. Even the clothing worn by inter-preters is authentic—right down to the fibers. School groups get a chance to dip candles or cut firewood in the authentic manner.

Also in the park, the adjacent Tyler Arboretum has an extensive col-lection of native and non-native plants. Highlights include a giant sequoia with a circumference of 9 feet and a unique fragrant garden designed specifically for the visually impaired. The arboretum is open daily at no charge, 8:00 A.M. until dusk. Call (610) 566–5431.

Swarthmore

SCOTT ARBORETUM (all ages)

Swarthmore College campus; (610) 328–8025. Open daily from dawn to dusk; Free.

One hundred and ten acres surrounding Swarthmore College consti-tute the college's Scott Arboretum. Come here for a quiet stroll through collections of flowering cherries, roses, conifers, daffodils, dogwoods, lilacs, hollies, rhododendrons, and more. Specialty gardens include the Theresa Long Garden of Fragrance, the Dean Bond Rose Garden, and the Winter Garden, which provides longed-for colors in the gray of winter.

Merion

THE BARNES FOUNDATION (ages 8 and up)

300 North Latches Lane; (610) 667–0290. Open Thursday 12:30 to 5:00 P.M., Friday 9:30 A.M. to 5:00 P.M., Saturday 9:30 A.M. to 5:00 P.M., and Sunday 12:30 to 5:00 P.M. Admission: $5.00 per person. Audio tour fee: $5.00 per person. Admission is by reservation only.

The art lovers in our family have always been awe-struck by the paintings at the Barnes Foundation, one of the nation's most amazing private collections of Impressionist and Post-Impressionist art. This collection remained one of the art world's best-kept secrets until a recent national tour took many of its masterpieces to several major museums.

The Barnes Foundation has undergone some changes lately, including a complete restoration, the addition of a gallery shop, and new audio tours. If you use the audio tour and take time to talk about the art with your children, this can be a wonderful learning experience.

Dr. Albert C. Barnes was a businessman by vocation, but art was his great love, and he held very definite opinions about it. He collected more than 180 Renoirs, seventy Cézannes, and many Matisses, including a mural specifically commissioned for his home. His walls are cluttered with the works of Manet, Van Gogh, Picasso, and Seurat hanging beside those of Titian and El Greco, interspersed with wrought-iron hinges and latches, African masks, and antiques. Every piece has its place, and Dr. Barnes chose that place for a reason.

Handicapped-accessible, with diapering facilities in the ladies' bathroom. The Barnes is within fifteen minutes of Suburban Square, Ardmore, for shopping or a bite to eat at Ruby's Diner.

Amazing Pennsylvania Facts

Henri Matisse In 1930 Dr. Albert Barnes commissioned the artist Henri Matisse to paint a mural for the Barnes Foundation in Merion. The wall space, however, was measured incorrectly, so when the mural arrived from France, it was 5 feet too short! Although he had spent more than a year on the first version, Matisse started all over again. The second version now decorates three arches above the main gallery in the Barnes Foundation.

Glenside

KESWICK THEATER (ages 6 and up)

Easton Road and Keswick Avenue; (215) 572–7650.

The Keswick Theater offers concerts, plays, and other productions year-round. Ticket prices vary.

Fort Washington

CHILDVENTURE MUSEUM (ages 2 to 10)

Fort Washington Office Campus, at 430 Virginia Drive; (215) 643–9906. Open Tuesday through Saturday 10:00 A.M. to 4:00 P.M., Sunday noon to 4:00 P.M. Closed Monday. Admission: $4.00 per person; infants who don't walk yet enter Free.

There are no "no-no's" at the Childventure Museum, a hands-on, imaginative learning environment aimed at kids 10 and under. This is a place for you to interact with your child. When Faith's two older kids were preschoolers, they loved playing on the safe, indoor climbing structures and trying on dress-up costumes in the Storybook Room, where everything is scaled down to fit younger children. Kids still flock to the Fairy Tale Theater, the "pretend" Main Street, and international music room.

Churchville

CHURCHVILLE NATURE CENTER (ages 6 and up)

501 Churchville Lane; (215) 357–4005. The Nature Center is open Tuesday through Sunday 9:00 A.M. to 5:00 P.M. The grounds are open dawn to dusk. Admission is Free.

Trails at the Churchville Nature Center are open from sunup to sundown daily. Inside the Nature Center you can view dioramas depicting local wildlife. There are also children's programs, such as nature crafts, junior naturalist hikes, and activities centered on the Lenape Native Americans.

Langhorne

 SESAME PLACE (all ages)

100 Sesame Road, Route 1 to Oxford Valley exit; (215) 752–7070; www. sesameplace.com. Operating days and hours vary, with the park opening in May for weekends only; starting in mid-May daily 10:00 A.M. to 5:00 P.M.; staying open later after Memorial Day and returning to weekend-only hours after Labor Day until mid-October, when it closes for the season. Regular admission (ages 3 to 54) costs $27.95. Discounts are available for families of four or more or during late-afternoon hours.

Just about any kid will have fun at Sesame Place. We've found that even kids too grown up for Cookie Monster can't help but enjoy many of the water rides and physical play environments. In 1998, Sesame Place introduced its first roller coaster, Vapor Trail, which is also the first mechanical ride at Sesame Place.

You can walk down Sesame Street, a full-sized replica of the thoroughfare seen on the popular TV show, and take pictures of your kids in front of Bert and Ernie's house. You'll love the Rock Around the Block parade and all the shows starring *Sesame Street* characters. There are

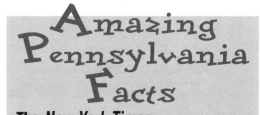

Amazing Pennsylvania Facts

The *New York Times* recently included Sesame Place on its list of best water parks in the United States.

more than fifty kid-powered physical play elements, such as Nets and Climbs and Ernie's Bed Bounce.

The *New York Times* recently included Sesame Place on its list of best water parks in the United States. The park has fifteen water attractions, and most will appeal to all members of your family. Big Bird's Rambling River is a winding, relaxing circular tube ride your kids can go around and around all afternoon. Even very young children have no fear on Teeny Tiny Tidal Waves and the Rubber Duckie Lake. Sky Splash is filled with giant-sized water adventures including an 8-foot-tall rubber duckie and huge tinker toys that spray water.

Sesame Place is located in Langhorne about thirty minutes from Philadelphia at Exit 29A on I-95 North. Most areas are accessible to the disabled, and special events include some designed for disabled children. Bathing suits are required for all water attractions.

A Paulsen Family Adventure In the summer of 1994, we visited Sesame Place and decided to go on "Big Bird's Rambling River." We climbed into our tubes, my younger son, Seth, with me and my older son, Judah, on his own. But, I forgot to take off Judah's glasses.

Being a kid, Judah paddled straight for the nearest jet of water, got doused and lost his glasses ten seconds into the ride. We had not brought his spares.

We reported the loss at the Guest Services office, but we didn't hold out much hope of finding them. We were told that it took around thirty minutes for the water to circulate through the system and all drains were checked periodically. We checked back at the desk a little later and, sure enough, there were Judah's glasses.

Morrisville

PENNSBURY MANOR (ages 8 and up)

400 Pennsbury Memorial Road; (215) 946–0400. Open Tuesday through Saturday 9:00 A.M. to 5:00 P.M. and Sunday from noon to 5:00 P.M. Last tour begins 3:30 P.M.

Pennsylvania was William Penn's "holy experiment," a colony founded on Quaker moral principles. Although he only lived here for a total of about four years, Pennsbury Manor was never far from his thoughts. Today his home has been restored, complete with icehouse, stable, smokehouse, garden, and livestock. The boathouse contains a replica of the vessel Penn used to commute to Philadelphia. The oven in the bake-and-brew house can bake up to thirty loaves of bread at a time.

On Sunday afternoons from April to October, Pennsbury Manor offers living history just for families. It has an activity room and a worker's cottage where kids can try seventeenth-century skills, such as writing with a quill pen. Geese, peacocks, sheep, and Red Devon cattle—authentic breeds wherever possible—populate the farm.

ALSO IN THE AREA

When William Penn was living at Pennsbury Manor, he attended Quaker Meeting at Falls Meeting in Fallsington, a town built around its meetinghouses. Guided tours start at the Gillingham Store and include several restored historic buildings: Moon-Williamson House; Burges-Lippincott House; and the Stage Coach Tavern. Fallsington is located on Route 13 off I-95. For details contact Historic Fallsington, Inc. at (215) 295-6567.

Washington Crossing

We picture "Washington's crossing" as in the famous painting by Emanuel Leutz, with George Washington standing heroically in the small boat as his troops row across the Delaware to surprise the Hessians on Christmas Day. The German artist had never seen Washington's Crossing when he painted it in the nineteenth century. It may not be safe to stand up in a small boat, but the image depicts an artist's impression of a historic event. In the Memorial Building at Washington Crossing Historic Park, you can see a copy of the painting (the original is owned by the Washington's Crossing Foundation). It's larger than life in more ways than one—the painting is 20 feet long, 12 feet tall.

WASHINGTON CROSSING NATIONAL HISTORIC PARK (ages 8 and up)

State Routes 32 and 532, 3 miles north of I-95 exit 31; (215) 493-4076; www.spiritof76.com. The Visitor Center and historic buildings are open Monday through Saturday 9:00 A.M. to 5:00 P.M. and on Sunday from noon to 5:00 P.M. There is a fee for the buildings ($4.00 for adults, $3.50 for seniors and AAA members, $2.00 for children 6 to 12). The park grounds, however, are open at no charge from 8:00 A.M. until sunset. Free.

A thirty-minute film at the Visitor Center describes the events of December 25, 1776, which led to the turning point of the Revolution. Washington planned his surprise attack from his headquarters in the Thompson-Neely House, and he ate dinner before the crossing at the Old Ferry Inn. In the Durham Boat House, you can see the boats that were actually used for the crossing.

Every year on Christmas Day the park hosts a reenactment of Washington's crossing. Other special events here include Gingerbread Days, Tavern Nights, and special activities in honor of Washington's birthday. Gazebo Games, another special event, lets kids try out the games and toys enjoyed by eighteenth-century children.

BOWMAN'S HILL TOWER and **BOWMAN'S HILL WILDFLOWER PRESERVE (all ages)**

Located on the grounds of Washington Crossing Historic Park; (215) 862–2924 or 862–3166. Open from 8:00 A.M. until sunset; Free.

During the Revolution sentries were posted in Bowman's Hill Tower, which has now been restored. Surrounding the tower you'll see breathtaking varieties of wildflowers. You can pick up a self-guided tour map that also includes a list of flowers currently in bloom.

New Hope

In summer the streets of New Hope bustle with people drawn to the more than 200 art galleries, craft shops, restaurants, and history this town offers. But New Hope welcomes visitors any time of the year. You can get more information about bed and breakfasts in New Hope by contacting the New Hope Information Center, 1 West Mechanic Street, New Hope 18938 (215-862-5880) or Village of New Hope, Greater New Hope Chamber of Commerce, P.O. Box 633, New Hope 18938 (215-862-3730).

 CORYELL'S FERRY HISTORIC BOAT RIDES (all ages)

Ferries leave Coryell's Ferry at Gerenser's Exotic Ice Cream, 22 South Main Street (215–862–2050; www.spiritof76.com) April through October starting at 11:00 A.M.

Artists began settling in New Hope in the late 1800s, but the town started out as Coryell's Ferry, which started carrying passengers across the Delaware in canoes in 1733. Ferries still operate here for half-hour tours; only now they use more commodious paddleboats. The longest ride on the river, aboard a 65-foot Mississippi riverboat, leaves at 11:00 A.M. daily, in season. Call for details or to find out about special kids' days on the ferry.

 COLONIAL NEW HOPE WALKING TOURS (ages 6 and up)

Gerenser's Exotic Ice Cream, 22 South Main Street; (215) 862–2050; www. spiritof76.com. Tours of New Hope are available April through October, starting at noon.

General Washington visited New Hope at least four times. To learn more about the history of this town, you can take a walking tour. Tickets and schedules for walking tours of New Hope are available here.

NEW HOPE MULE BARGES (all ages)

New Street; (215) 862–2842 or (800) 59–BARGE. Open from April through November. Boat fares on weekends are $5.00 for adults, $3.00 for children. On weekdays, fares are $5.00 for adults, $4.00 for seniors, $2.00 for children.

You can take a ride on a mule barge, sailing past eighteenth-century homes, gardens, and workshops. Many barges are equipped with folk singers or historians. The Delaware Canal became operational in 1840, and, at its height, mules hauled thousands of barges, carrying loads of coal and limestone. The canal includes twenty-five lift locks, nine aqueducts, and 106 bridges.

BOAT RIDES AT WELLS FERRY (all ages)

At the end of Ferry Street on River; (215) 862–5965. Open May through October 11:00 A.M. to 6:00 P.M. Admission: adults $6.00, children $4.00, seniors $5.00.

The *Star of New Hope* carries thirty-six passengers at a time on a guided tour. Tour guides offer a little history, as well as a glimpse at New Hope's varied architecture. Some tour guides play guitar music as well.

NEW HOPE AND IVYLAND RAILROAD (all ages)

Station at Bridge and Stockton Streets; (215) 862–2332. Trains run daily from April to November, weekends only from January until March. In December, special Santa Claus rides are offered. Tickets are $9.50 for adults, $8.50 for seniors, $5.50 for kids 3 to 11, and $1.50 for children under 3. The train operates seasonally.

The New Hope and Ivyland Railroad, built in 1889, eventually made the canal obsolete. If you take this train on its 45-minute narrated trip to Lahaska, you will notice a curved trestle bridge. If this bridge looks like something right out of *The Perils of Pauline,* that's because this actually was the bridge that was used in those movies.

ALSO IN THE AREA

The **Bucks County Playhouse** offers a series of plays for children on Fridays and Saturdays, at reasonable prices. Call (215) 862-2041 for a schedule, or check the website at buckscountyplayhouse.com.

If you wish to take any kind of ride or tour, including walking tours, check at **Gerenser's Exotic Ice Cream** at 22 South Main Street, where tickets and schedules are available. You can purchase tickets for a **colonial walking tour** (215-862-2050). This is also where you get tickets for **Coryell's Ferry** (see page 56). Have some ice cream while you're here! To find out about **Ghost**

Tours, call (215) 357-5637 or (215) 957-9988. You can also find out about different tours and boat rides by checking out the website at bctc.org/. We especially enjoy just strolling along the canal, watching the barges go by. Some of the restaurants here have views of the canal.

Lahaska

Sad to say, the wonderful Carousel World is no longer open. However, Peddler's Village outside New Hope on Routes 202 and 263, does have an antique Grand Carousel and is planning to open a new kid fun center soon. While in Peddler's Village, take a look at some of the unusual shops and restaurants.

Point Pleasant

The signers of the Declaration of Independence had to sweat it out in the notorious Philadelphia humidity, but you don't have to. Point Pleasant, north of Lahaska and New Hope, offers some great ways to cool off in its inviting, kid-friendly rapids. Several outfitters rent canoes, tubes, and rafts from April through October. To make reservations (which are required) or to find out about prices and special Pedal and Paddle trips, call Bucks County River Country (215-297-5000).

 BUCKS COUNTY RIVER COUNTRY (ages 6 and up)
Route 32, Upper Black Eddy; (215) 297–5000. Call for days, hours, prices, and river conditions.

Our kids spent a carefree summer afternoon riding the current in tubes, occasionally dunking each other or taking time to see how deep the water was (not very). To protect your feet, remember to wear old sneakers that can get wet, and don't forget the sunscreen. Bucks County River Country also presents other events in the woods, such as the nation's largest haunted-woods hayride.

Doylestown

A wonderful choice for a day-trip, Doylestown will charm you with its cast-iron lampposts, neat nineteenth-century houses, and unusual shops and galleries. You can walk to the Mercer Museum and James A. Michener Museum. Also within walking distance is the County Theater, showing art and vintage, as well as first-run, movies; the picturesque Doylestown Inn; as well as many other restaurants and shops. A short drive out of town, you may also wish to visit Fonthill and the Moravian Pottery and Tileworks. For information about Historic Doylestown, call (215) 345-0788.

MERCER MUSEUM (ages 6 and up)

84 South Pine Street, near Ashland; (215) 345–0210. Open Monday through Saturday 10:00 A.M. to 5:00 P.M., Sunday noon to 5:00 P.M. On Tuesdays, the museum closes at 9:00 P.M. Closed New Year's Day, Thanksgiving, and Christmas. Admission is $5.00 for adults, $4.50 for seniors, $1.50 for youth ages 6 to 17, children under 6 enter Free.

On Pine Street in the charming town of Doylestown, stands what can only be described as a castle, not of stone but of poured concrete, brainchild of Henry Chapman Mercer (1856-1930).

In 1916 Mercer built what is now the Mercer Museum, with its turrets and parapets, to house his collection of more than 50,000 artifacts and tools of more than sixty different American trades. Entering the central court of the museum, you find yourself surrounded by odds and ends hanging over your head: a Conestoga wagon; a whaling skiff; wooden buckets. Then, take the elevator up to the top floor and walk down, working your way through the implements left behind by shoemakers, bakers, candlemakers, milliners, and farmers of America's past.

Our kids felt that the highlight of the collection was the vampire-killing kit. They also enjoyed hunting for the footprints left in the concrete by Mercer's pet dog. The museum is unheated, so bring a sweater. There are special children's programs, as well as FolkFest in May.

Our Tubing Trip —*by Seth Paulsen-Sacks, at age 10*

We had to wait in a line and tell the people how much we weighed. Then they gave us the inner tubes. All the kids in my group tied their tubes together with a camp counselor. The current was strong. We had to paddle so the current wouldn't pull us away. Luke and Paul fell off their tubes so the counselor got off, held onto our tubes, and waited for them to get back on. When we were waiting, it felt like we were still moving because of the current.

We saw a hot dog guy on a motorboat with big balloons on a string. You could buy hot dogs from him if you had money.

When we got back we found little frogs the size of ants and I caught three.

JAMES A. MICHENER MUSEUM (all ages)

138 South Pine Street; (215) 340–9800. Open Tuesday through Friday 10:00 A.M. to 4:30 P.M., Saturday and Sunday 10:00 A.M. to 5:00 P.M. Open until 9:00 P.M. on Wednesdays. Admission is $5.00 for adults, $4.50 for seniors, $1.50 for students; children under 12 are Free.

Across the street from the Mercer Museum, the James A. Michener Museum has recently opened the Mari Sabusawa Michener Wing, named for James Michener's wife. The novelist James Michener was born and raised in Doylestown and was closely involved with the museum from its inception until his death in 1997. The museum, which was recently profiled in the *New York Times,* focuses on Bucks County artists, authors, and playwrights. Bucks County's fertile soil has nourished Broadway luminaries like George S. Kaufman, Moss Hart, Oscar Hammerstein II, writers like Michener and Pearl S. Buck, and artists such as George Nakashima and Edward Hicks.

All ages love the interactive exhibits in the new wing, including puzzles and Discovery Boxes. A small theater shows clips from movies associated with Bucks County. For example, did you know the author of the Lassie books was from Bucks County? Kids are allowed to hug and pet the outdoor sculpture of Lassie.

MORAVIAN POTTERY AND TILE WORKS (ages 8 and up)

East Court Street; (215) 345–6722. Open daily except major holidays, 10:00 A.M. to 4:45 P.M. Self-guided tours leave every thirty minutes, with the last tour departing at 4:00 P.M. Admission is $3.00 for adults, $2.50 for seniors, $1.50 for youth ages 7 to 17. The tile shop, open daily 10:00 A.M. to 4:45 P.M., can be entered without admission.

The Moravian Pottery and Tile Works is the legacy of Mercer's effort to preserve an American craft. You can purchase Moravian tiles here, or take a tour to see how the tiles are made.

FONTHILL (ages 8 and up)

East Court Street and Route 313; (215) 348–9461. Open Monday through Saturday 10:00 A.M. to 5:00 P.M. and Sunday noon to 5:00 P.M. Reservations are required. Admission for adults is $5.00, seniors $4.50, youth 6 to 17 $1.50. Children under 6 are Free.

Mercer's home, Fonthill, has forty-four rooms, eighteen fireplaces, and thirty-two staircases. Tours have recently been revamped to capture the interests of children. Be sure to check it out.

ALSO IN THE AREA

Gardeners get a breath of fresh air at **Henry Schmieder Arboretum of Delaware Valley College** (on Route 202; 215-345-1500) and the nearby **Inn at Fordhook Farm** (a bed and breakfast; call 215-345-1766). The Burpee family (of Burpee Seeds) developed many well-known seed varieties in this area.

Another fun idea: Try ballooning. For information, call Color the Sky, Inc. at (215) 340-9966.

Chalfont

 BYERS' CHOICE LTD. (ages 6 and up)

4355 County Line Road; (215) 822–6700. The factory is open at no charge Monday through Saturday, 10:00 A.M. to 4:00 P.M. Understandably, it is closed January (to recover) and major holidays.

At Byers' Choice Ltd. the Byers family and their employees hand-sculpt thousands of delightful Caroler figurines every year, giving a percentage of their profits to charity. They invite visitors to watch the delicate faces molded and painted and to tour their gallery of little carolers in various costumes and settings. Children's eyes grow wide when they see these tiny landscapes filled with doll-like figures, each one unique, each one singing a Christmas carol. There is also a gift shop and a short movie about the history of the company.

ALSO IN THE AREA

Ballooning adventures are available in Pipersville by contacting **Keystone State Balloon Tours, Inc.,** P.O. Box 162, Pipersville 18947; (610) 294-8034.

At **Malmark, Inc. Bellcraftsmen** (Bell Crest Park, Route 611, in Plumsteadville), the world's largest manufacturer of tuned handbells offers tours of their factory by appointment only. Call (215) 766-7200 for an appointment.

Amazing Pennsylvania Facts

Bucks County's fertile soil has nourished Broadway luminaries like George S. Kaufman, Moss Hart, Oscar Hammerstein II; writers like James Michener and Pearl S. Buck; and artists such as George Nakashima and Edward Hicks.

Hilltown

 GREEN HILLS FARM (PEARL BUCK HOUSE) (ages 10 and up)
520 Dublin Road, 1 mile southwest of Route 313; (215) 249–0100 or (800) 220–BUCK. Guided tours are available March through December, Tuesday through Saturday, at 10:30 A.M., 1:30 P.M., and 2:30 P.M. On Sunday, tours leave at 1:30 P.M. and 2:30 P.M. only. Admission is $5.00 for adults, $4.00 for seniors and students, $\mathbf{Free}$ *for children under 6.*

Perhaps you or your kids have read *The Good Earth* or other books by Pearl S. Buck. The author settled in the 1835 farmhouse at Green Hills Farm. In her office here she wrote more than one hundred novels. Buck is admired not only for her writing but for her work to help Amerasian children through the Pearl S. Buck Foundation, which still has offices at the farm. The home is filled with Chinese art, including a 500-year-old Buddha and a wall hanging that was a gift from the Dalai Lama.

Worcester

 PETER WENTZ FARMSTEAD (ages 6 and up)
Off Route 73 at Scheare Road; (610) 584–5104. Open year-round Tuesday to Saturday 10 A.M. to 4:00 P.M. and Sunday 1:00 to 4:00 P.M.; closed Monday, Thanksgiving, and Christmas. Donations are accepted.

The historians at Peter Wentz Farmstead have done an exceptional job researching and restoring this farm to its appearance in 1777.

If you thought colonial farms were painted in subdued tones, you'll be amazed at the paint colors and wild patterns on the walls: dots, zig-zags, stripes, and more.

Come on a Saturday afternoon and you can watch staff members demonstrate colonial crafts using authentic techniques. You can watch spinning, weaving, candle making, and cooking, as well as unusual arts such as *scherenschnitte,* the German art of paper cutting. The kids especially like the farm animals.

ALSO IN THE AREA

Only a few blocks away, on Weikel Road, you can see the **Morgan Log House,** built in 1695 and more than 90 percent intact. The Morgans, who lived here, had ten children, one of whom grew up to become the mother of Daniel

Boone. Open April to November weekends only, noon to 5:00 P.M., or by appointment. Call (610) 368–2480.

Skippack

Come to Skippack Village to shop in the country-style crafts shops and boutiques. The Village attracts many visitors around the holidays when you can walk the streets by the light of luminaria.

ALSO IN THE AREA

In Centre Point near Skippack, on Route 73, you can visit the **Ironmaster's House.** The hours vary, so call ahead to make sure they're open (610–584–4441). You can visit an actual iron shop where the ironmaster creates lamps, toys, and other objects. The museum portion is no longer open.

Schwenksville

 ### PENNYPACKER MILLS (ages 8 and up)
Route 73 and Haldeman Road; (610) 287–9349. Open Free *of charge Tuesday through Saturday 10:00 A.M. to 4:00 P.M. and on Sunday from 1:00 to 4:00 P.M. Last daily tour begins at 3:30 P.M. It is closed Monday and major holidays.*

Seven miles down Skippack Pike (Route 73) from the Peter Wentz Farmstead, you can see an excellent example of Colonial Revival architecture. Pennypacker Mills was owned by the Pennypacker family as early as 1747. In 1900 Samuel W. Pennypacker purchased it and added onto the home, making a turn-of-the-century mansion. The mansion retains original furnishings. Pennypacker was governor of Pennsylvania from 1903 to 1907, as well as a respected historian, collector, and farmer. The home is surrounded by fifteen acres of gardens landscaped in the English "natural" style. At present the site is preserved by Montgomery County as a turn-of-the-century country gentleman's estate.

Pennypacker Mills hosts special events for children, including a Halloween celebration with horse-drawn hay rides. Special children's events re-create the neighborhood parties once held by the Pennypacker daughters. There are also living-history events including a Civil War re-enactment and Christmas holiday celebrations. Call for details about these events and others for adults, families, and young children.

ALSO IN THE AREA

The **Philadelphia Folk Festival,** soon to celebrate its fortieth birthday, is one of the oldest and best folk festivals in the country. The Folk Festival brings music, crafts, dancing, and thousands of people to Old Pool farm in Schwenksville every August. New in 1999, it is a smoke-free event. For information, call (800) 556-FOLK or check out the website at www.folkfest.org.

Alburtis

The anthracite iron industry played an important role in the development of this area, beginning in 1839.

 LOCK RIDGE FURNACE MUSEUM (ages 6 and up)
Franklin Street; (610) 435–4664. Open May through September, weekends 1:00 to 4:00 P.M. Admission is Free.

Lock Ridge Furnace operated as a furnace until 1914 and is now one of the sites administered by the Lehigh County Historical Society.

Breinigsville

 TERRY HILL WATERPARK (all ages)
On Route 222 in Breinigsville; (610) 395–0222. Open noon to 6:00 P.M. daily beginning in June. In July and August, open to 7:00 P.M. weekdays and noon to 8:00 P.M. weekends. Admission is $12.50 for persons under 48 inches tall and $15.00 for all others.

Terry Hill Waterpark has three pools, nine water slides, a kiddie area, refreshments, and more. Call for details.

Allentown

On the waterfront in Allentown, long-quiet historic transportation and industrial buildings are being transformed into Lehigh Landing. The eleven-acre project will eventually include a vistor center for the region, playground, baseball field, riverfront walk, and more. Slated for opening in 2001, America on Wheels calls itself "a museum of over-the-road transportation." Exhibits will teach about carriages, bicycles, automobiles, and visions of the future. An exhibit of Mack trucks is expected to be a highlight.

Lehigh Landing will be located immediately north of the Hamilton Street Bridge, a short walk east of downtown Allentown. Keep up-to-date on new developments by checking the Web site at www.americaonwheels.org.

MUSEUM OF INDIAN CULTURE AND LENNI LENAPE HISTORICAL SOCIETY (ages 5 and up)

2825 Fish Hatchery Road; (610) 797–2121. Open Tuesday through Sunday noon to 3:00 P.M. Admission is $2.00; students and seniors $1.50; special group rates are available. Wheelchair-accessible.

As the saying goes, you can't understand another person until you've walked a mile in his moccasins. The Museum of Indian Culture and Lenni Lenape Historical Society gives kids just this kind of opportunity. Children will enjoy the many hands-on exhibits that illuminate Native American culture, as well as the exhibits of tools, baskets, and crafts. Three ceremonies are held annually: Corn Planting in May; Roasting Ears of Corn in August; and Time of Thanksgiving in October. There are also picnic facilities, two nature trails, and a fish hatchery.

ALLENTOWN ART MUSEUM (ages 5 and up)

Fifth and Court Streets; (610) 432–4333. The museum is open Tuesday through Saturday 11:00 A.M. to 5:00 P.M. and Sundays noon until 5:00 P.M. Admission is $3.50 for adults, $3.00 for seniors, $2.00 for students, and **Free** *for kids under 12. Admission is also* **Free** *on Sunday if you enter between noon and 1:00 P.M.*

The Max Hess Junior Gallery at the Allentown Art Museum offers hands-on art activities and touchable sculpture for children. The museum also shows family-oriented films.

HAINES MILL (ages 8 and up)

3600 Haines Mill Road; (610) 435–4664. Open weekends from May until September, 1:00 to 4:00 P.M. Admission is **Free***.*

The mill was built in 1760 and operated until 1956, after having been renovated in 1909 with a water-turbine power source.

LEHIGH COUNTY HISTORICAL MUSEUM (ages 10 and up)

Fifth and Hamilton Streets; (610) 435–4664. The museum and library are open 10:00 A.M. to 4:00 P.M. Monday through Saturday. The museum is also open Sunday 1:00 to 4:00 P.M. Admission is **Free***.*

Housed in Allentown's Old Courthouse, the Lehigh County Historical Museum displays artifacts from the earliest inhabitants of the Lehigh Valley, the Lenni Lenape, as well as from the Pennsylvania Germans and other settlers who came to this area. The museum also includes the Scott Andrew Trexler II Memorial Library, an extensive collection of county and genealogical records.

 LIBERTY BELL SHRINE (ages 8 and up)
Zion Church at 622 Hamilton Mall; (610) 435–4232. Open Monday through Saturday noon to 4:00 P.M. and on Sunday from 2:00 to 4:00 P.M. Admission is Free.

Did you know that during the Revolutionary War, when the British occupied Philadelphia, all the bells in the city were removed so that the British would not be able to melt them down for ammunition? From September 1777 to June 1778, the Liberty Bell was hidden under the floor of Allentown's Zion Church at 622 Hamilton Mall, 1 block away from the Lehigh County Historical Museum. At present the Liberty Bell Shrine includes an exact replica of the famous bell, as well as flags, maps, weapons, uniforms, and a 46-foot mural showing scenes from the Revolution.

Amazing Pennsylvania Facts

Liberty Bell During the Revolutionary War, when the British occupied Philadelphia, all the bells in the city were removed so that the British would not be able to melt them down for ammunition. So from September 1777 to June 1778, the Liberty Bell was hidden under the floor of Allentown's Zion Church.

 DORNEY PARK and WILDWATER KINGDOM (all ages)
Near Exit 16 on Route 309 South, at 3700 Hamilton Boulevard. For more information call (610) 395–3724. Hours for both parks vary according to season. Dorney Park is open weekends only in May and September, then daily from Memorial Day to Labor Day. Wildwater Kingdom is open mid-May to Labor Day and

selected weekends in September. At the height of the season, tickets cost $29.50 for anyone 48 inches or taller, $6.00 for anyone under 47 inches and seniors, and are **Free** *for children under 3. These prices include admission to both parks. There is a $5.00 parking fee.*

Dorney Park's latest attraction is "Dominator," a three-story tower structure featuring two rides. One tower blasts riders 16 stories into the air before it unceremoniously drops them. The other tower lifts riders slowly up 175 feet, then sends them downward at "faster-than-free-fall" speed.

In spring of 1997, Steel Force, the tallest, longest, and fastest steel roller coaster on the East Coast, made its debut at Dorney Park. Willing passengers (some would call them victims) lined up to be lifted up 200 feet in the air, hurled 205 feet to the ground, then raced through a 120-foot tunnel and up a hill 161 feet high, all before speeding through a maze of twists, turns, camelbacks, and a second tunnel.

Dorney Park also has three other world-class roller coasters, and Wildwater Kingdom has eleven water slides. Younger children will love meeting the Berenstain Bears, playing in the TotSpot, and cooling off in two water park areas specifically for small fry. Our kids could have spent the whole day in the giant wave pool.

ALSO IN THE AREA

The Lehigh County Historical Society administers a number of sites, including several historic homes. **Trout Hall** (414 Walnut Street; 610–435–4664) is Allentown's oldest home, built in 1770 by the son of the city's founder, William Allen. The **Troxell-Steckel House** in nearby Egypt (4229 Reliance Street; 610–435–4664) is an excellent example of a rural German-style farmhouse. Its barn contains a collection of old buggies and wagons. Trout Hall is open April through November, Tuesday through Saturday, noon to 3:00 P.M. and on Sunday from 1:00 to 4:00 P.M. The Troxell-Steckel House is open weekends only 1:00 to 4:00 P.M.

Frank Buchman, founder of the world-wide Moral Rearmament Movement, who was nominated for two Nobel prizes, lived at 117 North Eleventh Street in Allentown. The **Frank Buchman House** displays some of Buchman's souvenirs from an extraordinary life. The house is open for tours weekends only 1:00 to 4:00 P.M.

Schnecksville

GAME PRESERVE (all ages)

5150 Game Preserve Road; (610) 799–4171; www.gamepreserve.org. Open April through October, 10:00 A.M. to 5:00 P.M., last admission at 4:00 P.M. Admission: adults 13 to 64, $5.00; seniors 65 and older and children 2 to 12, $3.00

The Game Preserve, formerly known as the Trexler-Lehigh County Game Preserve, is actually a zoo featuring a wide variety of wildlife in naturalistic habitats. There's a butterfly garden, pony rides, animal contact area, a new birds of prey exhibit, and the zoo's newest residents: Arctic wolves. Stay tuned for exciting renovations in upcoming years.

Claussville

CLAUSSVILLE ONE-ROOM SCHOOLHOUSE (ages 6 and up)

Route 100; (610) 435–4664. From May through September, open on weekends 1:00 to 4:00 P.M. Admission is Free.

Children can picture what school must have been like in the Claussville One-Room Schoolhouse, in which children learned from 1893 until 1956. They can imagine kids sitting at these very desks, reading the very books displayed there. The schoolhouse is one of the Lehigh County Historical Society sites.

Hellertown

If your kids are fascinated by crystal formations, rocks, minerals, and stalagmites and stalactites, don't miss Lost River Caverns, located in Hellertown.

LOST RIVER CAVERNS (ages 6 and up)

726 Durham Street, south of Bethlehem on Route 412, off I–78 Exit 21; (610) 838–8767; fax (610) 838–2961. Open all year. From Memorial Day to Labor Day, open 9:00 A.M. to 6:00 P.M.; the rest of the year, 9:00 A.M. to 5:00 P.M. Closed major holidays.

Take an underground tour of a natural limestone cavern with crystal formations and a crystal chapel. There is also a museum, gift shop, and picnic grove.

Bethlehem

The Star of Bethlehem shines on Star Mountain every night of the year, watching over this city founded by Moravian settlers and named "Bethlehem" on Christmas Eve, 1741. You may wish to visit during Christkindlmarkt, in December, when lanterns are lit, or in August, when Musikfest is held. But no matter when you visit, start out at the Visitor Center, where you can see a film and multimedia presentation about the city. You can pick up a schedule of events and walking-tour map, or you can schedule a guided tour. The Visitor Center is in the Historic Area, off Route 378, at 52 West Broad Street. Call (610) 868-1513, 867-0173, or (800) 360-8687.

 ### GEMEIN HAUS (ages 8 and up)

66 West Church Street; (610) 867–0450. Open Tuesday through Saturday, 1:00 to 4:00 P.M. Closed in January. Free *admission.*

A log cabin five stories tall, built entirely without nails, Gemein Haus served as the Moravians' church when they first came to Bethlehem. It was also their sleeping quarters and their workshop. Now it serves as a museum of Moravian history, exhibiting Moravian furniture, needlework, toys, and art.

 ### COLONIAL INDUSTRIAL QUARTER (ages 6 and up)

459 Old York Road; (610) 691–0603. Open for self-guided tours, Free*, daily from dawn to dusk.*

There is a self-guided walking tour of the quarter. Pick up a walking-tour brochure at the Luckenback Mill. Groups can call ahead to arrange a tour of the buildings. On selected Saturdays and Sundays in summer, and for other special events, costumed interpreters host your visit.

 ### KEMERER MUSEUM OF DECORATIVE ARTS (ages 8 and up)

427 North New Street; (610) 868–6868. Open Tuesday through Sunday noon to 5:00 P.M. Admission: $3.00 for adults, $1.00 for students; family rate is $7.00.

The Kemerer Museum features eighteenth- and nineteenth-century decorative arts such as furniture, folk art, textiles, paintings, and toys. Call for a schedule of changing exhibits.

BURNSIDE PLANTATION (all ages)

1461 Schoernersville Road, next to the Bethlehem Racquet Club; (610) 868–5044. Open for free *self-guided tours Monday through Sunday 8:30 A.M. to 5:00 P.M.*

Seven acres of James Burnside's original farm are being developed as a living history museum to interpret farming between 1748 and 1848. The farmhouse, built in 1748, has recently been restored to its 1818 appearance. A nature trail will soon link Burnside Plantation to the 18th-century Moravian Industrial Quarter about a 10-minute walk away. The plantation hosts an annual Blueberry Festival on the last weekend in July and a Harvest Festival in fall.

THE DISCOVERY CENTER OF SCIENCE AND TECHNOLOGY (all ages)

511 East Third Street; (610) 865–5010; www.discovery-center.org. Open Tuesday through Saturday, 9:30 A.M. to 4:30 P.M., Sunday noon to 4:30 P.M. Admission: adults 13 and older, $4.50; seniors 62 and older, $4.00; children 3 to 12, $3.50. Children under 3 enter free. *There are additional fees for the Laser Theater shows and for selected special exhibits and shows.*

"Discover the fun of learning," is the slogan of the Discovery Center, where over ninety hands-on interactive exhibits cover many science and technology topics. Kids can crawl through a 76-foot-long tunnel using only the senses of touch, smell, and hearing. They can take a ride with "Dr. Bones" to learn about the body's skeletal system. There's also a Science Playground, Hologram Gallery, Workbench, and more. The Center offers educational programs, scout badge days, summer camp, birthday parties, and other activities.

BANANA FACTORY (ages 5 and up)

211 Plymouth Street; (610) 332–1300; www.bananafactory.org.

The mission of the Banana Factory is "to kindle, support, and celebrate the artistic, cultural, and creative spirit of the Lehigh Valley." Located in a former warehouse for bananas, the Banana Factory offers classes for children and adults, as well as art exhibits. There are twenty-three artists' studios in the building, which is also home to the Pennsylvania Youth Theater and the Bethlehem Musikfest Association.

ALSO IN THE AREA

For ten days every August the streets, plazas, and historic places of Bethlehem vibrate with music from all over the world. Bethlehem's Musikfest attracts hundreds of musicians and music lovers to performances at thirteen outdoor and six indoor venues. Specially for the children, clowns, jugglers, and magicians roam the streets. There is also an interactive theater for kids and parents. Hands-on crafts, an outdoor art studio call "Muralplatz," and both regional and international foods, plus a fireworks display complete the festivities.

Nazareth

Like Bethlehem, Nazareth was founded in the 1700s by Moravian settlers. At present Nazareth is also the home of Martin Guitars.

MARTIN GUITAR FACTORY (ages 8 and up)

510 Sycamore Street; (610) 759–2837. Free *guided tours Monday through Friday at 1:15 P.M. For groups of ten or more, reservations are required and a $2.00 fee per person is charged.*

A small museum displays limited edition guitars made for people like Gene Autry and Johnny Cash. The Free tour takes about an hour, and brings you close-up to the craftspeople who create the instruments.

ALSO IN THE AREA

Other sites in Nazareth include **Moravian Historical Society** and **Whitefield** (pronounced wit-field) **House Museum** (214 East Center Street; 610–759–5070) and **Nazareth Speedway** (located on Highway 191 in Nazareth; call 610–759–8000 for tickets).

Easton

Did you know that the average child in the United States will wear down 730 crayons by his tenth birthday? Your children won't want to miss out on the Crayola Factory at Two Rivers Landing, 30 Centre Square.

CRAYOLA FACTORY (all ages)

30 Centre Square; (610) 515–8000; www.crayola.com. Open Tuesday through Saturday 9:30 A.M. to 5:00 P.M. and Sunday from noon to 5:00 P.M. Longer hours from Memorial Day through Labor Day, 9:00 A.M. to 6:00 P.M. on weekdays, 11:00 A.M. to 6:00 P.M. on Sundays. Closed on Mondays except for the following holidays: Martin Luther King, Jr. Day, Presidents Day, Memorial Day, Labor Day, Columbus Day, and the Monday after Christmas. Closed New Year's Day, Easter, Thanksgiving, Christmas Eve, and Christmas Day. Admission price includes access to the Crayola Factory and the National Canal Museum. Admission: $6.00 for adults and children, $5.50 for seniors 65 and over; children under 3 are admitted Free.

In July 1996 something new and colorful came to Easton: the Crayola Factory, a 20,000-square-foot family discovery center filled with dozens of hands-on activities designed to get kids to "think outside the lines." Already more than 400,000 visitors of all ages have seen the brightly colored liquid wax molded into crayons, expressed their creativity with markers on giant glass walls, made rubbings and transfers, and mixed colors of light.

In The Factory Floor exhibit, an expert crayon maker mixes the hot wax and pigments to mold your own souvenir four-pack of crayons. You can also see how Crayola markers are made and take home a souvenir marker. Learn about the history of Binney & Smith in the Crayola Hall of Fame, where you can see the sweater that TV's "Mr. Rogers" wore when he molded the 100-billionth Crayola crayon. And remember those eight colors that were retired in 1990? They're here, too. In The Creative Studio, you can decorate a sidewalk with chalk and literally write on the walls. In Bright Ideas you can explore the science of color and light, using Crayola products such as Changeable markers and Silly Putty. In The Imagination Station, you can work with other visitors to build a huge sculpture.

The Crayola Factory is housed on the second floor of the Two Rivers Landing cultural center in downtown Easton. The National Canal Museum is on the third floor, and one admission gets you into both. The National Heritage Corridor Visitors Center, on the first floor, is open to the public Free of charge. There's also a McDonald's in the building!

NATIONAL CANAL MUSEUM (ages 8 and up)

30 Centre Square; reservations and information (610) 515–8000, office (610) 559–6613. Open year-round Tuesday through Saturday 9:30 A.M. to 5:00 P.M.,

Sunday noon to 5:00 P.M. Closed Mondays except for the following holidays: Martin Luther King, Jr. Day, Presidents Day, Memorial Day, Labor Day, and Columbus Day. See Crayola Factory above for admission fees.

The Delaware Canal runs from Easton to Bristol, and its area has recently become a National Heritage Corridor. There are opportunities to learn about the canal's place in history in Bristol, New Hope, and other towns.

Here at the National Canal Museum, interactive exhibits allow you to operate a lock model or pilot your boat through the lock. Artifacts, photomurals, and life-sized figures create a sense of "being there" as a canal boatman recounts tales of canal life interspersed with traditional canal songs.

THE WELLER CENTER (all ages)

325 Northampton Street; (610) 258–8500; www.wellercenter.org. Admission: $5.00 per person.

The Carl and Emily Weller Center for Health Education has for some years served school groups only. In October 1999 the Weller Center opened its doors to the general public, becoming the first interactive museum in the United States to focus on health education. Kids can walk through a giant model of the human brain. There's also a giant nose that actually sneezes. ("Oooh, gross!" they'll say, but they'll love it.) Other exhibits focus on nutrition, human growth and development, and drug abuse. Located adjacent to the Crayola Factory and the National Canal Museum, the Weller Center also has a very nice gift shop.

JOSIAH WHITE II CANAL BOAT RIDES and HUGH MOORE PARK (all ages)

Hugh Moore Park (look for CANAL BOAT signs); (610) 559–6613. Rides available May 3–26, Tuesday through Friday 9:30 A.M. to 3:30 P.M. and Saturday, Sunday and Memorial Day 1:00 to 4:30 P.M.; May 27 to September 1, Tuesday through Saturday 10:30 A.M. to 4:30 P.M., and Sunday and Labor Day 1:00 to 4:30 P.M.; September 2 to 28 Saturday and Sunday only 1:00 to 4:30 P.M. Fares: adults, $5.00; children 3 to 15, $3.00.

A costumed interpreter takes you on a forty-minute ride on a mule-drawn canal boat. Special evening rides with dinner and music are available, as are charter rides for groups.

While in Hugh Moore Park, you may wish to take advantage of the park's trails, pavilions, picnic areas, and playground. The Locktender's House Museum re-creates the life of a locktender and his family.

Where to Stay

IN BUCKS COUNTY

Best Western New Hope Inn, *6426 Lower York Road, New Hope; (215) 862–5221 or (800) HOPE–202.* Country setting, pool, restaurant.

The Warrington, *Routes 611 and 132, Warrington; (800) 333–1827.* Pool, playground, restaurant.

Holiday Inn Select–Bucks County, *4700 Street Road, PA Turnpike, exit 28, Trevose; (215) 364–2000 or (800) HOLIDAY.* Indoor pool. Sesame Place packages available.

IN MONTGOMERY COUNTY

The Inn at King of Prussia By Best Western, *127 South Gulph Road, King of Prussia; (610) 265–4500.* Convenient to Valley Forge National Historic Park as well as King of Prussia shopping. Outdor pool.

McIntosh Inn, *260 North Gulph Road, King of Prussia; (800) 444–2775.* Next to King of Prussia mall. Great rates for families.

McIntosh Inn, *Route 1 and Route 352 South, Media; (800) 444–2775.* Convenient to Brandywine River Museum, Brandywine Battlefield, Chadds Ford, etc.

Doubletree Guest Suites, *Plymouth Meeting, 640 West Germantown Pike, Plymouth Meeting; (610) 834–8300 or (800) 222–TREE.* Suite accommodations, restaurant, indooor pool.

The Philadelphia Marriott West, *111 Crawford Avenue, West Conshahacken; (610) 941–5600.* Convenient to Valley Forge, Philadelphia, Main Line, and Manayunk.

For More Information

Bucks County Tourist Commission, Inc., *(800) 836–BUCKS or (215) 345–4552; www.bctc.org.*

Bucks County, *(800) 836–2825; www.bctc.org.*

Chester County Tourist Bureau, Inc., *(800) 228–9933 or (610) 344–6365; www.brandywinevalley.com.*

Delaware County Convention and Visitors Bureau, Inc., *(800) 343–3983 or (610) 565–3679; www.libertynet.org/-delcocvb.*

Lehigh Valley Convention and Visitors Bureau, Inc., *(800) 747–0561 or (610) 882–9200; www.travelfile.com/get?lvcv.*

Montgomery County Historic Sites, *www.montcopa.org.*

Nazareth Area Visitor Center, *201 North Main Street, Nazareth 18064; (610) 759–9174.*

New Hope—Village of New Hope, Greater New Hope Chamber of Commerce, *P.O. Box 633, New Hope 18938; (215) 862–3730.*

Valley Forge Convention and Visitors Bureau, *(888) VISIT–VF or (610) 834–1550; www.valleyforge.org.*

New Hope Information Center, *1 West Mechanic Street, New Hope 18938; (215) 862–5880.*

Hershey–Pennsylvania Dutch Country

Hershey–Pennsylvania Dutch Country beckons with amusement parks, historical sites, Pennsylvania Dutch arts and crafts, and lots of train rides. This is the Keystone State's classic countryside, with Amish farms and roadside markets. It was also the site of the Battle of Gettysburg, where more American lives were lost than in any other single battle in U.S. history.

Harrisburg, the state capital on the shores of the Susquehanna, is in the midst of a renaissance under its active mayor, Steven Reed. City Island, once abandoned, has been transformed into a family-entertainment spot, with miniature golf, the *Pride of the Susquehanna* riverboat, Class AA baseball, a children's railroad, and more.

Kids delight in Hershey, ChocolateTown USA, with its streetlights shaped like chocolate kisses and its triple helping of kid-friendly attractions—Hersheypark, ZooAmerica, and Chocolate World.

Faith & Emily's
Favorite Hershey–Pennsylvania Dutch Country Attractions

1. Hersheypark
2. Strasburg Railroad
3. National Railroad Museum
4. Museum of Scientific Discovery
5. State Museum of Pennsylvania
6. *Pride of the Susquehanna* Riverboat
7. Fishing on the Yellow Breeches
8. Herr Food Factory
9. Gettysburg National Military Park
10. Middletown & Hummelstown Railroad

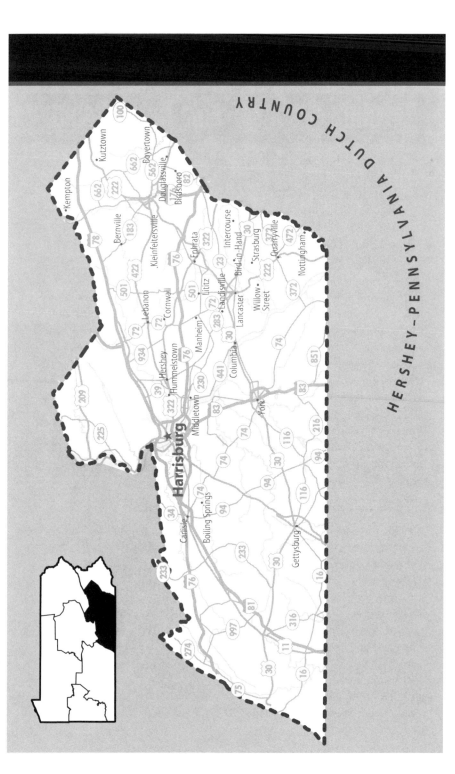

Some 70,000 Plain People live in Lancaster County, members of communities such as the Amish, Brethren, and Mennonites. Plain People appreciate it when tourists respect their privacy and dislike of cameras. Visits to The People's Place, the Amish Farm, and "The Amish Experience" will present important opportunities to teach your children sensitivity.

Families who visit Pennsylvania Dutch Country often comment on the food: It's abundant and inexpensive. Family-style restaurants abound, with diners seated at large tables and delicious, simple food passed around in large bowls.

A reader recently asked about driving on country roads in Lancaster County. If you take Route 772 starting in Intercourse and continuing toward Columbia, this well-marked road loops through the county, past Amish and Mennonite farms. You can stop at a farm stand and buy vegetables or preserves from an Amish child. You'll poke through little towns like Lititz, stumble upon quilt and craft shops, and admire scenic overlooks. The staff at the Pennsylvania Dutch Convention and Visitors Bureau can help you map out your own route, taking into consideration your own interests and the season.

The Pennsylvania Dutch area is a great place for a farm vacation. For more information on a vacation of any type in Pennsylvania Dutch Country, call the Pennsylvania Dutch Convention and Visitors Bureau at (717) 299-8901. To learn about farm vacations, write to the Pennsylvania Farm Vacation Association, Pennsylvania Department of Agriculture, Marketing Department, 2301 North Cameron Street, Harrisburg 17110-9408. A list of farm B&Bs is included in this chapter.

Faith & Emily's
Favorite Hershey–Pennsylvania Dutch Country Events

- **Kutztown Folk Festival,** Schuylkill County Fairgrounds, Summit Station (nine days surrounding July 4); (610) 683-8707.
- **Pennsylvania Renaissance Faire** (summer); (717) 665-7021.
- **Charles Dickens Victorian Christmas** (November through December); (717) 665-7021.
- **Fort Hunter Day** (September); (717) 599-5751.
- **Hersheypark Christmas Candylane** (November through December); (717) 534-3860 or (800) HERSHEY.
- **Hersheypark Creatures of the Night** (October); (717) 534-3860 or (800) HERSHEY.
- **Greater Harrisburg Arts Festival** (Memorial Day weekend); (717) 238-5180.

Kempton

HAWK MOUNTAIN SANCTUARY (ages 8 and up)

Five miles east of Route 61, north of Hamburg, off Route 895. Call (610) 756–6961 for more information. www.hawkmountain.org. The Visitor Center is open daily year-round 9:00 A.M. to 5:00 P.M.; extended hours in fall. Admission is $6.00 for adults, $4.00 for seniors, $3.00 for children 6 to 12.

Hawk Mountain Sanctuary's twin missions are conservation and education. This nature-observation area attracts bird-watchers from up and down the East Coast to Berks County to watch the many species of hawks and eagles that pass through the area on their annual migrations. Some trails are rocky, so younger children may not be able to keep up.

Children should be reminded that noise may frighten the birds. At the height of migration, North Lookout becomes almost like a theater with a crowd of onlookers, so children should be instructed to keep their voices low. Parents should use their best judgment; if your child won't be able to be quiet, wait a few years. Bring binoculars, wear a jacket, and check the website or call ahead for a brochure that gives timetables of migration. Spring and summer are great times for family outings at Hawk Mountain.

WK&S RAILROAD LINE (all ages)

Take Route 143N or 737N into Kempton and follow signs to WK&S Railroad. Call for schedules and more information: (610) 756–6469. The steam train runs on Sunday from May through October and on Saturday during June, July, August, and October. The diesel train runs on Saturdays in June and August. Fares are $5.00 for adults, $3.00 for children ages 3 to 11.

The train ride on the Wanamaker, Kempton, and Southern is about 6 miles round-trip and takes about forty minutes. Pack a picnic and have the train drop you off at a trackside grove. You can ride all day if you like. A Santa Claus Special rides the rails in December; in October, it's time for the Harvest Moon Special. Please note that although the train is sometimes known as the Hawk Mountain Line, it does not actually go to Hawk Mountain.

Kutztown

CRYSTAL CAVE (ages 8 and up)

Situated between Allentown and Reading off Route 222 at Crystal Cave and Valley Roads. For information and the schedule of guided tours, call (610) 683–6765; www.crystalcavepa.com. Admission: $8.00 for adults, $4.75 for children ages 4 to 11.

Just use your imagination and you can see the ice-cream cone, the crystal ballroom, the giant's tooth, and the prairie dogs inside the geological formations at Crystal Cave. After your underground adventure, try some of the **free** activities such as the nature trail, picnic area, and Amish buggy display.

This cave is probably less strenuous than some, with railings and walkways. No strollers are permitted in the cave, so put the baby in a backpack, if possible. The Main Inn has a large rest room and lounge, but no changing table. Picnic tables are available, some covered. You can eat at the Pennsylvania Dutch Fast Food Restaurant, Sugar Shack, and ice-cream shop, open seasonally.

Boyertown

BOYERTOWN MUSEUM OF HISTORIC VEHICLES (all ages)

28 Warwick Street; (610) 367–2090; www.boyertownmuseum.org. Open 9:30 A.M. to 4:00 P.M. daily except Monday. Admission: $4.00 for adults, $3.50 for seniors, $2.00 for children 6 and over.

The Boyertown Museum of Historic Vehicles is devoted to local transportation history, showcasing Duryeas, Daniels, Biddles, and many other vehicles produced in Southeastern Pennsylvania. The museum also has a collection of horse-drawn vehicles such as carriages and sleighs, and what may be the largest collection of electric vehicles in the area. In early 2000, the Museum will move to a new location at Third and Walnut Streets, where visitors will enjoy an expanded exhibition area, a theater, and an improved gift shop.

Douglassville

 MARY MERRITT DOLL MUSEUM and **MERRITT'S MUSEUM OF EARLY CHILDHOOD (ages 10 and up)**

Located between Pottstown and Reading on Route 422. Call (610) 385–3809 for the Doll Museum and (610) 385–3408 for the Museum of Early Childhood. Open Monday through Saturday 10:00 A.M. to 5:00 P.M.; Sunday and holidays 1:00 to 5:00 P.M. Combination admission to both museums: $3.00 for adults, $1.50 for children 5 to 12.

At the Doll Museum, your children can see thousands of antique dolls, the oldest dating from the 1660s. More than fifty doll houses are on display. Just stroll around the toy trains, toy boats, rag dolls, pull toys, baby dolls, hobby horses, and paper dolls. We recommend that parents consider their children's maturity level; very little children will be frustrated that they can't touch the displays.

The Museum of Early Childhood was designed to give other family members something to do while the doll enthusiasts were in the Doll Museum. It includes Colonial and Victorian antiques and Native American relics. Each museum has its own gift shop. Handicapped-accessible.

Birdsboro

 DANIEL BOONE HOMESTEAD (all ages)

400 Daniel Boone Road; (610) 582–4900. Open Tuesday through Saturday, 9:00 A.M. to 5:00 P.M., Sunday noon to 5:00 P.M. year-round. Admission is $4.00 for adults, $2.00 for children 6 to 12, $3.50 for seniors. There is a family rate of $10.00.

Daniel Boone was born and grew up in a log cabin at Daniel Boone Homestead. Only the foundation of the orginal cabin remains, but the oldest section of the log cabin that stands here now was built in 1750, around the time the Boones moved away. Here you can see a blacksmith's shop, smokehouse, bake oven, and sawmill. Children especially enjoy the horses and sheep. Facilities available for picnicking and camping. The second floor of the house is not handicapped-accessible, but disabled visitors may view a video of it.

Bernville

KOZIAR'S CHRISTMAS VILLAGE (all ages)

782 Christmas Village Road, 7 miles past the Reading Airport in Bernville, off Route 183; (610) 488–1110. Open evenings only from October through New Year's Day. Admission: $5.50 for adults, $4.00 for children ages 6 to 12, $4.50 for seniors.

Over fifty years in the making, Koziar's Christmas Village is a holiday tradition—and every year it's new, improved, and all handmade. More than 500,000 lights sparkle on the lakeside house, along with its walkways, trees, and ten outbuildings including Santa's post office and toy shop. There are more than thirty buildings, about eight of which can be entered, but Koziar's is mostly an outdoor experience, so dress accordingly.

Kleinfeltersville

MIDDLE CREEK WILDLIFE MANAGEMENT AREA (ages 8 and up)

Hopeland Road. Visitor Center: (717) 733–1512. Open February 1 to the day before Thanksgiving, Tuesday through Sunday 8:00 A.M. to 4:00 P.M. and Sunday noon to 5:00 P.M. **Free**.

Bundle up, bring your binoculars, and come to the Middle Creek Wildlife Management Area in February or March and you can see thousands of tundra swans! In spring and fall there are many other species of migrating waterfowl. There are also 6,254 acres of state game land, with seven trails, plus fishing and hunting in designated areas only, including one trout stream that's accessible to the disabled. Picnic areas are available, but you must not feed the birds. Administered by the Pennsylvania Game Commission.

There are a number of annual events at Middle Creek. The first full weekend in August brings their annual art show. During the third full weekend in September, you can see an exhibit of woodcarving including decoys. Also in September is the annual Pennsylvania State Goose-Calling Championship.

Lebanon

THE DANIEL WEAVER COMPANY (ages 8 and up)

Located at the corner of 15th and Weavertown Road, ½ mile off Route 422 in Lebanon. For more information call (717) 274–6100 or (800) WEAVERS. Open Monday through Saturday 9:00 A.M. to 4:00 P.M.; Free *admission.* Free *tours also are available.*

Lebanon is the one town where you can see how genuine Lebanon bologna is made. The Daniel Weaver Company, which produces both Weaver's famous Lebanon Bologna and Baum's Bologna, is the oldest commercial manufacturer of Lebanon bologna in the United States. Here you can see the outdoor smokehouses, visit exhibits, enjoy Free samples, and visit their retail store.

Cornwall

CORNWALL IRON FURNACE (ages 8 and up)

Call (717) 272–9711 for information. The furnace is open daily Tuesday through Saturday 10:00 A.M. to 4:00 P.M., Sunday noon to 4:00 P.M. It is open Memorial Day, Independence Day, and Labor Day. Admission is $3.50 for adults, $1.50 for children.

The most important difference between Cornwall Iron Furnace and Hopewell Furnace (see Philadelphia Countryside, page 45) is that most of Cornwall is original, whereas Hopewell is reconstructed. Cornwall Iron Furnace operated from the 1740s until the 1880s. A guide takes you through the iron-making complex, pointing out the 32-foot-tall furnace itself.

MOUNT HOPE ESTATE, PENNSYLVANIA RENAISSANCE FAIRE (all ages)

Mount Hope Estate. Call (717) 665–7021 for details on schedules and admission.

On weekends from August through mid-October, join the raucous revelry of the Pennsylvania Renaissance Faire. Meet sixteenth-century knaves and wenches, jesters, pirates, princesses, and knights who will immerse your family in a spectacle of living theater. Events include jousting, human chess, children's games, crafts, short plays such as *Robin Hood,* and dancing. From the end of October through mid-November, you can be mystified at "Edgar Allan Poe Evermore."

("Edgar Allan Poe Evermore" is macabre and includes direct readings from Poe. It is recommended for older children, from 13 up.) From Thanksgiving weekend until after Christmas, the estate is decked out quite differently for a festive "Charles Dickens Victorian Christmas," recommended for all ages.

Lititz

JULIUS STURGIS PRETZEL HOUSE (ages 6 and up)
219 East Main Street, Lititz; (717) 626–4354. Open year-round Saturday 9:30 A.M. to 4:30 P.M. From April 1 to December 1, also open Monday through Saturday 9:30 A.M. to 4:30 P.M. Admission: $2.00 per person.

You can actually twist your own pretzel here at the first pretzel bakery in the country.

Ephrata

Ephrata is an interesting town where you may wish to browse in the art galleries and craft shops. Stop by at **Artworks at Doneckers,** 100 North State Street (717-738-9503).

EPHRATA CLOISTER (ages 10 and up)
632 West Main Street (Routes 272 and 322); (717) 733–6600. Open Monday to Saturday 9:00 A.M. to 5:00 P.M. and Sunday from noon to 5:00 P.M. On Monday through Saturday, tours leave at 10:00 and 11:00 A.M., 1:00, 2:00, 3:00, and 4:00 P.M. Admission is $5.00 for adults, $4.50 for those 60 and older, $3.00 for ages 6 to 12.

Older children may be interested in learning about a true alternative life-style at one time practiced in the eighteenth century at Ephrata Cloister. Here you can step into another reality in twelve restored buildings where hymns still seem to echo.

Intercourse

THE PEOPLE'S PLACE (ages 5 and up)
3510 Old Philadelphia Pike; (800) 390–8436. Open Monday through Saturday 9:30 A.M. to 8:00 P.M. Memorial Day through Labor Day. Off-season the museum is open 9:30 A.M. to 5:00 P.M. Admission to the movie Who Are the Amish? *is*

$4.00 for adults and $2.00 for children 5 to 11. Admission to the museum is $4.00 for adults, $2.00 for children. A combination ticket is $7.00 for adults, $3.50 for children.

Kids have lots of questions about the Pennsylvania Dutch. What's it like to dress in Amish clothes? How does it feel to ride in an Amish buggy? And deeper questions: What do the Amish believe? Why do they live differently from most of us? Their questions will be answered here.

After viewing the three-screen, twenty-five-minute film *Who Are the Amish?*, kids in first through eighth grade can actually try school lessons used by Amish children their age. They can also learn to work the signal indicators on an Amish carriage. Hands-on exhibits and a collection of folk art help build an understanding of the life-style chosen by the Amish and Mennonites.

"20Q" is a new museum on the second floor of The People's Place. It answers the twenty most-often-asked questions about the Amish and Mennonites, both the Old Order and modern groups. Interactive exhibits are on two tracks: one for adults, one for children. Kids love finding Plain Pig, a character who appears throughout the exhibits.

The People's Place Quilt Museum is adjacent. Behind People's Place you'll find the collection of more than thirty craft shops called Kitchen Kettle Village (800–732–3538). You can see fudge being made and Shaker-style furniture being built.

Plain & Fancy Farm Attractions

PLAIN & FANCY FARM

3121 Old Philadelphia Pike on Route 340 between Bird-in-Hand and Intercourse; (717) 768–4400; www.800padutch.com/millers.html. Open daily. Call ahead for hours.

Easily accessible to Mt. Hope on the opposite side of Route 340 between Bird-in-Hand and Intercourse, you'll find Plain & Fancy Farm with its buggy rides and Pennsylvania Dutch crafts and food. There are a lot of things to do at Plain & Fancy, including buggy rides, "The Amish Experience," and

Amish Buggy Rides

- Abe's Buggy Rides (717–392–1794)
- Ed's Buggy Rides (717–687–0360)
- Aaron and Jessica's Buggy Rides, at Plain & Fancy Farm; (717) 768–4400

Amish dining. Also at Plain & Fancy, you can visit the Amish Country Homestead (717–392– 8622).

You can also take a guided bus tour of Amish country starting at Plain & Fancy Farm. Admission to each attraction may be purchased separately or you may choose a combination ticket to the theater and homestead, or even a super-saver ticket that includes the theater, homestead, and guided bus tour.

AMISH COUNTRY HOMESTEAD (all ages)

Plain & Fancy Farm, 3121 Old Philadelphia Pike; (717) 768–8400. Hours subject to change seasonally. Admission to the homestead is $5.00 for adults, $3.25 for seniors. Combination tickets available for homestead, theater, and bus tours.

AARON AND JESSICA'S BUGGY RIDES (all ages)

Plain & Fancy Farm; (717) 768–4400.

Lancaster County offers several opportunities to ride in a Pennsylvania Dutch buggy, but only one ride is owned and operated by an Amish family. This is Aaron and Jessica's Buggy Rides at Plain & Fancy Farm.

THE AMISH EXPERIENCE (ages 7 and up)

Plain & Fancy Farm; (717) 768–8400 or 768–3600. Hours subject to change seasonally. Admission to theater only is $6.50 for adults, $3.75 for children 4 to 11. Combination tickets available to homestead, theater and bus tour.

This new multimedia interactive "experiential theater" defies easy labeling. Opened in July 1996, this well-researched, twenty-seven-minute program immerses the audience in the world of the Amish, in a unique theater with some live actors, five different image areas showing different pictures, and special effects. The show *Jacob's Choice*, introduces a fictional Amish teenager and his family. Although younger kids will be entertained, children aged 7 and up will get the point of what it means to be Amish.

Manheim

KREIDER FARMS

Route 72 (ten minutes from Route 283) at 1461 Lancaster Road; (717) 665–5039. Farm tour hours: Monday, Wednesday, and Friday 9:30 A.M. and 11:30 A.M. by reservation only.

"Daddy, where does milk come from?" Here's a great way to answer this perennial question. At Kreider Farms you can pet young calves, see cows milked on a carousel, and learn how the milk gets from the farm to the supermarket shelf. You can also visit the egg-packaging plant, then top off your visit with lunch or dinner at Kreider Farms restaurant adjacent to the farm tour. (Kreider Farms also has restaurants at three other locations in the area.)

Bird-in-Hand

 AMERICANA MUSEUM IN BIRD-IN-HAND (ages 6 and up)
Route 340 East (2709 Old Philadelphia Pike); (717) 391–9780. Open April through November, Tuesday through Saturday 10:00 A.M. to 5:00 P.M. (Last tour begins at 4:40 P.M.) Admission: adults $4.00, children 8 to 12 $2.00, seniors 60 and up $3.00.

The Americana Museum focuses on American life from 1890 to 1930. Touring this indoor complex with a self-guided tour pamphlet, you can stroll through a re-created town of the period including a fully-stocked country general store and eight shops common to the era. A children's activity sheet is available.

  here to Eat Amish Style with Kids

- **Amish Barn Restaurant,** *Route 340 between Bird-In-Hand and Intercourse;* *(717) 768–8886.* Kids eat Free.
- **Bird-in-Hand Family Restaurant,** *Old Philadelphia Pike, 5 miles east of Lancaster on Route 340; (717) 768–8266.* Menu-style.
- **Harvest Drive Family Restaurant,** *Intercourse; (717) 768–4510.* Full menu or family-style.
- **Zinn's Diner,** *Route 272, Denver; (717) 336–2500.*
- **Plain & Fancy Farm,** *3121 Old Philadelphia Pike; (717) 768–4400.*

 WEAVERTOWN ONE-ROOM SCHOOLHOUSE (all ages)
Route 340, east of Bird-in-Hand; (717) 768–3976 or (717) 291–1888; www.800paductch.com/wvrtown.html. Open Good Friday through Thanksgiving, starting at 10:00 A.M. Closing time changes seasonally. Hours and days vary seasonally. Admission is $2.75 for adults, $2.25 for seniors, $1.75 for children.

Class is in session, with animated figures of a teacher and pupils in the Weavertown One-Room Schoolhouse. The building, desks, and blackboard are original.

ABE'S BUGGY RIDES (all ages)

2596 Old Philadelphia Pike; (717) 392–1794. Open year-round, but closed on Sunday.

Paradise

AMAZING MAIZE MAZE (All ages)

Cherry-Crest Farm; (717) 687–6843; www.amazingmaze.com. Open seasonally. Call ahead for current admission prices.

This large corn maze was cut in the shape of the Liberty Bell for its 1999 season. Watch for different designs in coming years. There are also four smaller mazes, a petting zoo, hay ride, and special events. Many people arrive to explore the maze by way of the Strasburg Rail Road!

Strasburg

A reporter for the *New York Times* has recently called the Strasburg area "command central for railroad buffs." Here in the town of Strasburg, transportation enthusiasts can learn about toy trains, real trains, classic cars, and more. It's the perfect place to take little boys who are "into" vehicles.

RAILROAD MUSEUM OF PENNSYLVANIA (all ages)

300 Gap Road, on Route 741 East; (717) 687–8628; www.rrhistorical.com includes this and other railroad museums. Open Monday through Saturday 9:00 A.M. to 5:00 P.M., Sunday noon to 5:00 P.M. Closed Monday from November through April. Admission is $6.00 for adults, $5.50 forseniors, $4.00 for children 6 to 12. A family rate is available.

Newly renovated to accommodate more trains and a hands-on learning center, the Railroad Museum of Pennsylvania will entrance your junior engineers. It's almost overwhelming to walk into the huge collection of locomotives and rolling stock at this museum, which specializes in railroad trains built or operated in Pennsylvania. Rolling Stock Hall is designed with a balcony and a pit so that you can see the forty-six locomotives and passenger cars from different angles. Outdoors you can see some thirty-three more cars. The HO-scale layout and hands-on learning center are open selected hours. There are changing tables in both the men's and women's rest rooms. Handicapped-accessible.

STRASBURG RAIL ROAD (all ages)

Route 741 East; (717) 687–7522. Hours vary seasonally. Fares are $8.25 for adults, $4.00 for children 3 to 11. Children under 2 ride Free.

After you've seen the Railroad Museum, cross the street for a forty-five-minute ride on the Strasburg Rail Road. Food service is available. The East Strasburg Rail Road Station was built in 1882 and includes railroad gift shops and the Dining Car restaurant. The Strasburg Rail Road is the nation's oldest short-line railroad. For an additional fee, you can ride in style in the first-class parlor car.

 ### CHOO CHOO BARN (all ages)

Route 741 East; (717) 687–7911. Open April through December 10:00 A.M. to 5:00 P.M. daily; in summer 10:00 A.M. to 6:00 P.M. Admission is $4.00 for adults, $2.00 for children 5 to 12.

Also within walking distance, you'll find the Choo Choo Barn, where eighteen miniature trains chug through 130 animated scenes. If your kids are like ours, you'll want to visit Thomas's Trackside Station, a shop devoted exclusively to Thomas the Tank Engine and his friends from the Island of Sodor. All displays and rest rooms are handicapped-accessible, but not all the shops. If you get hungry, there's a picnic area, candy shop, and Isaac's Restaurant and Deli.

 ### NATIONAL TOY TRAIN MUSEUM (all ages)

300 Paradise Lane; (717) 687–8976; www.traincollectors.org. Open May through October 10:00 A.M. to 5:00 P.M. In April, November, and December the museum is open weekends only. Admission is $3.00 for adults, $1.50 for children 5 to 12.

This museum features metal electric trains: five operating layouts with buttons for the kids to push. There is also a short video, plus display cases full of trains.

 ### ED'S BUGGY RIDES (all ages)

Route 896; (717) 687–0360. Fares: $7.00 for adults, $3.50 for children 6 to 12.

Now that you've seen trains and cars, you can include horse-drawn vehicles by taking a 3-mile ride at Ed's Buggy Rides.

AMISH VILLAGE (all ages)

Two miles north of Strasburg on Route 896; (717) 687–8511. Hours vary seasonally. Admission to the Amish Village is $5.50 for adults, $1.50 for children 6 to 12.

Tours of the Old Order farmhouse at the Amish Village, which dates back to 1840, emphasize the culture of the Plain People. There's also a one-room school, a windmill, and a blacksmith shop. The smokehouse sells specialty foods like apple butter, candies, and cider. There is a handicapped-accessible rest room with a changing table, but the second floor of the house is not accessible. In December special house tours feature hot mulled cider.

SIGHT & SOUND THEATRES (ages 8 and up)

Route 896; reservations: (717) 687–7800; www.noahonstage.com. Tickets range from $33.00 to $38.00 for adults and $7.00 to $15.50 for children.

In 1999 the American Bus Association named Sight & Sound Theatres the "Best New Attraction for Groups." The specifically Christian shows at Sight & Sound's two huge theaters will remind you of something from the glory days of Radio City Music Hall. Recent spectacular productions have included "Noah," "Behold the Lamb," and "The Miracle of Christmas." "Noah," for example, featured a four-story ark, 56 actors, 100 live animals, and 125 animatronics (animated figures).

Quarryville

ROBERT FULTON BIRTHPLACE (ages 10 and up)

North of Goshen on Route 222; (717) 548–2679. Open Memorial Day to Labor Day, Saturday 11:00 A.M. to 4:00 P.M. and Sunday 1:00 to 5:00 P.M. Admission is $1.00 for adults; children 12 and under enter Free.

Your kids have probably heard about Robert Fulton and his steamboat *Clermont*, nicknamed "Fulton's Folly." But few people realize how wide-ranging Fulton's interests were. Famous for his fine portraits, Fulton was also a respected scientist who patented many different devices.

Nottingham

HERR FOODS, INC. (preschool and up)

At intersection of Route 272 and Route 1 in Nottingham. For details and reservations call (800) 284–7488; www.herrs.com. Tours are Free*, but reservations are highly recommended. Open daily 8:00* A.M. *to 5:00* P.M. *Tours are conducted Monday through Thursday, 9:00* A.M. *to 3:00* P.M.*; Friday 9:00* A.M. *to noon.*

You can see how potato chips are made, and then try some chips still warm from the cooker at Herr Foods, Inc. Cutting-edge tour technology uses DVD screens to show you production areas in detail never before available. Kids also enjoy seeing Chipper, the company's mascot, who appears in the video and sometimes in person. Chipper's Cafe offers hot dogs, chicken nuggets, PB&J, and cookies. Handicapped-accessible, with a changing table in the women's room.

Willow Street

HANS HERR HOUSE (ages 8 and up)

1849 Hans Herr Drive; (717) 464–4438. Open April through December, Monday through Saturday 9:00 A.M. *to 4:00* P.M. *Open by appointment only in the off-season. Admission to the Hans Herr House is $3.50 for adults, $1.00 for children 7 to 12.*

The date 1719 appears on the door lintel of the Hans Herr House. Check with the Visitor Center first for information about the home, garden, blacksmith's shop, and more. Call for information about special events such as the Hans Herr Heritage Day in August and the Snitz Fest (an apple festival) in October.

Lancaster

Many of the non-profit museums in the Lancaster area have cooperated in a joint ticketing program. Save your ticket stub from one museum and when you go to another, you'll get a reduced rate. These museums include the Railroad Museum, Heritage Center of Lancaster County, Ephrata Cloister, Wrights Ferry Mansion, National Association of Watch and Clock Collectors Museum, and many more.

Amazing Hershey–Pennsylvania Dutch Facts

Lancaster For exactly one day in 1777, Lancaster served as the U.S. capital.

DUTCH WONDERLAND (ages 3 to 12)

2249 Route 30 East; (717) 291–1888; www.dutchwonderland.com. Open weekends in spring and fall and daily from Memorial Day to Labor Day. Admission includes everything but food and the monorail, and runs $15.95 to $20.95 for children over 3 and adults. Handicapped-accessible.

Your 6-year-old can drive an old-fashioned motorcar, your 12-year-old can brave the Sky Princess roller coaster, your family can take a walk in the botanical gardens, and everyone can grab a carpet square and race down the giant slide. There are changing tables in both men's and women's rooms, and food offerings include chicken, pizza, and sandwiches.

Dutch Wonderland is next door to the Discover Lancaster County History Museum and within minutes of the Amish Farm and House, the Weavertown One-Room School, the Old Mill Stream Camping Manor, and a great deal of outlet shopping.

NORTH MUSEUM OF NATURAL HISTORY AND SCIENCE (all ages)

400 College Avenue; (717) 291–3941; www.fandm.edu/NorthMuseum. Open Tuesday through Saturday 9:00 A.M. to 5:00 P.M., Sunday 1:30 P.M. to 5:00 P.M. Admission: $2.00 for adults and children over 4.

The North Museum, on the campus of Franklin and Marshall College, offers collections of Native American artifacts, birds, fossils, minerals, and a planetarium. Children especially enjoy the Discovery Room and hands-on science and nature exhibits, and the herpetarium with over forty live reptiles.

DISCOVER LANCASTER COUNTY HISTORY MUSEUM (all ages)

2249 Route 30 East; (717) 393–3679; www.800padutch.com/museum.html. New hours for 2000: From Memorial Day to Labor Day, open 9:00 A.M. to 8:00 P.M. daily. From November through March, open 9:00 A.M. to 5:00 P.M. daily. In September, October, April, and May, open Sunday to Friday 9:00 A.M. to 5:00 P.M., Saturday 9:00 A.M. to 8:00 P.M. Closed Christmas. Abridged hours on Thanksgiving and New Year's. Admission is $6.50 for adults, $3.75 for children ages 5 to 11, $5.75 for seniors 60 and over. Children 4 and under enter **Free.**

After $300,000 in renovations, the former Wax Museum of Lancaster County has emerged with a new name and many new exhibits. The original thirty-two wax tableaux are still here, newly restored and expanded. Now, when you see the animated exhibit in which Daniel Boone grows up before your eyes, you can also put on a Daniel Boone hat and, using one-way mirror imaging, observe yourself transforming into Daniel Boone, too. New interactive exhibits include touch-screen computers. You can learn to count tree rings and twist pretzels. Employees are now dressed in period costume, and more educational items are offered in the gift shop.

 AMISH FARM AND HOUSE (ages 6 and up)

2395 Route 30 East, ½ mile east of Dutch Wonderland; (717) 394–6185; www.800padutch.com/afh.htm. Open seven days a week at 8:30 A.M., the site closes at 4:00 P.M. in winter, 5:00 P.M. in spring and fall, and 6:00 P.M. in summer. On selected dates in September and October, hours are extended for kerosene-lamp tours. Admission is $5.75 for adults, $5.25 for seniors, $3.25 for children 5 to 11.

This is the only operating Amish farm open to the public. The farm itself dates from the 1700s, the house from 1805. Guided tours show the house and describe the history, culture, and clothing of Old Order Amish. You can take a self-guided tour of the farm with its barns, carriage sheds, springhouse, and animals. Come on the last Thursday and Friday in April and see the sheep shearing. A food pavilion is open seasonally, and there are changing tables in both men's and women's rooms.

 HANDS-ON HOUSE, CHILDREN'S MUSEUM OF LANCASTER (ages 2 through 10)

721 Landis Valley Road; (717) 569–KIDS; www.800padutch.com/handson. html. Admission is $4.00 for both adults and children. Open Tuesday through

Thursday 11:00 A.M. to 4:00 P.M., Friday 11:00 A.M. to 8:00 P.M., Saturday 10:00 A.M. to 5:00 P.M., and Sunday noon to 5:00 P.M.

The museum has eight interactive areas for children ages 2 through 10, including the new exhibit "E-I-E-I-KNOW," which teaches kids about farming in Lancaster County through computer touch-screens, interactive games, and hands-on exhibits. The Hands-On House is now in its new quarters on the grounds of the Landis Valley Museum. The new building is twice the size of the old one, all on one level, completely wheelchair- and stroller-accessible.

 ## LANDIS VALLEY MUSEUM (elementary-school age)

2451 Kissel Hill Road; (717) 569–0401. Open March through December, Monday through Saturday 9:00 A.M. to 5:00 P.M., Sunday noon to 5:00 P.M. Closed some holidays. Admission to the Landis Valley Museum is $7.00 for adults, $6.50 for seniors, $5.00 for children 6 to 12.

This museum has an extensive collection of Pennsylvania Dutch items that range from pottery to tools to guns. There are fifteen historic buildings including a farmhouse, a tavern, a country store, and a hotel.

Downtown Lancaster

Downtown Lancaster is worth a visit, offering the Central Market, Lancaster Newspapers' "Newseum", Steinman Park, and more. A walking tour is available. For information contact the Pennsylvania Dutch Convention and Visitors Bureau at (717) 299-8901 or (800) PA–DUTCH, ext. 4255.

 ## HERITAGE CENTER MUSEUM OF LANCASTER COUNTY (all ages)

Penn Square; (717) 299–6440; www.heritagemuseum.com. The museum and hands-on room are open **Free** *January through November, Tuesday through Saturday 10:00 A.M. to 5:00 P.M. Open seven days a week from the day after Thanksgiving until the end of the year. Donations accepted.*

The Heritage Center Museum collects, preserves, and interprets the decorative arts of Lancaster County. In the midst of all the furniture, silver, paintings, needlework, folk art, and rifles, kids will be attracted to the Museum Classroom, where ten different stations will have them doing puzzles, playing games, cutting paper, naming quilt patterns, and more. A new children's guide to the museum poses a series of questions to get kids started hunting for answers.

CENTRAL MARKET (all ages)

West King Street; (717) 291–4739. Open Tuesday and Friday 6:00 A.M. to 4:30 P.M. and Saturday from 6:00 A.M. to 2:00 P.M.

Next to the Heritage Center, breathe in the delicious smells of Amish baked goods coming from the Central Market, which has been operating as a farmers' market since the 1730s.

JAMES BUCHANAN'S WHEATLAND (ages 10 and up)

1120 Marietta Avenue; (717) 392–8721. Open daily April through November 10:00 A.M. to 4:00 P.M. Admission is $5.50 for adults, $4.50 for seniors, $3.50 for students, $1.75 for children 6 to 11.

In spite of the pivotal role that Pennsylvania played in our history, the Keystone State produced only one U.S. president, James Buchanan. Located on the outskirts of downtown Lancaster, James Buchanan's Wheatland, Buchanan's home, has been furnished with memorabilia of his life and career.

Landisville

1852 HERR FAMILY HOMESTEAD (ages 6 and up)

1756 Nissley Road; (717) 898–8822. Hours vary seasonally.

Although open only seasonally, the folks at the 1852 Herr Family Homestead do a nice job for children. There is a pleasant park nearby if you'd like to pack a picnic lunch.

Columbia

NATIONAL ASSOCIATION OF WATCH AND CLOCK COLLECTORS MUSEUM (ages 8 and up)

514 Poplar Street, just off Route 30; (717) 684–8261; www.nawcc.org. Open Tuesday through Saturday 9:00 A.M. to 4:00 P.M. and Sunday from noon to 4:00 P.M. from May to September. Closed Monday and holidays. Admission is $3.00 for adults, $1.00 for children 6 to 17.

Water clocks, candle clocks, sundials, musical clocks, grandfather clocks, wristwatches, pocket watches . . . . You've never seen so many kinds of timepieces as you'll find at the National Association of Watch and Clock Collectors Museum. Parents of school-morning slugabeds will get inspiration from the alarm-clock collection. For example, there's one alarm clock that gives the sleepyhead's big toe a yank. One tall musical clock runs seven days and plays seven different tunes.

WRIGHT'S FERRY MANSION (ages 10 and up)

Second and Cherry Streets; (717) 684–4325. Open May through October, Tuesday, Wednesday, Friday, and Saturday from 10:00 A.M. to 3:00 P.M. Last tour begins at 3:00 P.M. Admission is $5.00 for adults, $2.50 for children ages 6 to 18.

Susanna Wright was known as the "bluestocking of the Susquehanna," but she was really more of a "Renaissance woman." (*Bluestocking* was a derogatory term for an intelligent unmarried woman.) Just a few blocks away from the Watch and Clock Museum at Wright's Ferry Mansion, you can get acquainted with this colorful but little-known character in American history. Wright operated a ferry here, drew up legal documents, raised silkworms, practiced medicine, and corresponded with people like Benjamin Franklin.

York

HARLEY-DAVIDSON, INC. ANTIQUE MOTORCYCLE MUSEUM (all ages)

1425 Eden Road, just off Route 30; (717) 848–1177. Museum tours are offered at specified times Monday through Friday. Plant tours are offered Monday through Friday 10:00 A.M. to 2:00 P.M. and are open to people over 12. No cameras, no sandals allowed on factory tours. Call ahead to check for times of museum-only tours or to make reservations for factory tours. Free.

Our 7-year-old was disappointed to learn that kids under 12 are not allowed on the factory tours at Harley-Davidson, Inc. All ages are welcome, however, at the adjacent Harley-Davidson Museum, where antique motorcycles on display include police bikes, army bikes, and bikes owned by celebrities. Handicapped-accessible.

Hershey

If ever there were a town made for family enjoyment, it's Hershey, Pennsylvania. What child could resist the city that chocolate built, with Hersheypark as its main attraction. Even the street lights are shaped like Hershey kisses! If you park your car at the Hersheypark entrance, you can get around town on foot.

CHOCOLATE WORLD VISITORS CENTER (all ages)

Hersheypark Drive; (717) 534–4900. Open year-round, **Free***, from 9:00 A.M. to 4:45 P.M.; in summer it stays open until 6:45 P.M. Admission to the chocolate tour is* **Free***.*

Enjoy a **Free** ride on the chocolate-making tour. Even when the line here is long, it keeps moving. The ride gives an introduction to today's candy-making processes, and you'll get a **Free** sample at the end. Of course, there's also a gift shop where you can buy Hershey products and merchandise.

HERSHEYPARK (all ages)

100 West Hersheypark Drive; (800) HERSHEY or (717) 534–3090; www. hershey.com. Hersheypark's season runs from mid-May through mid-September. The gates open at 10:00 A.M., and the rides open at 10:30 A.M. Closing times vary from 6:00 to 11:00 P.M. Admission plans range from regular (ages 9 to 54) at $24.95 to junior and senior, both at $15.95. Children 2 and under are **Free***, and the sunset savings plan (after 5:00 P.M.) is $13.95. Admission includes all rides, all live performances and a same-day visit to ZooAmerica, (see page 97). There is a separate charge for paddleboats and miniature golf.*

In the summer of 1999, our kids were eager to try the Wild Mouse, Hersheypark's seventh roller coaster. They love it!

In 1998, Hersheypark introduced Great Bear, a steel, inverted looping coaster that is the first of its kind in Pennsylvania. For persons who understand roller-coaster jargon, the Great Bear has multiple high-speed turns; a spiral; a loop; an immelmann (which is like a loop except that you change direction and then complete a barrel roll as you head out of the immelmann); a zero-G roll; a flat spin; and a corkscrew.

As you enter Herheypark, have your kids stand next to the "measure-up" signs. Kids of a certain height are "Hershey Kisses" and can ride Hershey Kiss rides. Taller kids are "Reese's Peanut Butter Cups," "Hershey Milk Chocolate Bars," "Twizzlers," or "Nutrageous." If your kids would like to get a bracelet that shows what candy-height they are, you can stop by the rides office in the operations building, located inside the park beside Swing Thing. (If you don't choose to get a bracelet, there are signs next to every ride.) This manageable theme park is divided into small sections, which are centered around a different theme—and there's something for everyone. This way, your family can stay together and everyone can stay happy. For example, little ones can ride the Swing Thing, which is a kid-sized version of Wave Swinger. The antique carousel will delight many visitors, whereas others flock to the Comet with its 95-foot drop. And don't stand anywhere near Tidal Force unless you don't mind getting wet! If you get hot and tired, a visit to the air-conditioned Music Box Theater may be just the ticket. If you do decide to split up, the Kissing Tower makes a good meeting spot.

You may choose to ride the water rides in your clothes or bathing suits, but shoes are required, so we recommend wearing something waterproof like flip-flops or water shoes.

Traveling with an infant, we were delighted to find that Hersheypark offers facilities for nursing mothers and baby food at the First Aid station. Even some of the men's rooms have changing tables.

Besides its regular season Hersheypark opens for two special family events: Creatures of the Night at Halloween, and Hersheypark Christmas Candylane. At each of these events the park is specially lighted and decorated, and most of the family-oriented rides are open.

What We Remember about Hersheypark
—by Judah (12½) and Seth (10)

Seth: At Hersheypark there was this booth with water guns and we had to shoot at a blue button. If you shot the blue button enough, a bell would go off and you could win a stuffed animal. Judah and I didn't win anything, but Judah's friend Gabbi won three times and she gave us each one of her prizes.

Judah: We went on a ferris wheel. The cars on the ferris wheel went around. When we got to the top, I said "AHHHH!" We all laughed.

 ZOOAMERICA NORTH AMERICAN WILDLIFE PARK (all ages)
Hersheypark Drive; (717) 534–3860. Open year-round. Hours vary seasonally; the zoo is open 10:00 A.M. to 8:00 P.M. whenever Hersheypark is open and 10:00 A.M. to 5:00 P.M. the rest of the year. Admission is $5.25 for adults 13 and up, $4.00 for children 3 to 12.

You can enter ZooAmerica North American Wildlife Park directly through Hersheypark, and admission to the zoo is included in your Hersheypark ticket. The zoo is open year-round, not just seasonally, and a separate admission is also available. ZooAmerica focuses on plants and animals from different regions in North America.

Many of Hershey's attractions grew out of Milton Hershey's special interests. The rose garden at the Hotel Hershey developed from his own passion for the flowers, ZooAmerica started out with the animals Hershey collected, and the Hershey Museum sprang from Hershey's original collection of artifacts.

THE HERSHEY MUSEUM (all ages)

170 Hersheypark Drive; (717) 534–3439. Open year-round. Admission to the museum is $4.25 for adults, $2.00 for youth, $3.75 for seniors.

Administered by the Hershey Foundation, The Hershey Museum is located at the west end of Hersheypark Arena. Its permanent exhibits celebrate the history of Hershey—the town, its founder, and its industries. Younger children will enjoy the Discovery Room, which has hands-on activities on these themes.

ALSO IN THE AREA

You may want to check the schedule of events at Hersheypark Stadium and Arena (717-534-3911). Hershey also offers several golf courses, Milton Hershey School, and the Derry One-Room School.

Hummelstown

INDIAN ECHO CAVERNS (ages 8 and up)

368 Middletown Road; (717) 566–8131. Open daily except some holidays. Admission is $8.00 for adults, $4.00 for children 3 to 11.

Your young geologists can have a forty-five-minute tour of Indian Echo Caverns. You can also pan for gemstones at Gem Mill Junction, take a ride in a horse-drawn buggy, and pet the animals. The cavern is open year-round, but most other attractions are open seasonally. You can also reach Indian Echo Caverns on the Middletown and Hummelstown Railroad.

Middletown

MIDDLETOWN AND HUMMELSTOWN RAILROAD (all ages)

136 Brown Street; (717) 944–4435. Operates seasonally. Call for fares and schedule.

All ages seem to get a kick out of this folksy ride in a 1920 vintage railroad coach. You take a guided scenic ride 11 miles to Indian Echo Caverns. Your train will cross Swatara Creek on a 35-foot-high bridge. You can get off at the caverns, if you like, and take a forty-five-minute tour. On your return trip an accordionist leads a sing-along.

Harrisburg

The bad new is that in May 1999 Harrisburg's Museum of Scientific Discovery closed its doors. The good news is that in September of that year the new Whitaker Center for Science and the Arts opened, dedicated to continuing the mission of its predecessor.

WHITAKER CENTER FOR SCIENCE AND THE ARTS (ages 6 and up)

The Kunkel Building, 301 Market Street; (717) 221–8201. Open Monday through Saturday 9:30 A.M. to 5:00 P.M., Sunday 11:30 A.M. to 5:00 P.M. IMAX theater shows begin at 5:30 P.M. A combination ticket to both the Science Center and the theater costs $9.75 for adults, $7.50 for children ages 3 to 12, and $9.00 for students and seniors. For tickets to the theater only, fees are: $7.00 for adults, $5.00 for children 3 to 12, and $6.25 for students and seniors. For tickets to the Science Center only, fees are: $6.75 for adults, $5.25 for children 3 to 12, and $5.25 for seniors and students. For all tickets, children under 3 enter **Free***.*

 Walking Tour of Downtown Harrisburg It's convenient to park your car at the Walnut Street parking garage, located right at Strawberry Square (North Third and Market Streets), an urban shopping mall with a food court and many shops. The new Whitaker Center is across the street in the Kunkel Building.

Look up and you'll see the dome of the State Capitol Building.

The circular building to the right as you leave the Capitol is the State Museum of Pennsylvania.

If your feet aren't sore yet, you can walk over to the riverfront and cross Walnut Street Bridge, now exclusively for pedestrians. The bridge spans the Susquehanna River from Riverfront Park to City Island. (At night this bridge is illuminated, adding to the nighttime view of the city.)

The new Whitaker Center describes its theme as "science through the arts," making science fun through dance, film, music, and more. The Center includes a state-of-the-art IMAX 3-D movie theater and a Broadway-size theater. If you park at Strawberry Square, you can enter the Whitaker Center by way of an enclosed walkway.

STATE CAPITOL BUILDING (ages 10 and up)

Third and State Streets; (717) 787–6810; www.pasen.gov. Open to the public seven days a week. Tours are given Monday through Friday, every half-hour from 8:30 A.M. to 4:00 P.M. and on Saturday and Sunday hourly from 9:00 A.M. to 4:00 P.M. with no tour between noon and 1:00 P.M. **Free**.

The dome of the State Capitol Building is said to be the most impressive one of any state capitol in the country. Inside, huge murals depict scenes such as Penn's treaty with the Indians, the signing of the Declaration of Independence, and Washington's troops at Valley Forge. The floors are made of tiles from the Moravian Pottery and Tileworks in Doylestown (see Philadelphia Countryside, page 60). The main floor of the rotunda displays more than 350 flags formerly carried by regiments from Pennsylvania.

In the East Wing visit the eighteen interactive exhibits of the Welcome Center, including a kinetic sculpture that depicts how a bill becomes law.

STATE MUSEUM OF PENNSYLVANIA (all ages)

Third and North Streets; (717) 787–4978. The State Museum of Pennsylvania is open Tuesday through Saturday 9:00 A.M. to 5:00 P.M. and Sunday from noon to 5:00 P.M. It is closed holidays except for Memorial Day and Labor Day. Admission is **Free***, but there is a small charge for Curiosity Corner and the planetarium show. Handicapped accessible.*

This museum strives to describe the entire history and prehistory of the state. You'll work your way down, starting at the third floor. There you'll begin with geology and the earth and go on through paleontology, archaeology, and the beginning of civilization. In Dino-Lab you can observe a real paleontologist at work, freeing a dinosaur skeleton from the rock. Using an intercom, you can ask questions about this painstaking process.

Going down to the second floor, you can see a series of life-sized dioramas that depict the life cycle of a Native American in this area. There are also displays about the Revolution and the Civil War, including a huge mural of the Battle of Gettysburg. One gallery re-creates a typical early American Main Street. In Curiosity Corner younger children can try on period clothing, handle birds' nests, and use interactive computers.

On the first floor the museum displays a facsimile of its treasure, the original charter from the British crown that gave Pennsylvania to William Penn in 1681. This charter granted William Penn "rights, privileges and obligations" to Pennsylvania, as a payment of debts owed to Penn's father by King Charles II.

Amazing Hershey-Pennsylvania Dutch Facts

William Penn The State Museum in Harrisburg displays the original charter that gave Pennsylvania to William Penn. It's amusing to note that Penn was to pay the king two beaver furs and all the gold and silver found in the colony. Of course, there was no gold or silver found in Pennsylvania.

CITY ISLAND ATTRACTIONS (all ages)

City Island sits in the middle of the Susquehanna, a spot of greenery amidst the water. Its sixty-three acres of parkland now include Riverside Stadium, where Class AA minor league baseball is played. You'll also find a steam-driven train for children, an arcade, miniature golf, jogging and skateboarding facilities, HarbourTown, and more.

PRIDE OF THE SUSQUEHANNA RIVERBOAT (all ages)

City Island; (717) 234–6500. Boat sails from May through October. Hours vary seasonally, with tours hourly in the summer. Fares are $4.95 for adults, $3.00 for children 12 and over. Children under 12 ride **Free**.

From City Island take a ride on the *Pride of the Susquehanna* (operated by Harrisburg Area Riverboat Society, 116 Pine Street).

The riverboat tour gives an excellent view of this riverside city. Kids love looking up at the underside of the six bridges under which you'll pass, including the Walnut Street Bridge. Take your choice: You may sit indoors, where there is a small snack bar, or on the lower or upper decks, where the wind blows through your hair.

From the riverboat you can see the wrought-iron railing around the grave of the city's founder, John Harris. You can visit his home, the John Harris/Simon Cameron Mansion, at 219 South Front Street. This historic home was built in 1766 and now houses the collection of the Historical Society of Dauphin County.

 ## FORT HUNTER MANSION (ages 8 and up)

5300 North Front Street; (717) 599–5751. Fort Hunter Mansion is open May through November, Tuesday through Saturday 10:00 A.M. to 4:30 P.M., Sunday noon to 4:30 P.M. Admission $4.00 for adults, $3.00 for seniors, $2.00 for students and children.

Just outside Center City, on a bluff overlooking the Susquehanna River, stands Fort Hunter Mansion, surrounded by its outbuildings and park. The Federal-style mansion, built in 1814 by Archibald McAllister, is in remarkably good condition. Touring the house, open the closet doors to discover surprises such as sets of china or collections of fashionable clothing left behind by Helen Reily, last owner of the house. In the guest-room closet, you can peek at Mrs. Reily's pantaloons, bonnets (she had some one hundred), fans, hat pins, and other accessories. She also left a collection of dolls, toy soldiers, and even paper dolls. The doll house features a tiny hobby horse, a little dog curled up in a minute dog bed, and postcards glued to the walls for paintings. And don't miss the garden with its spicebush, smokebush, and boxwoods.

In December, when the mansion is decorated for Christmas, it is open daily from noon to 7:00 P.M. In September Fort Hunter Day brings the whole park alive with bagpipe music (in honor of the McAllisters), colonial art and crafts, food, and more. Demonstrations of open-hearth baking are offered periodically, as are other special programs.

 # Farm Bed and Breakfasts in Pennsylvania

- **Cedar Hill Farm,** Mt. Joy; (717) 653–4655.
- **Elver Valley Farm,** Cochranville; (717) 529–2803.
- **Highland Farm,** Emmaus; (610) 965–3843.
- **Meadow Spring Farm,** Kennett Square; (610) 444–3903.
- **Olde Fogie Farm,** Marietta; (717) 426–3992.
- **Spruce Edge Guest House,** Christiana; (717) 529–3979.
- **Sweetwater Farm,** Glen Mills; (610) 459–4711.

Carlisle

The town of Carlisle is known for country inns and antiques shops—not exactly what most kids want to see. Perhaps more kid-friendly are attractions such as the Carlisle fairgrounds (depending on what's going on this weekend), and, for older children interested in history, the Carlisle Barracks.

 CARLISLE BARRACKS (ages 10 and up)

Entrance located on Hanover Street. The post is open seven days a week. The Military History Institute and Bradley Museum are open weekdays only, 8:00 A.M. to 4:30 P.M. Closed weekends and federal holidays. Hessian Powder Magazine is open daily 10:00 A.M. to 4:00 P.M. Admission is **Free***. For information call the Public Affairs office at (717) 245–4101.*

At Carlisle George Washington founded the Army's first arsenal and school, the Carlisle Barracks. Later this site served as the Indian School where Jim Thorpe received his education. At present the Carlisle Barracks houses the U.S. Army War College.

Walking tours of the barracks begin with the newly restored Hessian Powder Magazine. History buffs won't want to miss the Military History Institute and Omar N. Bradley Museum, both in Upton Hall. The Military History Institute offers **Free** tours of its collection of rare military books. Family historians can research family members who served in the armed forces. (It's helpful to know not only the name but the unit of your family member.)

 CARLISLE FAIRGROUNDS (ages 8 and up)

1000 Bryn Mawr Road; (717) 243–7855.

Maybe somebody in your family is nuts about cars or antiques. The eighty-two-acre Carlisle Fairgrounds hosts major collector events on many weekends throughout the year. The antiques shows take advantage of the abundance of antiques dealers based in this area, plus many from outside the county. The automobile shows offer car flea markets and car corral, as well as "new old stock," parts, and memorabilia. Special events include Kids at Carlisle, in which children 3 to 8 can show off their own miniature pedal-, battery-, or gas-powered cars. For a schedule of events, contact Carlisle Productions at (717) 243–7855.

ALSO IN THE AREA

For hiking, cross-country skiing, hunting, and other outdoor activities, contact King's Gap Environmental Center on Route 174 West (500 Kings Gap Road) at (717) 486–5031.

Boiling Springs

This lovely lakeside town is the home of the Allenberry Resort Inn and Playhouse. The Allenberry stretch of the Yellow Breeches River attracts many families to try their hands at fly-fishing. Here, the rules are "catch and release" and "artificial lures only." It's a little different on the Letort Spring Run (pronounced *lee-tort*), which is considered more challenging, and attracts devotees of *A River Runs Through It*.

 ### ALLENBERRY RESORT INN
Route 174; (717) 258–3211.

 An eighteenth-century estate where you can enjoy professional theater, fishing, and special events. Call for a list of upcoming dinner theater productions.

Gettysburg

Every schoolchild in America should get the chance to experience Gettysburg. Before your visit older kids and parents can prepare by watching either Ken Burns's PBS *Civil War* series or the 1993 movie *Gettysburg*. The better prepared they are, the more they'll get out of it.

You may also plan ahead by choosing a tour ahead of time. A tour will help you get a handle on this remarkable shrine. To find the one that best suits your needs and to receive a sixty-four-page booklet about Gettysburg, contact the Gettysburg Travel Council, Department R-67, Gettysburg 17325; (717) 334–6274.

You may choose a bus tour, bicycle tour, a tour on tape, or a tour on horseback.

- Bus tours on a double-decker bus or an air-conditioned enclosed bus are available through Gettysburg Battlefield Bus Tours (717–334–6296).
- Tours on a Yellowstone Park bus are available through Historic Tours (717–334–8000).

Our Class Trip to Gettysburg

—by Judah Paulsen-Sacks, age 12½

When I was in the fifth grade, my classmates and I went to Gettysburg. Our social studies teacher was telling us about the Civil War. Each of us brought some lunch and money. I also brought my camera.

First we went to a museum of the Civil War. We came to see a special room. The walls were electronic. They showed in pictures the story of the Battle of Gettysburg.

We ate lunch in the van. (We were careful not to get the car messy.) Then we went to a horse stable. My horse was named Cowgirl. Anthony's horse was Bubblegum, and Mike's was Abbey. I've forgotten the other horses' names. Abbey was always leaving the trail. Bubblegum kept eating off the trees. The owner of the stable had warned us not to let our horses eat leaves or grass because once they'd started, they'd never stop. Even though the horses didn't always behave right, it was fun. I mean, who doesn't like horseback riding? It was that trip that inspired me to someday get a horse.

Later we went to the Tower. The tower was taller than a whale! Okay, maybe not that tall, but it *looked* that way. Some kids chose the stairs but Gabbi and I chose the elevator. The inside part isn't at the top. The top's an outside balcony. I didn't want to go up to the top but we couldn't find Mike and we thought he might be up there. I was scared out of my wits! Everything on the ground looked so small. I was scared the wind would blow me off the tower and I'd meet my death! Then we went down the stairs and found Mike sitting there!

My favorite part of the trip was Devil's Den. That's a place where many people claimed to have seen ghosts and demons and things like that. Me and Anthony went exploring there. We found a little cave-type place that I was just thin enough to squeeze through. We all went inside. I was the leader. In the dark, we thought we saw two green eyes!

None of us are quite sure whether what we saw was a demon or not. It could have been a ghost. Or maybe a hoax.

The trip to Gettysburg was one of the funnest, most memorable trips I've ever taken and it really made me think, "Ain't this a great planet?"

- Tours on tape are available from Gettysburg Battlefield Tape Tours (717–338–0631), CC Inc. Auto Tape Tours (717–334–6245), or Battlefield Driving Tours (717–334–8838).

- Tours on horseback, called "Ride Into History," are available through National Riding Stables (717–334–1288). Two-hour tours include a history of the battle; one-hour tours leave the history lesson out. Reservations six to eight weeks in advance are highly recommended. Tours are $20.90 for one hour, $42.00 for two hours. Ninety percent of tour riders have never been on a horse before, so have no fear.

- For your own personal tour, contact the Association of Licensed Battlefield Guides at (717) 334–1124.

- If you are interested in an 8-mile educational tour on a mountain bike, call Battlefield Bicycle Tours. Information is available at (800) 830–5775 or (717) 691–0236 or teribiker@aol.com.

The Gettysburg Travel Council recommends a minimum visit of three days to see all that Gettysburg has to offer. To prevent an overdose of history, plan for breaks and vary your activities. Here are some highlights.

GETTYSBURG NATIONAL MILITARY PARK (ages 8 and up)
Steinwehr Avenue (Business Route 15 South); (717) 334–1124; www.nps.gov/ gett. The Visitor Center is open daily 8:00 A.M. to 5:00 P.M. Although admission to the park and Visitor Center are **Free**, *there is a small charge for the Cyclorama and Electric Map attractions. Twenty-minute Cyclorama showings are offered every half hour from 9:00 A.M. to 4:30 P.M. The thirty-minute Electric Map showings are given every forty-five minutes from 8:15 A.M. to 4:15 P.M. For either show the fees are the same: adults 16 and over, $2.00; seniors, $1.50; children 15 and under,* **Free***; group rate, $1.50.*

A walk or horseback ride across this ghostly battlefield can be a truly moving experience.

Gettysburg National Military Park brings to life the story of three days in July 1863. About 400 artillery guns stand along the Union and Confederate battle lines, and more than 1,000 monuments help visitors picture what happened here.

Plan to stop at the Visitor Center first thing. Don't miss the *Cyclorama,* a 356-by-26-foot circular painting by Paul Phillippoteaux. You'll feel as if you're standing on the battlefield just before Pickett's charge. (Just think what an effect this painting must have had when it was completed in the 1880s!) At present a sound-and-light program brings the painting to life and adds to the experience. The Visitor Center also has an Electric Map of the battlefield and the Museum of the Civil War, the largest collection of Civil War artifacts anywhere.

Walking Tour of Downtown Gettysburg After you've

toured Gettysburg National Military Park and, optionally, Eisenhower
National Historic Park, you may think you've "done" Gettysburg. Well,
think again because you've only just begun!

Downtown Gettysburg offers an array of museums, shops, and
attractions.

Start at the town's official Information Center, located at 35 Carlisle
Street, across Lincoln Square from the center of town.

Cross Lincoln Square from the Information Center to visit the Lincoln Room Museum.

After the Lincoln Room Museum, you may choose to turn left down
Baltimore Street, where most of the museums and sights are, or turn
right for a ride on the Gettysburg Steam Train.

Going down Baltimore Street away from Lincoln Square, you can
stop at points of interest such as Schriver House Tour, Farnsworth
House, and Greyston's Story Theater.

Baltimore Street then forks. The left fork is the continuation of Bal-
timore Street where you'll find such sites as the Confederate States
Armory Museum, Jennie Wade House and Olde Town, Soldiers National
Museum, and Hall of Presidents and First Ladies.

The right fork is Steinwehr Avenue, where you'll find Magic Town,
the National Civil War Wax Museum, the Lincoln Train Museum, and
the Conflict Theater.

There is a self-guided driving tour that takes about two or three
hours. The park roads are open 6:00 A.M. to 10:00 P.M. Hikers, bikers,
and horses are welcome. Licensed battlefield guides are also available
from the National Park Visitor Center. Tours begin at 8:00 A.M. and
depart hourly. The fee is $30 per car for each two-hour tour. Boy Scouts
can earn a special merit badge by completing a 10-mile historic hike at
Gettysburg.

We found that when children have prepared by studying the battle
before their trip, many are able to imagine themselves as soldiers on the
field. When "reenacting" Picketts' Charge with our kids, we heard them
say, "That was really hard! Imagine how hard it would be if we were carrying rifles and surrounded by cannon smoke!"

EISENHOWER NATIONAL HISTORIC PARK (ages 10 and up)

Located on Business Route 15 South, adjacent to the battlefield; (717) 344–1124; www.nps.gov/eise. The farm is open daily from April through October. It is closed Monday and Tuesday from November through March, and for thirty-one days beginning the Sunday after New Year's Day.

Adjacent to the battlefield you'll find the Eisenhower National Historic Site, the 189-acre retirement home and farm of President and Mrs. Dwight Eisenhower. If you wish to tour the home, pick up tickets at the Gettysburg National Park Visitor Center, and then take a shuttle bus to the Eisenhower farm.

Pace yourself, because you've only just begun! You may wish to take a walking tour of downtown Gettysburg to get yourself oriented before visiting some of the many sites in town. The town's official Information center is located at 35 Carlisle Street, across from Lincoln Square in the center of town.

Cross Lincoln Square from the Information Center to visit the Lincoln Room Museum.

LINCOLN ROOM MUSEUM (ages 7 and up)

12 Lincoln Square; (717) 334–8188. Open in summer Monday through Thursday 9:00 A.M. to 7:00 P.M., Friday and Saturday 9:00 A.M. to 8:00 P.M. In the off-season, the museum is open Monday through Friday 10:00 A.M. to 3:00 P.M. Admission is $3.25 for adults, $1.75 for children.

This is the room where Abraham Lincoln spent the night before he delivered the Gettysburg Address. The room is still furnished as it was that night. You can follow in Lincoln's footsteps with a ten-minute sound-and-light program, and you can view original drafts of the famous speech.

JENNIE WADE HOUSE (ages 8 and up)

758 Baltimore Street; (717) 334–4100. Admission is $5.25 for adults, $3.25 for children. The Jennie Wade House and Olde Town are open daily. In summer hours are 9:00 A.M. to 9:00 P.M. and in the off-season 9:00 A.M. to 5:00 P.M.

In addition to the thousands of men who died at Gettysburg, there was one woman. Twenty-year-old Jennie Wade was baking bread for the Union soldiers when she was hit by a stray bullet. You can see the bullet hole. A clever holographic display tells Jennie's story. Jennie Wade's house is adjacent to Olde Town, where the streets of Gettysburg of 1863 are re-created.

HALL OF PRESIDENTS AND FIRST LADIES (ages 8 and up)

Baltimore Street; (717) 334–5717. Open daily 9:00 A.M. to 5:00 P.M. Admission $5.25 adults, $3.25 students.

You can hear U.S. presidents "speak" at the Hall of Presidents and First Ladies. A series of life-sized mannequins and taped messages can help kids learn the difference between Andrew Jackson and Andrew Johnson. The first ladies appear in reproductions of their inaugural gowns.

THE CONFLICT THEATER (ages 8 to 15)

213 Steinwehr Avenue; (717) 334–8003. Hours vary with season, so be sure to call ahead. Admission is $5.00 for adults, $4.00 for children.

The Conflict Theater presents a variety of different Civil War programs, including a new theatrical program, *Gettysburg: A Study in Valor,* which is the most in-depth study of the battle in town. For children ages 8 to 12, the best choice is *Adventure in Gettysburg.* For reservations or a schedule of performances, call (717) 334–8003.

THE NATIONAL CIVIL WAR WAX MUSEUM (ages 8 and up)

297 Steinwehr Avenue; (717) 334–6245. Hours vary seasonally, but usually 9:00 A.M. to 5:00 P.M. daily. Admission: adults, $4.50; young adults 13 through 17, $2.50; children 6 through 12, $1.75; children 5 and under, Free.

The National Civil War Wax Museum has organized its more than 200 life-sized figures into an audiovisual presentation including thirty different scenes. You can see animated figures reenact the Battle of Gettysburg and an animated Lincoln deliver the Gettysburg Address. On weekends from May until Labor Day, special events include living reenactments.

LINCOLN TRAIN MUSEUM (ages 8 and up)

Steinwehr Avenue; (717) 334–5678. Open in summer from 9:00 A.M. to 9:00 P.M. and in spring and fall 9:00 A.M. to 5:00 P.M. The museum is closed during the winter months. Admission to the Lincoln Train Museum is $5.25 for adults, $3.25 for children.

You can join Lincoln for the train ride to Gettysburg on a twelve-minute simulated trip at the Lincoln Train Museum. The museum also exhibits a toy train collection including a model-railroad layout that represents the Civil War.

GETTYSBURG SCENIC RAIL TOUR (all ages)

106 North Washington Street; for schedules and fares, plus information about theme trains, call (888) 94–TRAIN. Open seasonally. Tickets cost $8.00 for adults, $4.00 for children.

Board the Gettysburg Railroad Train about 2 blocks from Lincoln Square and choose between the 16-mile and 50-mile trips on trains that pass by the Gettysburg Battlefield.

Lighter Attractions in Gettysburg

Okay, so your younger ones have had enough history. Now's the perfect time for some lighter fare. For something spookily different, hear stories by candlelight at **Farnsworth House Ghost Stories** at 401 Baltimore Street. In season, stories are given Tuesday through Friday at 9:30 P.M. and Saturday at 8:00 and 9:30 P.M. Hours vary seasonally. Call (717) 334–8838 for details and the current schedule. Tickets are $6.00 for adults; children under 6 are **free**. Not recommended for children who are afraid of the dark or for very young children.

Younger kids will enjoy a break from history at **Magic Town,** 49 Steinwehr Avenue. You'll want to look very closely at the minute details and "magic" illusions that make this tiny town seem so real. Open evenings. Call (800) 878–4276 or (717) 337–0492.

In season you can enjoy these lighter attractions: **The Gettysburg Family Fun Center,** 1 mile from Town Square on Route 30 East (717-334-GOLF), has miniature golf, batting cages, an arcade, and a snack bar. **Mulligan McDuffer Adventure Golf,** adjacent to the battlefield, offers miniature golf and ice cream. Call (717) 337–1518.

Land of Little Horses is outside Gettysburg at 125 Glenwood Drive. The smallest Falabella horses may weigh seventy pounds and stand less than 20 inches high. Kids under eighty pounds can climb up on their backs (for an additional fee). The horses perform tricks three times a day from Memorial Day through Labor Day. There's also a carousel, train tram, nature area, gift shop, and snack bar. The Land of Little Horses is open 10:00 A.M. to 5:00 P.M., weekends only in April and May, September through October. Open daily in summer. Call (717) 334–7259. Admission is $6.50 for adults, $4.50 for children 2 to 12. "Herd" rates are available. Handicapped-accessible. Web site: www.littlehorses.com.

CONFEDERATE STATES ARMORY AND MUSEUM (ages 8 and up)

529 Baltimore Street; (717) 337–2340. Hours vary seasonally, closed for winter. Admission $1.50, all ages.

This museum features many original Confederate weapons.

SOLDIERS NATIONAL MUSEUM (ages 10 and up)

777 Baltimore Street; (717) 334–4890. Hours vary seasonally. Admission $5.25 adults, $3.25 children.

Ten Civil War dioramas are housed in the building that was General Howard's headquarters during the battle and later the Soldiers' National Orphanage.

GENERAL LEE'S HEADQUARTERS (ages 10 and up)

Route 30 West, 8 blocks west of Lincoln Square; (717) 334–3141. Hours vary seasonally. Admission $3.00 adults, $.50 children.

In this house General Lee and his staff made plans for the battle. Now the building houses a collection of Civil War relics.

Where to Eat

IN READING/BERKS COUNTY

These non-fast food restaurants offer kid-friendly dining:

Arner's Family Restaurants, *four convenient locations throughout Berks County: 2101 Howard Boulevard, Reading; (610) 779–6555; 9th and Exeter Street, Reading; (610) 929–9795; 1714 State Hill Road, Wyomissing Hills; (610) 372–6101; and 4643 Pottsville Pike, Route 61, Reading; (610) 926–9002. Casual atmosphere.*

Peanut Bar and Restaurant, *332 Penn Street, Reading; (610) 376–8500.* Lunch through late night, it's one of the few places where parents can enjoy gourmet selections while youngsters eat more kid-friendly choices. Besides, where else can you tell the kids, "go ahead, throw the peanut shells on the floor."

Cracker Barrel, *21 Industrial Drive, Hamburg; (610) 562–3622.* Home-style country cooking and a front porch with rocking chairs.

IN GETTYSBURG

These non-fast food restaurants in Gettysburg offer children's menus.

Dobbin House Tavern, *89 Steinwehr Avenue; (717) 334–2100.* A historic building including country store, bakery, and underground slave hideout.

Farnsworth House Inn, *401 Baltimore Street, (717) 334–8838.* An historic building with one hundred bullet holes. Gettysburg's only Civil War dining.

General Lee's Family Restaurant, *US 30, (717) 334–2200.* Casual, country dining rooms.

Where to Stay

IN LANCASTER AND PENNSYL-VANIA DUTCH COUNTRY

Bird-in-Hand Family Inn, *2740 Old Philadelphia Pike, Bird-in-Hand; (800) 537–2535.* Indoor/outdoor pools, free bus tour, restaurant, bakery.

Fairfield by Marriott—Lancaster, *150 Granite Run Drive, Lancaster; (717) 581–8122 or (800) 228–2800.* New in 1997. Indoor pool.

Quality Inn & Suites, *2363 Oregon Pike, Lancaster; (717) 569–0477.* Restaurant, outdoor pool.

Red Caboose Motel, *P.O. Box 303, Strasburg; (717) 687–5000.* Sleep in authentic cabooses and dine in authentic dining car. Seasonal buggy rides, petting zoo, flea market, country music.

Historic Strasburg Inn, *1 Historic Drive off Route 896, Strasburg; (800) 872–0201.*

IN HERSHEY

The Hotel Hershey, *Hotel Road, Hershey; (717) 533–2171 or (800) 533–3131.* Luxurious resort hotel with indoor/outdoor pool, children's pool, and **Free** shuttle buses to Hersheypark. Has two restaurants to suit different tastes. Choose the Fountain Cafe is you're traveling with young children.

The Hershey Lodge, *West Chocolate Avenue and University Drive, Hershey; (717) 533–3311 or (800) 533–3131.* Casual resort with indoor/outdoor pool, a playground, children's pool, and **Free** shuttle buses to Hersheypark.

Chocolatetown Motel, *1806 East Chocolate Avenue, Hershey; (717) 533–2330.* Good location.

Cocoa Nights Motel, *1518 East Chocolate Avenue, Hershey; (717) 533–2384.*

IN HARRISBURG

Ramada Inn on Market Square, *23 South 2nd Street, Harrisburg; (800) 2–RAMADA or (717) 234–5021.* Restaurant, indoor pool. Minutes from Hershey, Lancaster, Gettysburg.

Best Western Hotel Crown Park, *765 Eisenhower Boulevard, Harrisburg; (717) 558–9500.* Convenient to Hersheypark, Amish Country. State capitol minutes away.

Double Tree Club Hotel Harrisburg, *815 Eisenhower Boulevard (exit 19 of the Pennsylvania Turnpike and Highway 283), Middletown; (717) 939–1600 or (800) 222–TREE.* Indoor pool, restaurant. Convenient to Hersheypark and Amish Country.

For More Information

While surfing the web, you may wish to check out the website of the Harrisburg-Hershey-Carlisle Tourist and Convention Bureau at www.visithhc.com or any of the websites given in this chapter.

Laurel Highlands Region

The beauty of the Laurel Highlands area of Pennsylvania will take your breath away. One hundred miles of countryside, mountains, and valleys, two mountain ridges, and thirteen state parks and forests provide the setting for golfing, skiing, fishing, and hiking. The Youghiogheny River (the "Yock") means white-water rafting, and Raystown Lake offers calmer boating, swimming, and more.

In this area the Rails-to-Trails Conservancy is converting old railroad paths to hiking and biking trails. (For information, contact Rails-to-Trails of Central Pennsylvania at 814–832–2400 or Rails-to-Trails of Pennsylvania at 717–238–1717.)

Here you'll find a masterpiece of modern architecture, Frank Lloyd Wright's Fallingwater. Old Bedford Village re-creates our history, and Idlewild Park takes us to the Land of Make-Believe.

The Laurel Highlands is rich in history, especially sites associated with the French and Indian War, such as Fort

Faith & Emily's
Favorite Laurel Highlands Attractions

1. Idlewild Park
2. Family Float Trip on Youghiogheny River
3. Laurel Caverns
4. Lincoln Caverns
5. Raystown Lake
6. Old Bedford Village
7. Bat Hike in Canoe Creek Park
8. Rockhill Trolley Museum
9. Horseshoe Curve Railroad
10. Johnstown Incline

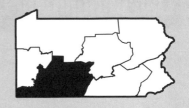

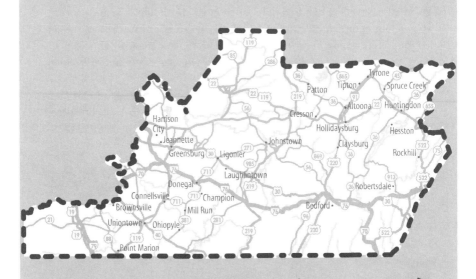

LAUREL HIGHLANDS REGION

Necessity and the authentically restored Fort Ligonier. In 1806 the National Road was built to link the East with what was then the Western frontier. This road is now Route 40, where every May wagoners with teams of horses commemorate the opening of the nation's first turnpike (the National Pike Festival). Two old tollhouses still exist along Route 40, which is also a great foliage route in October.

This area saw remarkable industrial development: coal mining, the steel industry, the growth of railroading, and the building of canals. Many families enjoy driving the 500-mile Path of Progress Heritage Route, which takes them past many of the sites described in this chapter. (For further information about the Path of Progress, call 800–898–3636 or check the website at www.allegheny.com.)

Faith & Emily's
Favorite Events in Laurel Highlands

- **Overly Country Christmas** (November through December), (412) 423–1400.
- **Hidden Valley Resort Winter Carnival** (late January), (814) 443–2600 or (800) 443-SKII.
- **Seven Springs Resort Spring Festival** (March), (800) 452–2223.
- **Ligonier Scottish Highland Games,** Idlewild Park (September), (412) 238–3666.
- **National Pike Festival** (October), (412) 329–1560.
- **Fort Ligonier Days** (October), (412) 238–4200.
- **Pioneer Days,** Old Bedford Village (September), (814) 623–1156.

Point Marion

FRIENDSHIP HILL NATIONAL HISTORIC SITE (ages 10 and up)
Off Route 119; (724) 725–9190; www.nps.gov/frn. Open daily year-round 8:30 A.M. to 5:00 P.M. Closed Christmas Day. **Free**.

Friendship Hill is the home of Swiss-born patriot Albert Gallatin, who was elected to the U.S. Senate and the House of Representatives, played an important role in the Whiskey Rebellion, was Secretary of the Treasury, a member of the team that negotiated the end of the War of 1812, and minister to France.

There are 8 miles of trails and a picnic area. You can take a pleasant walk to the grave of Gallatin's first wife, Sophia Allegre. The site overlooks the Monongahela River, but watch out for the steep banks. Also, be aware that there may be potential dangers in old buildings and mine works that have not yet been restored. Since the house is sometimes closed for restoration work, it's wise to call ahead: (412) 725-9190.

Uniontown

In the Uniontown area, you can visit Searights Tollhouse, Fort Necessity National Battlefield, and Laurel Caverns.

SEARIGHTS TOLLHOUSE (ages 8 and up)

Route 40 West; (724) 439–4422. Open Tuesday through Saturday 10:00 A.M. to 4:00 P.M. and, from mid-May to mid-October, Sunday 2:00 to 6:00 P.M. Hours subject to change due to restoration work. Admission is $1.00 for adults, children enter Free.

The U.S. government authorized construction of the National Road in 1806 to connect the East and the West. Even today it is the only road system constructed completely by the federal government. One of the National Road's tollhouses, Searights Tollhouse is open to the public and is administered by Fayette County Historical Society. Inside the tollhouse, you can visit the toll keeper's office, kitchen, and living room.

FORT NECESSITY NATIONAL BATTLEFIELD (ages 9 and up)

On Route 40 (the National Road), 11 miles east of Uniontown; (724) 329–5512. The fort building is open every day from dawn to dusk. The Visitor Center and Mount Washington Tavern are open 8:30 A.M. to 5:30 P.M. Closed Christmas Day. Extended hours in summer.

At Jumonville Glen, 5 miles from here, the young George Washington met with his first experience of battle, during the French and Indian War. Washington's forces won the first encounter. The fort was built afterward in expectation that the French would return, which they did, but this time Washington was forced into the only surrender of his career. Here you can also visit the grave of General Braddock.

Fort Necessity was reconstructed in 1952. At the Visitor Center here, you can view an audiovisual presentation about the fort, the battle, and the research behind the reconstruction effort. You'll probably be surprised when you see the size of the reconstructed fort. The circular stockade is 53 feet in diameter. The gate is only 3½ feet wide.

While you're in the neighborhood, you may wish to visit the Mount Washington Tavern, built in the 1820s on land once owned by George Washington himself. The tavern has been restored to look as it might have in the period when it was constructed to serve travelers along the new National Road, which was built in 1818.

LAUREL CAVERNS (all ages)

Located 5 miles east of Route 40, at the crest of Summit Mountain; (724) 438–3003 or (800) 515–4150; laurelcaverns.com. Open daily from May to October, 9:00 A.M. to 5:00 P.M., and weekends only in March, April, and November. Family guided tours leave every twenty minutes. Tours: adults, $9.00; seniors, $8.00; youth grades 6 through 12, $7.00; children grades K through 5, $6.00; preschoolers are Free*. Group rates are available with advance notice. Indoor miniature golf course: $5.00 per person, $4.00 group rate.*

Located on a mountainside, Pennsylvania's largest cave offers not only the underground caves but a breathtaking view. Although the adventurous may choose the challenging Caving Adventure, the guided family tour is recommended for families with children under 12 and the physically challenged. Watch your step in the narrow passageways.

At the end of the tour, don't miss the sound-and-light show, sort of an underground *Fantasia*. There's even "Cavern Putt," a handicapped-accessible miniature golf course housed in a huge man-made cave!

Bring a jacket and a flashlight. Rappelling and climbing sessions are available to groups inside the caverns, as are fossil-hunting excursions. Bathrooms in the Visitor Center are handicapped-accessible and include changing tables. There is a picnic shelter, or you can pick up Zeb's Pizza nearby.

Brownsville

 ### NEMACOLIN CASTLE (ages 8 and up)

Front Street in Brownsville; (724) 785–6882. Open 11:00 A.M. to 5:00 P.M. Easter weekend through October. In June, July, and August, it's also open Tuesday through Friday 11:00 A.M. to 4:30 P.M. Admission: adults $5.00, seniors $4.00, children 12 and under $2.00.

Despite its name, Nemacolin Castle is not a castle but the home of Jacob Bowman, who opened a trading post in Brownsville in 1786. It does look a little like a castle, though, with its turreted tower and battlements. You can take a guided tour of more than twenty furnished rooms. Around the holidays Christmas candlelight tours are offered.

Connellsville

 CRAWFORD CABIN (ages 6 and up)

North Seventh Street at the Youghiogheny River; (724) 628–5640; www.faywest.com. Open Monday through Wednesday 9:00 A.M. to 5:00 P.M., Thursday and Friday 9:00 A.M. t o 3:00 P.M. Free.

The Connellsville Area Historical Society (275 South Pittsburgh Street; 412–628–5640) administers Crawford Cabin. George Washington visited his lifelong friend Colonel William Crawford in this humble log cabin, 14 by 16 feet, built in 1765. Colonel Crawford and his men served Washington at the crossing of the Delaware and the battles of Trenton, Princeton, Brandywine, and Germantown.

Ohiopyle

Ohiopyle State Park's Youghiogheny River (affectionately nicknamed the Yough, pronounced "Yock") offers a wide range of river adventures. From March into October, thousands of vacationers challenge the Yough. Find the guided or unguided trip that suits your family's taste and ages.

 RAFTING ON THE YOUGHIOGHENY (ages 4 and up for the Middle Yough only)

For novices or families with younger children, the **Middle Yough** is the best choice, with its gentler Class I and II rapids and relaxing scenery. Laurel Highlands River Tours offers a guided trip on the Middle Yough, which they call their Family Float Trip, for families with children ages 4 and up. (Many seniors also enjoy this trip.) Wilderness Voyageurs rents easily maneuverable rafts for unguided rafting. (See below for information on these establishments.)

The **Lower Yough's** Class III and IV rapids are a little wilder. The minimum age for this 7.5-mile stretch of the river is 12 years of age. Mountain Streams offers a minitrip on the Lower Yough that lasts about two hours. Many of these organizations also provide bike rentals, kayaks, or "duckies." A duckie is sort of an inflatable kayak, used with a double-ended paddle, available with one or two seats. Most outfitters recommend duckies rather than canoes. A Thrillseeker, also used with a double-ended paddle, is made of a harder plastic.

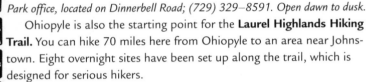

Amazing **L**aurel **H**ighlands **F**acts

This region includes twenty-three state parks and forests.

Teenagers with a taste for adventure can take on the **Upper Yough**. This 11-mile stretch of the river includes Class IV and V rapids and is recommended for experienced paddlers only. The minimum age is 16.

OHIOPYLE STATE PARK (all ages)

Park office, located on Dinnerbell Road; (729) 329–8591. Open dawn to dusk.
Ohiopyle is also the starting point for the **Laurel Highlands Hiking Trail.** You can hike 70 miles here from Ohiopyle to an area near Johns- town. Eight overnight sites have been set up along the trail, which is designed for serious hikers.

There are flush toilets and shower facilities in Ohiopyle State Park, and **Fox's Pizza** not far away. **Mountain Streams & Trails Outfitters** offers a licensed day-care center for children under the minimum rafting age of 4.

Any of the following outfitters can help you select your trip:

- **Laurel Highlands River Tours,** P.O. Box 107, Ohiopyle 15470, (800) 4-RAFTIN or (724) 329-8531; www.laurelhighlands.com

- **Mountain Streams and Trails Outfitters,** P.O. Box 106, Route 381, Ohiopyle 15470, (800) RAFT NOW (723-8669); www.mtstream.com

- **White Water Adventurers, Inc.,** P.O. Box 31, Ohiopyle 15470, (800) WWA-RAFT; www.wwaraft.com

- **Wilderness Voyageurs, Inc.,** P.O. Box 97 Department PA, Ohiopyle 15470, (800) 272-4141 or (724) 329-5517; www.wilderness- voyageurs.com

KENTUCK KNOB (ages 9 and up)

Kentuck Road, Chalk Hill; (724) 329–1901. Open Tuesday through Sunday. Regular tours depart from 10:00 A.M. to 4:00 P.M. Reservations are suggested. Tours are $10 on weekdays, $15 on weekends and holidays. Longer, in-depth tours are $30 and depart at 8:30 A.M. or by reservation.

Opened in May 1996, this home designed by Frank Lloyd Wright is a great side trip if you enjoyed Fallingwater. Children 9 and up are welcome to join the regular tour. There are no day-care facilities for younger ones.

Mill Run

 ### FALLINGWATER (ages 9 and up except for children's tours for ages 5 to 9)

Route 381; (724) 329–8501. Open for guided tours April to mid-November, Tuesday through Sunday 10:00 A.M. to 4:00 P.M. In December tours are offered weekends only 11:00 A.M. to 3:00 P.M. Closed January and February. On weekends, tours are $12.00; on weekdays, tours are $8.00. Children under 9 are not permitted on the regular tour. Special tours for children ages 5 to 9; call for schedules and admission prices.

The story goes that Frank Lloyd Wright told Edgar Kaufmann, "I want you to live with the waterfall, not just look at it." Because of the technology of cantilevers, Wright was able to do just that.

In a beautiful wooded setting, Wright placed Fallingwater, one of his most significant architectural achievements. It seems as if it has always been here, with the waterfall cascading from it. Inside the house walls of windows look out into the woods. The American Institute of Architects has called Fallingwater "the best all-time work of American architecture."

The regular tour takes about forty-five minutes to an hour, but if you like, you may make a reservation for a longer tour, which is very detailed and can take up to two hours. (These in-depth tours are available at 8:30 A.M. and carry a fee of at least $33 per person.) Tours do require a fair amount of walking. Only the first floor is handicapped-accessible.

Please note that children under 9 are not permitted to take the regular tour of the house. If you wish to see it yourself, however, you may take advantage of child care provided here ($2.00 per child per hour). If you have children 5 to 9 who might like to see the house, call to find out when special children's tours are scheduled. Reservations are strongly recommended for both children's and adult tours. Lunch is available in Fallingwater's restaurant.

If you would like to see more of Wright's work, try Kentuck Knob in Ohiopyle.

ALSO IN THE AREA

Fallingwater is operated by the Western Pennsylvania Conservancy, which also runs **Bear Run Nature Preserve,** one-half mile away. It is very convenient to Ohiopyle.

The family can camp at **Yogi Bear's Jellystone Park,** but even if you're not camping here, you can take advantage of the water slides, playground, and other recreational activities. For information and pricing schedule, call (800) HEY-YOGI.

Mill Run Water Slides (724–455–2929) offers two 400-foot slides to cool you off.

Champion

 SEVEN SPRINGS MOUNTAIN RESORT (all ages)
Located between exits 9 and 10 on the PA Turnpike; (800) 452–2223.

Ski magazine has rated Seven Springs Mountain Resort among the top fifty ski resorts in North America. This large facility offers lodging for more than 5,000 people in hotel rooms, condos, and chalets. Besides ski and snowboard rentals and ski lessons, the resort offers snowtubing (eight chutes), swimming, bowling, indoor miniature golf, and game rooms.

Donegal

 CADDIE SHAK FAMILY FUN PARK (all ages)
Located 1.5 miles east on Route 31 off Exit 9 of the Pennsylvania Turnpike; (724) 593–7400; www.caddieshak.com. Open daily March through October. Admission and parking are Free.

You can't drive past Caddie Shak Family Fun Park without a reaction from your kids. ("Their tongues hang out," says one parent.) Convenient to the turnpike, Caddie Shak has three go-cart tracks, miniature golf, batting cages, games, and food. Recently added attractions include bumper cars with water cannons, a petting zoo, paint ball, and horseback riding. A nice way to break up the trip. The rides and attractions are moderately priced, and family discounts are available. Handicapped-accessible.

Hidden Valley

HIDDEN VALLEY SKI (all ages)
4 Craighead Drive; (814) 443–2600 or (800) 443–SKII;
www.hiddenvalleyresort.com.

The instructors at Hidden Valley Ski want you to learn to ski with them. One of the mid-Atlantic's most popular family ski resorts, Hidden Valley has twenty-five ski slopes and trails, over 30 miles of cross-country ski trails, and a half-pipe for snowboarders. They also have kids' camp, indoor and outdoor pools, boating, fishing, tennis, and more.

In spring and summer, there's still a lot to do, such as golfing, mountain-biking, and swimming. The many restaurants cater to a variety of tastes, and all are kid-friendly with the possible exception of the Snow Shoe Lounge (kids may be served with parents, but it is a lounge). Mountain Munchkins Child Care offers baby-sitting for children 18 months to 8 years. There are changing tables in both men's and women's rest rooms.

Greensburg

HANNA'S TOWN (ages 8 and up)
951 Old Salem Road; (724) 836–1800. Open Memorial Day through Labor Day, Tuesday through Sunday 1:00 to 5:00 P.M. In May, September, and October, it is open on weekends only.

Archaeological research in Greensburg has revived Hanna's Town. A stockade fort, the home of Robert Hanna, the town jail, and a wagon shed are reconstructed. Klingensmith House has been moved here. You can visit the field museum and see archaeological artifacts unearthed here.

ALSO IN THE AREA
You may want to check out the **Westmoreland Museum of Art** (221 North Main Street, 412-837-1500) or the **Westmoreland Symphony Orchestra** (412-837-1850).

Jeannette

Depending on how you look at it, Bushy Run Battlefield is in either Jeannette or Harrison City. Either way, it's about 11 miles northwest of Greensburg, and it's an interesting place to visit.

BUSHY RUN BATTLEFIELD (ages 8 and up)

Route 993; (724) 527–5584. Visitor Center: April through October, Wednesday to Saturday 9:00 A.M. to 5:00 P.M. and Sunday noon to 5:00 P.M. Battlefield: Wednesday to Sunday 9:00 A.M. to 5:00 P.M. year-round. From November to March the museum is closed. Admission: $2.00 for adults, $1.50 for seniors and students, $1.00 for children under 12.

Here's an opportunity to acquaint your family with a lesser-known conflict: Pontiac's War. In 1763 Native American forces, under the command of war chief Pontiac, struggled against the British, eventually occupying Fort Detroit and Fort Pitt. At the Bushy Run Battlefield, the British turned the tide against this rebellion.

At the Visitor Center a fiber-optic map helps you get your bearings. Take some time to observe the new interactive exhibits, maps, flags, and weapons and learn about this episode in our history. In the Kids' Corner you can try on a reproduction uniform. Then you can take a guided tour of the battlefield. There are 3 miles of historic hiking trails, education programs, and special events. On the Edge Hill Trail, each stop represents one aspect of the Battle of Bushy Run, including the Flour Bag Entrenchment in which flour bags were used to protect the British wounded. There is also a gift shop. Handicapped-accessible.

Another trail, the Flour Sak Discovery Trail, focuses on how humans have used things from the forest. For example, the black walnut tree provided food, dye, insect repellent, gunstocks, and furniture.

The Iroquois Nature Trail was designed by the Boy Scouts to demonstrate the changes in the environment between the nineteenth and twentieth centuries. There are thirteen stations, such as Beauty in Nature Through Adaptation, where you can see how nature has healed itself in what was once a stone quarry.

Ligonier

IDLEWILD PARK (all ages)

Route 30 West; (724) 238–3666; www.idlewild.com. The park is open Tuesday through Sunday, June through August, on weekends only mid-May to June and on holiday Mondays. The gates open at 10:00 A.M., and closing times vary. Admission to Idlewild Park, which includes all rides and attractions, is a real bargain: $15.95 for anyone ages 2 to 54; $11.50 for seniors; children 2 and under are Free.

"America's Most Beautiful Theme Park," Idlewild Park is the home of Mister Rogers' Neighborhood of Make-Believe, complete with the Neighborhood Trolley your preschoolers have always wanted to see. Fred Rogers himself served as creative consultant for this charming replica with the castle, King Friday, Queen Sarah Saturday, and all the details you'll recognize right away. In July, characters such as Mr. McFeeley may appear in person.

This relaxing and manageable park, nestled in the woods, is perfect for children 12 and under. But it also has rides for older kids such as the new Wild Mouse and the Rollo Coaster, built in 1938. Located about 50 miles east of Pittsburgh and also a sister park to Kennywood and Sandcastle, it began as a picnic area in 1878. At present the three-row carousel, built by Philadelphia Toboggan Company in the 1930s, still entrances children of all ages.

You'll literally step through the pages of a Story Book to visit the homes of "Peter, Peter, pumpkin eater," "The Three Little Pigs," and the "Little Crooked Man," among others. The beloved Story Book Forest was added in 1956, with its more than forty scenes and characters from fairy tales and nursery rhymes. It takes about an hour to explore the Story Book Forest.

Jumpin' Jungle gets families climbing and crawling and, well, jumping. Climb up the netting; jump in the ball room. H2Ohhh Zone is a giant water attraction for all ages. It has body flumes, "shotgun" slides, and a huge swimming pool, plus Little Squirts, wet fun for younger ones. Bring your bathing suit if you plan to go on any of the water slides or swim in the pool.

FORT LIGONIER (ages 8 and up)

Intersection of Routes 30 and 711; (724) 238–9701. The fort is open daily April to October, Monday through Saturday 10:00 A.M. to 4:30 P.M., and Sunday noon to 4:30 P.M. Admission is $5.00 for adults, $2.75 for children 6 to 14 years old.

Fort Ligonier was built by the British during the French and Indian War. The entire fort, except for its foundation, was destroyed by 1800, but it has been carefully reconstructed. It has gun batteries and a retrenchment. The Visitor Center offers exhibits and a film. You can visit several restored buildings such as a quartermaster's storehouse, magazine, hospital, and commissary.

Every October, on the anniversary of its most famous battle, the fort celebrates Fort Ligonier Days.

WINDSWEPT 'HOT AIR BALLOON' ADVENTURES
(ages 8 and up)

303 Chrisner Road; (724) 238–2555. Call for reservations and for pricing schedule.

This beautiful area is really something to see from the air. Windswept 'Hot Air Balloon' Adventures offers morning and evening flights. Children 8 to 12 must be accompanied by an adult, and children weighing under sixty pounds fly at half-price. If one member of your family doesn't want to fly, he or she can follow the balloon with the chase crew, which is also fun.

Amazing Laurel Highlands Facts

Mt. Davis in Somerset County is the highest peak in Pennsylvania.

Laughlintown

COMPASS INN MUSEUM (ages 8 and up)

Three miles east of Ligonier, on Route 30 East; (724) 238–4983. Open May through October, Tuesday through Saturday 11:00 A.M. to 4:00 P.M. and Sunday noon to 4:00 P.M. Admission is $4.00 for adults, $2.00 for students, Free *for children under 5.*

If you want to get a picture of what it was like in a typical roadside inn of the eighteenth and nineteenth centuries, visit the Compass Inn Museum. The log part was built in 1799, and the stone addition in 1820. The Ligonier Valley Historical Society has restored the building, and the kitchen, blacksmith's shop, and barn, have been reconstructed on their original sites.

You can find out where terms like "upper crust" and "toasting" came from. You can see how travelers spent the night crammed into beds with other guests. You can visit the family's quarters, as well as the barn, where old horse-drawn and ox-drawn vehicles still remain, and sometimes a blacksmith is on duty, demonstrating the craft. You can also see tools of the period.

During summer living-history days are held on the third weekend of each month. In November and December candlelight tours are offered on weekends only.

Johnstown

The town of Johnstown will always be remembered as the site of the tragic flood that occurred on May 31, 1889. The stress of a storm proved too much for the town's neglected dam, which broke, sending a wall of water down the mountain and through the town, killing more than 2,000 people.

But Johnstown is not just a place of tragedy; it is a town full of life. In late June, Johnstown hosts "Thunder in the Valley," an unusually family-oriented motorcycle rally. In August, the Cambria County Ag-Tour offers a day in the country with 𝓕𝓻𝓮𝓮 refreshments at several area farms. The Log House Arts Festival, during Labor Day weekend, has many activities for children. Also, the Pasquerilla Performing Arts Center has "Sydney's Series" of plays for children. Besides these annual events, Johnstown has the new BOTTLEWORKS Ethnic Arts Center.

JOHNSTOWN FLOOD NATIONAL MEMORIAL (ages 8 and up)

Located in St. Michael, 10 miles northeast of Johnstown; (814) 495–4643; www.nps.gov/jofl. Open from Memorial Day to Labor Day, 9:00 A.M. to 6:00 P.M. During the rest of the year, it is open 9:00 A.M. to 5:00 P.M. It is closed on Thanksgiving, Christmas, and New Year's Day. Admission $2.00. Call for details. Take U.S. 219 to the St. Michael/Sidman Exit. Head east on PA 869, and turn left onto Lake Road at the sign.

The Johnstown Flood began on the site in Saint Michael where you can see the Johnstown Flood National Memorial, administered by the National Park Service. In fact, you can see what little is left of the South

Fork Dam from here. A weakness in this dam is suspected of having made the flood so disastrous.

An award-winning documentary, *Black Friday,* brings the events to life. The thirty-five-minute film puts you inside the terror of the flood. In fact, it is so effective parents are warned that it may be too frightening for young children.

In summer you can see reenactments of some of the events surrounding the flood. You can also take a tour around the dam. The flood happened on Memorial Day, so every year during that holiday weekend, the abutments of the dam glow with the light of thousands of luminaries. Special presentations are offered, including *Tales of the Great Flood.*

JOHNSTOWN INCLINE (all ages)

711 Edgehill Drive; easily accessible to Routes 56 and 403, and Route 271; (814) 536–1816; www.inclineplane.com. Weekdays the ride runs from 6:30 A.M. to 10:00 P.M. On Saturday hours are 7:30 A.M. to 10:00 P.M., and on Sunday, 9:00 A.M. to 10:00 P.M. Call for fares and schedules. **Free** *parking is available at both the top and the bottom.*

After visiting the Memorial, you'll want to complete the story with a tour of the Johnstown Flood Museum. But first you might want to break up the seriousness with an exhilarating ride on the Johnstown Inclined Plane. You'll travel up on an amazing 71.9 percent grade, the steepest vehicular inclined plane in the world. Your car can ride the incline with you, if you desire, so that you can drive around the town of Westmont.

After the Johnstown Flood, the frightened residents of the area wanted to live at the top of the hill, but they needed a way to commute to and from the city, so this incline was built. An "incline" is an unusual kind of cable railway found in Johnstown and Pittsburgh. During Johnstown's two subsequent floods (1962 and 1977), the incline became the people's escape route. At night, when both the tracks and the cars are lit up, the incline is a spectacular sight.

At the top of the incline, 634 feet above the city, there is an observation deck, visitor center, and the Incline Station Restaurant and Pub. The view of the Conemaugh Valley is spectacular, as seen from the glass-walled Plane Visitor Center. From this vantage point you can see one of the largest American flags anywhere.

THE JOHNSTOWN FLOOD MUSEUM (ages 6 and up)

304 Washington Street (P.O. Box 1889); (814) 539–1889; www.ctcnet.net/ jaha. Open May though October, Sunday to Thursday 10:00 A.M. to 5:00 P.M.; Friday and Saturday 10:00 A.M. to 7:00 P.M. From November through April open daily 10:00 A.M. to 5:00 P.M. Call for information and admission charges.

The museum, located in a former Carnegie Library, tells the story of the Johnstown flood disaster. Photos show how the town looked before the waters came, and after. An animated map with light and sound effects shows how the water swept through Johnstown, destroying thousands of homes and businesses.

First, see the documentary film *The Johnstown Flood,* which won the Academy Award for Best Documentary Short Subject in 1989. This twenty-five-minute movie is shown hourly and was made using black-and-white still photos taken after the flood. A longer version of this movie has been shown on PBS's *The American Experience.*

Then visit the two floors of permanent exhibits. The third floor is used for temporary exhibits, such as one describing Johnstown's many ethnic "clubs." The museum store offers a large selection of books and gifts.

BOTTLEWORKS ETHNIC ARTS CENTER (ages 6 and up)

411 Third Avenue; (814) 536–3699. Open Tuesday through Friday 10:00 A.M. to 4:00 P.M., and Saturday 11:00 A.M. to 3:00 P.M. Admission is Free. *Some special events have additional fees.*

In 1998 the old Tulip Bottling Company building was converted into the BOTTLEWORKS, whose mission is "to educate, preserve, and celebrate the ethnic heritage of the people of the Johnstown region." The Tulip Bottling Company was founded by a family of Russian and Hungarian Jews. In just a few years, the BOTTLEWORKS has become well known in the area, primarily for three festivals: Ethnic Celebration, on the first Sunday in June; Oktoberfest in late September to October; and the Ethnic Wedding during Labor Day weekend.

ALSO IN THE AREA

Every September, the Johnstown Area Heritage Association hosts **Johnstown FolkFest,** three days of music and culture reflecting the historical and ethnic heritage of the area. For information call (888) 222–1889.

Stackhouse Park offers many special programs for children in its 277 acres of wooded land.

The all-new **Windber Coal Heritage Center,** in the nearby mining town of Windber, offers an interesting interactive view of the everyday life of a coal mining family. Open 10:00 A.M. to 5:00 P.M. daily May 1 to October 31. Adjacent to outdoor Miner's Park and within walking distance of the shops and restaurants of Windber. Call (814) 467–6680 for admission fees and information, or check the website at www.allegheny.org/windber.

Claysburg

 BLUE KNOB RECREATION (all ages)
Route 20 North (from Pennsylvania Turnpike, Exit 11). For details call in-state (800) 822–3405 or (814) 239–5111; out-of-state, call (800) 458–3403; www.bedfordcounty.net/blueknob.

One of the top ski resorts in the area, Blue Knob offers a KinderSki program, a ski school, an outdoor ice rink, swimming pools, and both junior and senior rates.

Cresson

ALLEGHENY PORTAGE RAILROAD NATIONAL HISTORIC SITE (ages 8 and up)
12 miles west of Altoona and 10 miles east of Ebensburg on Route 22, off the Gallitzin exit; (814) 886–6150; www.nps.gov/alpo. Open Memorial Day through Labor Day 9:00 A.M. to 6:00 P.M. The rest of the year it is open 9:00 A.M. to 5:00 P.M. Closed Christmas Day. Admission: $2.00.

In the middle of the nineteenth century, when Philadelphia was being linked to Pittsburgh by rail and canal, this portion of the Allegheny Mountains between Hollidaysburg and Johnstown seemed impassable. So someone came up with a "portage railroad." A series of inclines carried the freight and passengers up the hills.

The Engine House Interpretive Building features full-scale models, a movie, and hands-on exhibits. The railroad no longer exists, but you can walk along a portion of its route and see one section of restored track. As you enjoy the view from the overlook, be sure to note Skew Arch Bridge, which is actually twisted so that a wagon road could pass over the track. Costumed presentations and ranger-led hikes are available during the summer months.

Amazing Laurel Highlands Facts

The Laurel Highlands get more than 100 inches of real snow per year, plus another 60 to 80 inches from man-made snow machines.

Hollidaysburg

TROUGH CREEK STATE PARK (all ages)

Route 994. Twenty-four hour access. **Free**. *For information and pricing schedule, call (814) 658–3847.*

If you want to stay in comfort in a beautiful forested setting, Trough Creek Cottage, at Trough Creek State Park, is available for rental year-round. It is a two-story home built in the 1800s as an ironmaster's house, and now completely renovated, including a modern eat-in kitchen, four bedrooms, a bathroom, and central heat.

CANOE CREEK STATE PARK (all ages)

On Route 22, about 13 miles east of Altoona, and about 7 miles east of Hollidaysburg or 11 miles west of Water Street; (814) 695–6807. The "day use" side is open 8:00 A.M. to sunset. The cabin area and east side have twenty-four-hour access. Admission is **Free**.

You can reserve either a rustic or modern cabin and enjoy a wide variety of nature education programs at Canoe Creek State Park, one of a few parks that offer bat hikes, a favorite with our boys. At Canoe Creek you can join in on a bat hike to look in on Pennsylvania's largest bat nursery colony (females and young) in the attic of an old church. As night falls, they emerge from their home—about 10,000 of them! Children under 12 must be accompanied by an adult. Bring a flashlight. Other programs teach about bluebirds, birds' nests, frogs and toads, and wildflowers. Persons with disabilities may call (814) 695–6807 if assistance will be needed to participate in the program.

Patton

SELDOM SEEN TOURIST COAL MINE (ages 8 and up)

Located on Route 36, 4 miles north of Patton, 7 miles from Prince Gallitzin State Park; (800) 237–8590 or mine phone in season only (814) 247–6305. Open Memorial Day, July 4th, and Labor Day, plus weekends throughout June and September, as well as Thursday and Friday in July and August. Hour-long tours are conducted daily from noon to 6:00 P.M. Admission: adults, $6.00; children under 12; $3.50.

Many of the coal mines in southwestern Pennsylvania were small, family-run mines like this one. This nonprofit educational attraction is one of the region's most popular sites. Many of the tour guides are former miners and descendants of immigrant miners. Somehow once your kids have imagined themselves hand digging and hand loading coal for 25 cents a ton, taking out the garbage doesn't seem so bad.

Altoona

Altoona has a lot to offer. Once known as a great railroad town, Altoona had several large railroad shops. Several of the shop buildings still remain.

ALTOONA RAILROADERS MEMORIAL MUSEUM (all ages)

1300 Ninth Avenue; (814) 946–0834; www.railroadcity.com. From November through March, open Tuesday through Sunday 10:00 A.M. to 5:00 P.M. from April through October, open seven days a week 9:00 A.M. to 5:00 P.M. Admission: adults, $8.50; seniors, $7.75; children 3 to 12, $5.00.

There are many museums devoted to the technology of railroading, but the Altoona Railroaders Memorial Museum tells the story of the people involved in this gigantic industry. Inside, a locomotive dominates the lobby. As you enter, you'll receive an ID card. You'll want to take in a theater presentation about the people of the Pennsylvania Railroad. Next, you'll really get a feel for what it was like to live in a railroad town. You can visit a typical railroader's home, or see how safety was maintained by testing in the Altoona railroad lab. You can hear the voices of the workers and their families.

A new interactive exhibit called All Aboard for Kids is aimed at children ages 2 to 9.

The museum is across from the Amtrak station, so real fanatics can come by train, see the trains, and go home by train. There are changing tables in the bathrooms only in the new building. If you get hungry, the shopping center next door has fast food, pizza, and Chinese food.

HORSESHOE CURVE NATIONAL HISTORIC LANDMARK (all ages)

Located 6 miles west of Altoona; (814) 946–0834; www.railroadcity.com. Open daily May through October 10:00 A.M. to 6:00 P.M. and November through April 10:00 A.M. to 3:30 P.M. Closed on Monday. Adults, $3.50; seniors, $3.00; children 3 to 12, $1.75. A yearly pass is $5.00.

At the Altoona Railroaders Museum, you can see a film that describes how the Horseshoe Curve Railroad was built. Then you can drive about 5 miles to watch the trains at Horseshoe Curve National Historic Landmark. Also administered by the Altoona Railroaders Museum, this incredible engineering feat made the Allegheny Portage Railroad obsolete (see page 129).

You can watch the trains go by from the Visitor Center, where you can also see a model of what the area looked like before the railroad changed the landscape. The best view of the trains is from above. You can get there by funicular or on foot (up 194 steps). One round-trip funicular ride is included in the admission.

There is a food concession open seasonally, and all bathrooms have changing tables.

QUAINT CORNER CHILDREN'S MUSEUM (ages 3 to 10)

On Route 36, at 2000 Union Avenue only a few blocks from the Railroad Museum; (814) 944–6830. Open Thursday, Friday, and Saturday from 1:00 to 5:00 P.M. Admission: $1.00 for children, $1.50 for adults.

Kids love exploring closets and attics, and they're welcome to snoop around in the Quaint Corner Children's Museum. Peek in the International Closet or the Amish Closet, and climb up the ladder to Grandma's Attic.

The Quaint Corner Children's Museum was designed as a place for families to explore together, promoting creative hands-on learning and an appreciation for art, history, and science. The house itself is charming with its stained-glass windows and fine woodwork. Children love the craft room, dress-up clothes, and the sandbox in the basement. There's even a player piano in the gift shop. The gift shop has a nice selection of 25-cent items. The bathroom, like the house, is old, with no changing or handicapped facilities. The bathtub is full of toy jewelry! The annual Quaint Corner Children's Fair comes in mid-August with puppet shows, games, and food.

BENZEL'S PRETZEL BAKERY (all ages)

5200 Sixth Avenue (Route 76); (814) 942–5062; www.benzels.com. Open Monday through Friday 9:00 A.M. to 5:00 P.M. and Saturday 9:00 A.M. to 1:00 P.M. Tours are Free.

You can walk to Benzel's from the Quaint Corner Children's Museum. Operated by a third generation of the Benzel family, Benzel's Pretzel Bakery makes about five million pretzels every day. At one time the pretzels were shaped by hand, but at present the dough goes through an extruder. To order pretzels by mail, call (800) 344–GIFT. There is a changing table in the handicapped-accessible rest room.

ALSO IN THE AREA

Cast your cares away at **Lakemont Park,** 700 Park Avenue. For details call (814) 949–PARK. Lakemont Park is open daily from June to August and open weekends in May and September, 11:00 A.M. to 9:00 P.M. There are water slides, bumper cars, go-carts, miniature golf, and rides of all types including Spins n' Grins Kiddieland. Facilities include bathrooms throughout the park and a comfort station for nursing mothers. A wide variety of foods are available, from pizza to funnel cake.

Sinking Valley

 ### FORT ROBERDEAU (ages 8 and up)

Open May 15 through September 30, Tuesday to Saturday 11:00 A.M. to 5:00 P.M. and Sunday 1:00 to 5:00 P.M. Closed on Monday. (814) 946–0048.

Sinking Valley, which is between Altoona and Tyrone, is the site of Fort Roberdeau. This 1778 stockade has been reconstructed, and it now offers living-history reenactments, tours, and a picnic area.

Tipton

BLAND'S PARK (all ages)

Old Route 220; (814) 684–3538. Open daily except Monday from early June through Labor Day, weekends in May and September. Admission is **Free**.

Located on I-99 just north of Altoona, this amusement park has something for everyone, even if your family includes a toddler. Rides, miniature golf, pony rides, bumper cars, and much more are available for family fun. Brand-new in 1999 are two water areas. Tipton Rapids includes five water slides. You have to be 42" tall to ride the red tower, 48" tall for the green one. Smaller kids will enjoy the interactive water play in Tipton Waterworks.

Tyrone

GARDNERS CANDIES (all ages)

30 West Tenth Street; (814) 684–0857. Open Monday through Saturday 9:30 A.M. to 9:00 P.M. and Sunday from 1:00 to 9:00 P.M. Admission is **Free**.

A sweet taste of nostalgia for children of all ages, Gardners Candies has been making candies for nearly a century. Inside its History of Candyland Museum, you can visit a penny-candy store, complete with big jars of colorful penny candies such as fireballs, licorice, and candy buttons. It looks right out of a picture book, with dark wood candy counter, Tiffany-style lamp, brass scales, and antique valentine hearts.

Spruce Creek

INDIAN CAVERNS (all ages)

Eleven miles east of Tyrone on Route 45, between Water Street and State College in Huntington County; (814) 632–7578. During June, July, and August, hours are 9:00 A.M. to 6:00 P.M. daily. In April, May, September, and October, hours are 9:00 A.M. to 4:00 P.M. daily. November through March, the cavern is closed. Admission is $8.00 for adults, $4.00 for children 6 to 12.

There are real cave paintings on the walls of Indian Caverns; a turtle, a tepee, a Mohawk chief.

More than 400 years ago, Native Americans used these caverns as a winter shelter, council chamber, and burial ground. Adjacent to Indian Caverns is a second cavern, Giant's Hall, where you can view the Grotto of the Wah Wah Taysee, a cave that glows, and the Frozen Niagara, more than two stories tall. Kids enjoy the sounds made by a musical rock.

The wide concrete walkways and Native American artifacts make this an excellent cavern if your family includes a wide range of ages, attention spans, and energy levels.

Amazing Laurel Highlands Facts

This region includes more than twenty golf courses (including the Latrobe Country Club owned by Arnold Palmer); 700,000 acres of game land; 120 lakes and streams; plus white-water rafting on the Youghiogheny River; and Raystown Lake, Pennsylvania's largest man-made lake.

Huntingdon

GREENWOOD FURNACE STATE PARK (all ages)

On PA Route 305, 5 miles west of Belleville; (814) 667–1800. The Visitor Center is open daily from Memorial Day weekend through Labor Day, 9:00 A.M. to 5:00 P.M. During spring and fall the center is open limited hours.

Less than forty minutes from Huntingdon, Lewistown, or State College is a green park area on the site of the Greenwood iron furnaces and the "village built around an inferno." You can take a one-hour, self-guided walking tour of a portion of the historic district and see parts of the town such as the tramway, historic roads, and charcoal hearths. Campsites are available.

LINCOLN CAVERNS AND WHISPER ROCKS (all ages)

On Route 22, 3 miles west of Huntingdon; (814) 643–0268. The cave is open daily Memorial Day through Labor Day 9:00 A.M. to 7:00 P.M. In April, May, September, October, and November, hours are 9:00 A.M. to 5:00 P.M. Admission: $8.00 for adults, $4.50 for children ages 4 to 14, and **Free** *for children 3 and under. A single admission fee gets you into Lincoln Caverns and Whisper Rocks.*

These two caverns are a bit more challenging than some other nearby caverns. The walkways are narrow, wet, and steep, but the rock formations are spectacular: flowstones, stalactites, calcite, and crystals.

Ann Dunlavy Molosky, third-generation manager of the cave, emphasizes education as well as fun. Many educational programs are available, including geology and speleology workshops, as well as programs focused on debunking common misconceptions about bats. Bring a sweater.

THE SWIGART MUSEUM (all ages)

Route 22 East, 4 miles east of Huntingdon; (814) 643–0885. Open daily Memorial Day through October, 9:00 A.M. to 5:00 P.M. Admission: adults $4.00, children ages 6 to 12 $2.00; children under 6 enter Free.

This museum is the oldest automobile museum in America, established by the late W. Emmert Swigart in 1920. The present owner, William E. Swigart, Jr., continued the collection upon his father's death in 1949. The Swigart collection emphasizes the era when America was first becoming a mobile society. Featured cars include a 1900 Winton, 1904 Rambler, and the only remaining Carroll. Other highlights include two Tuckers and Herbie, the "Love Bug." About thirty-five cars from the collection of 200 are on display at any given time. Supporting these is an outstanding collection of license plates and name plates. Children will enjoy seeing the exhibits of antique toys, trains, and bicycles.

Going Batty For Judah's tenth birthday, we took about twelve of his friends on a bat hike. We also brought Seth, who was seven and a half and Gideon, a newborn in a baby sling. Judah was very interested in bats.

The guide told us that July was a good time for a bat hike because the bats would recently have had young, and the colony would be at its largest.

As the sun set we waited outside the dilapidated barn that was the bats' home. The kids were all impatient to see the bats fly out to feed on the millions of insects that congregated over the nearby field.

Our guide had brought a device that amplified the bats' sonar sounds. He explained how to distinguish the sounds the bats made as they located and devoured their prey.

As darkness fell, first one bat emerged from a crack in the roof of the barn. Then another. Then another, then more and more until we counted more than 200, then lost count. The sky over the field was dark with bats.

Hesston

Area residents believe that Raystown Lake doesn't get the attention it deserves. This huge man-made lake is located in Huntington County, surrounded by two state forests, trout-stocked streams, museums, historic sites, campgrounds, and lots of family recreation. Call (814) 658-0060 or (800) RAYSTOWN.

 ### SEVEN POINTS CRUISES (all ages)

Raystown Lake, Seven Points Marina, off Route 26; (814) 658–3074 for departure times and details; www.7pointsmarina.com. The boats operate for both private charter and for the public, April through October. Public cruises depart up to three times a day at the height of the summer season, and cost $6.00 for adults, $5.00 for seniors, and $2.50 for children under 12.

There are several ways to see the lake and its countryside. Seven Points Cruises offers a number of different cruises, including special Kidz Kruz on its two excursion boats, the *Raystown Belle* and the *Raystown Queen*. You get a view of the lake including Sheep Rock Cliffs, a box lunch, a chance to feed the fish, and a demonstration of the "rack storage" building, in which more than 200 hundred boats are kept.

Seven Points Marina also offers Seven Points Eatery, pontoon boats, ski boats, jet skis, and parasailing, plus a beach and water trampolines.

Entriken

 ### *PROUD MARY* PADDLEWHEEL BOAT (all ages)

Raystown Lake; for information call (814) 658–3500, (800) RAYSTOWN, or (800) 628–4262. Lake Raystown Resort & Lodge Marina cruises April through October. Sightseeing cruise $6.50 adults, $3.25 children. Dinner and brunch cruises available.

You can take a paddlewheel boat ride on the *Proud Mary*, which sails on Raystown Lake. This is also a great spot for recreation like swimming, fishing, hiking, and more. Lake Raystown Resort and Lodge, where the *Proud Mary* docks, also has a water park, an inner-tube ride, and a children's activity pool.

Rockhill

EAST BROAD TOP RAILROAD (all ages)

Route 994, 1 mile west of Orbisonia in Rockhill; (814) 447–3011. Open from June to mid-October, Saturday and Sunday, with three train trips daily. Trains depart at 11:00 A.M., 1:00 P.M., and 3:00 P.M. Fares: $9.00 for adults, $6.00 for children 2 to 11. Group rates available for groups of twenty or more.

East Broad Top Railroad once carried coal and other raw materials. At present it is the most complete and authentic rail site in North America.

Board the train for a ride on the only narrow-gauge railroad in the East still running at its original site. The narrated train ride takes about fifty minutes and carries you past countryside that is virtually unchanged since the days when East Broad Top Railroad transported coal along these tracks. If you like, bring along a picnic lunch. You can get off at Colgate Grove, picnic, and go back on a later train.

Every year during Columbus Day weekend, railroad buffs come from all over the United States to East Broad Top's Fall Spectacular. For this event all four locomotives operate at once and scheduled shop tours are available.

 ### ROCKHILL TROLLEY MUSEUM (all ages)

Meadow Street (Route 994); on weekends the number to dial is (814) 447–9576; other days call (717) 263–3943 or (610) 965–9028 for information. Open daily from Memorial Day to mid-October, 10:30 A.M. to 4:30 P.M., plus some weekends and holidays. Trolleys operate 11:00 A.M. to 4:30 P.M. Fares are $3.00 for adults, $1.00 for children. For more information write to Railways to Yesterday, Inc., P.O. Box 1601, Allentown 18105.

Adjacent to East Broad Top Railroad, you can visit the Rockhill Trolley Museum. This museum has twenty-six trolleys and streetcars, including cars from Norristown, Philadelphia, Johnstown, Harrisburg, Scranton, and York. You can take a 2½-mile ride on a restored trolley, passing the Rockhill Iron Furnace.

Like the National Trolley Museum near Pittsburgh, the Rockhill Museum is staffed by volunteers who love what they're doing. Volunteers here are members of Railways to Yesterday, Inc. Your trolley ticket is good for unlimited rides on the date purchased. Most days, you can try out two or three different cars. You can bounce along on the "Toonerville Trolley" or enjoy the fresh air in "1875," which is open on the sides.

Robertsdale

In the town of Robertsdale, you'll find the Broad Top Area Coal Miners Museum and Entertainment Center.

BROAD TOP AREA COAL MINERS MUSEUM AND ENTERTAINMENT CENTER (ages 8 and up)

Reality Theater, Main Street; (814) 635–3807, 635–3220, or 635–2013. Open Friday and Saturday 10:00 A.M. to 5:00 P.M. and Sunday 12:00 to 5:00 P.M. Admission is $3.00 for adults, $1.50 for children 12 and under. On show nights, tickets are $6.00 for adults, $3.00 for children.

This museum offers exhibits about coal mining and railroading in the area.

Bedford

If you like the tradition of stealing a kiss on a kissing bridge, you'll love Bedford County. It has fourteen covered bridges, and you can cuddle your toddlers and embarrass your older kids on every one of them.

OLD BEDFORD VILLAGE (all ages)

Business Route 220, one-half mile south of Pennsylvania Turnpike Exit 11; (814) 623–1156. Open daily starting on the second Sunday in April until the last Sunday in October, 9:00 A.M. to 5:00 P.M. Admission is $6.95 for adults, $5.95 for seniors, $4.95 for children 6 and over.

Drive over the Claycomb Covered Bridge to Old Bedford Village. (The village is also reachable via Route 30, the scenic Lincoln Highway.)

This restored village of more than forty log structures is beautifully laid out to re-create a typical village of the mid-1790s, with homes, schools, a church, and shops. Interpreters in authentic costumes bake bread and make brooms, baskets, and pottery. About fourteen indigenous crafts are represented. The kids will love stopping for ice cream or donuts as you tour the town.

Call (814) 623-3335 if you wish to see a play in the village's Log Opera House. Meals are available at Pendergrass Tavern in the village. Dress comfortably and wear walking shoes. Wheelchair-accessible. The Village Craft and Gift Shop offers many unusual crafts made in the Village.

Annual special events include a crafts festival in June, gospel music in August, Civil War reenactments in September, pumpkin festivals in October, and a holiday celebration in December. In 1995, for the first time, the village offered a storytelling festival in August.

You can take a pleasant walking tour of Historic Downtown Bedford, including several historic houses and the Fort Bedford Museum.

FORT BEDFORD MUSEUM (ages 8 and up)

Fort Bedford Drive; (814) 623–8891 or (800) 259–4284. Open daily May through October, except Tuesday in May, September, and October, 10:00 A.M. to 5:00 P.M. Call for admission rates.

Old Fort Bedford was a British stockade built in 1758 during the French and Indian War. Later it was used as a British outpost on the frontier until the 1770s. Fort Bedford is gone, but you can learn about its past by touring the Fort Bedford Museum. The museum includes a large scale model of the fort, Native American artifacts, weapons, uniforms, a Conestoga wagon, and children's toys of the period.

Where to Eat

IN JOHNSTOWN AREA

Applebee's Neighborhood Grill & Bar, 425 Galleria Drive; (814) 269–4500.

Capri Pizza & Restaurant, Richmond Mall; (814) 535–8914.

Coney Island Lunch, 127 Clinton Street; (814) 535–2885.

Fazoli's Italian Restaurant, 1419 Scalp Avenue; (814) 269–3403.

Incline Station Restaurant & Pub, 713 Edgehill Drive; (814) 536–1816.

Johnnie's Restaurant & Lounge, 415 Main Street; (814) 536–9309.

Where to Stay

IN OHIOPYLE

Yough Plaza Motel, (800) 992–7238. Within walking distance of the river.

Scarlett Knob Campground, Inc., Route 381 North; (412) 329–5200. Adjoining Ohiopyle State Park. Both campsites and cabins available.

Ohiopyle State Park Kentuck Campground, (729) 329–8591.

IN JOHNSTOWN

Comfort Inn Ebensburg, Route 22 West, Ebensburg; (814) 472–6100 or (800) 221–2222. Suites available, indoor pool, complimentary continental breakfast.

Days Inn Johnstown, *1540 Scalp Avenue; (814) 269–3366.*

Comfort Inn Johnstown, *455 Theatre Drive, Johnstown; (814) 266–3678 or (800) 228–5150.* Centrally located near all major attractions.

Holiday Inn, *downtown, 250 Market Street, Johnstown; (814) 535–7777.* Indoor pool, Harrigan's restaurant, sidewalk cafe.

Sleep Inn Johnstown, *453 Theatre Drive, Johnstown; (800) 753–3746.*

IN RAYSTOWN LAKE AREA

Lake Raystown Resort & Lodge, *100 Chipmunk Crossing, Route 994, Entriken; (814) 658–3500.* Wild River Waterpark, *Proud Mary* Paddlewheel Boat, miniature golf, hiking, fishing, picnic areas, camping, and restaurants all nearby.

Seven Points Marina/Houseboat Rental, *Seven Points Marina, off Route 26; (814) 658–3074.* Fully equipped houseboats for rent. Cruises aboard the *Raystown Bell* and *Queen.*

For More Information

Allegheny Mountains Convention and Visitors Bureau, *Logan Valley Mall, Route 220 & Goods Lane, Altoona 16602; (800) 84–ALTOONA or (814) 943–4183; www.alleghenymountains.com.*

Bedford County Visitors Bureau, *141 South Juliana Street, Bedford 15522; (800) 765–3331 or (814) 623–1771; www.bedfordcounty.net.*

Fulton County Tourist Promotion Agency, *112 North Third Street, P.O. Box 141, McConnellsburg 17233; (717) 485–4064.*

Greater Johnstown/Cambria County Convention and Visitors Bureau, *111 Market Street, Johnstown 15901–1608; (800) 237–8590 or (814) 536–7993; www.visitjohnstownpa.com.*

Greene County Tourist Promotion Agency, *17 South Washington Street, Waynesburg 15370; (412) 627–TOUR; www.greenepa.net.*

Indiana County Tourist Bureau, *Indiana Mall/2090 Route 286 South, Indiana 15701; (724) 463–7505; www.indiana-co-pa-tourism.org.*

Laurel Highlands Visitors Bureau, *120 East Main Street, Ligonier 15658; (800) 925–7669 or (724) 238–5661; www.laurelhighlands.org.*

Raystown Country Visitors Bureau, *241 Mifflin Street, Huntingdon 16652; (800) 269–4684 or (814) 643–3577; www.raystown.org.*

Pittsburgh and Environs

From the dizzying height of one of its two inclines, with the city spread below you, to the *Gateway Clipper* riverboat, from which you see the city at the confluence of the Monongahela, Allegheny, and Ohio Rivers, Pittsburgh comes as a pleasant surprise. As the boat passes the tip of Point State Park, you'll see a striking fountain that shoots a blast of water straight up into the sky.

Entering Pittsburgh through the Fort Pitt Tunnel, you'll see why the *New York Times* has called this "the only city in America with an entrance." Pittsburgh has the Golden Triangle (downtown area) with the cleanest Free subway system in the United States, and the Wayfinder system of 1,500 brightly colored signs to help you navigate.

For one hundred years the names Pittsburgh and Carnegie have been inextricably linked. Andrew Carnegie believed that wealth should

Faith & Emily's
Favorite Pittsburgh Attractions

1. Kennywood Park
2. Sandcastle Park
3. Carnegie Science Center
4. Pittsburgh Children's Museum
5. Carnegie Museums of Art and Natural History
6. Duquesne or Monongahela Incline
7. Pittsburgh Zoo
8. Gateway Clipper
9. National Trolley Museum
10. Children's Studio at Society for Contemporary Crafts

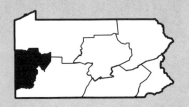

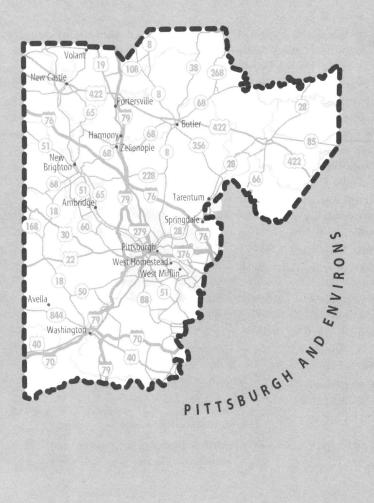

Volant
New Castle
Portersville
Butler
Harmony
Zelienople
New Brighton
Ambridge
Tarentum
Springdale
Pittsburgh
West Homestead
West Mifflin
Avella
Washington

PITTSBURGH AND ENVIRONS

be used to benefit the public. Thanks to Andrew Carnegie, and the museums he helped to create, your trip to Pittsburgh can include dinosaur bones, paintings, sculpture, a submarine, and more. Celebrating its centennial in 1996, the Carnegie museums include the Carnegie Science Center, Museum of Art, Museum of Natural History, Library of Pittsburgh, Music Hall and Performing Arts Center, and the Andy Warhol Museum.

You'll also benefit from the legacies of some of Pittsburgh's other leading families: the Mellons, Fricks, and Phippses.

You won't want to miss the latest addition to Pittsburgh's impressive list of museums, the Senator John Heinz Regional History Center, opened in 1996. Its Children's Discovery Place uses hands-on activities to teach about the everyday life of children from the region's history.

And then, within minutes, you can be squealing with excitement at America's favorite traditional amusement park or at an outstanding water park. If you're looking for a decidedly different way to tour Pittsburgh, check out Just Ducky Tours, Inc. They offer tours aboard a World War II military amphibious vehicle. Call (412) 928-2489 for information.

When planning your visit, you may want to check out the Greater Pittsburgh Convention and Visitors Bureau website at www.pittsburgh.net or any of the websites of the museums and attractions listed in this chapter.

Faith & Emily's
Favorite Pittsburgh Area Events

- "Pumpkin Patch Trolley" (October); (412) 228-9256.
- "Fireworks Capital of the World" July Fourth Celebration in New Castle; (412) 654-5593.
- Holidays at the Carnegie (November through December); (412) 622-3131.
- Pittsburgh Children's Festival, Pittsburgh's North Side (mid-May); (412) 321-5520.
- Greater Pittsburgh Renaissance Festival; (412) 282-2070.
- Three Rivers Arts Festival; (412) 481-7040.

Pittsburgh's North Side

Start your adventure in downtown Pittsburgh's North Side with a stop at the Visitor Center on Liberty Avenue near Stanwix Street, a handy place to pick up maps, brochures, and advice. Just a few blocks away is the Pittsburgh Children's Museum (PCM).

THE PITTSBURGH CHILDREN'S MUSEUM (ages 12 and under)

10 Children's Way; Allegheny Square–North Side; (412) 322–5059; www. pittsburghkids.org. Open Tuesday through Thursday and Saturday 10:00 A.M. to 5:00 P.M., Friday 10:00 A.M. to 8:00 P.M.; Sunday noon to 5:00 P.M. Open Mondays from mid-June through August. Admission: adults $5.00; children 2 to 18 and seniors $4.50; children under 2 are Free.

The Pittsburgh Children's Museum is reaching "great heights" with exciting exhibits and programs for the young and young-at-heart. Visitors can scale the two-story Kids' Climber, build and launch airplanes from Flying Machines, and raise themselves up in human-powered elevators. Get creative in the multimedia studio: Create silkscreen prints, play with clay, paint a masterpiece, and design on a computer. Learn about health and anatomy with 7-foot-tall blue-haired mascot Stuffee; and explore the basics of car, bicycle, bus, and pedestrian safety on Safety Street. Put on a puppet show at one of four stages and enjoy the original puppets from Mister Rogers' Neighborhood. There are even areas for the youngest visitors to explore and learn.

This hands-on museum, located in the historic Old Post Office building, is a top attraction for family fun in Pittsburgh. The Children's Museum also offers fun, unique educational programs, outreach performances, and classes.

POINT STATE PARK (all ages)

Point State Park is at the tip of Pittsburgh's "Golden Triangle." The 36-acre park is accessible from the east and west by I–376 and I–279, from the north by PA Route 8 and from the south by PA Route 51.

You can stroll the park's paved promenade along the riverfront, enjoying the view. At the tip of the park, you can see the fountain also known as "The Point." The sites of both Fort Duquesne and Fort Pitt are located in Point State Park.

Fort Duquesne was built by the French and destroyed by the British in 1758. Today only a bronze marker shows where that fort once stood.

FORT PITT MUSEUM (ages 8 and up)

Point State Park; (412) 282–9284. Open in winter, Wednesday to Saturday 10:00 A.M. to 4:30 P.M., and Sunday noon to 4:30 P.M. In summer it is open Tuesday as well. Admission is $4.00 for adults, $2.00 for children 6 to 12. If you bring in a losing Pennsylvania lottery ticket, you can save $1.00. Maximum family rate is $10.00.

The British occupied Fort Pitt until 1772, when the Americans took over. You can see the Fort Pitt Blockhouse and the Fort Pitt Museum. Here you can view exhibits that describe Pittsburgh's early years.

CARNEGIE SCIENCE CENTER (all ages)

One Allegheny Avenue; (412) 237–3400; www.csc.clpgh.org. Open Sunday through Friday 10:00 A.M. to 5:00 P.M., Saturday 10:00 A.M. to 9:00 P.M. The Omnimax Theater also has a special double feature at 7:00 and 8:00 P.M. Friday and Saturday, with laser shows following until 11:00 P.M. on Friday and midnight on Saturday. Call for titles, times, and special extended summer and holiday hours. Tickets can be purchased separately for the exhibits, Omnimax, laser shows, and the submarine, or you may select from two different "combo" tickets. Handicapped-accessible.

Pitch a fast ball, climb an ice wall, enter the world of virtual reality, watch a balloon shatter, hear lightening spark, feel an earthquake, see a tornado.

Come to the Carnegie Science Center and travel the world in a four-story Omnimax Theater, explore the universe in the planetarium, take a tour aboard a World War II submarine, and interact with more than 250 hands-on exhibits.

Carnegie Science Center's permanent exhibits include: Science and Sport, SciQuest, The Miniature Railroad and Village, Ports of Discovery, the USS *Requin,* The Kitchen Theater, The Works, and The Blue Cross Health Science Theater. Enjoy the ultimate audiovisual experience at the four-story-tall Omnimax Theater.

Now open throughout the year, you can visit Pittsburgh's famous Great Miniature Railroad and Village. This replica of western Pennsylvania of the 1920s includes a minute Ferris wheel, a circus parade, and real smoke puffing out of the steel mill.

NATIONAL AVIARY (all ages)

Allegheny Commons West; (412) 323–7235; www.aviary.org. Open 9:00 A.M. to 5:00 P.M. seven days a week. Closed Christmas. Admission: $5.00 for adults, $4.00 for seniors, $3.50 for children 2 to 12.

There are nearly 500 live birds of more than 220 species, many of them endangered, at the National Aviary. You'll see birds of all sizes and colors, from a tiny hummingbird to an Andean condor with a 10-foot wingspan, and more, including highly endangered red-crowned cranes. The aviary itself presents a lush green indoor oasis, with few obstructions between you and the birds' habitats.

Open exhibits, free-flight atriums, and hands-on demonstrations bring excitement and fun to the experience. The Animal Encounters program introduces visitors to the birds up-close in informal presentations. Guided tours by reservation. Educational programs are available for children and adults, and new interactive graphics will invigorate your imagination. The entire facility and spacious parking lot are handicapped-accessible.

 THE ANDY WARHOL MUSEUM (all ages)

117 Sandusky Street, on Pittsburgh's north side near the cultural district, and across the Seventh Street Bridge from downtown; (412) 237–8300; www.warhol.org. Open Wednesday and Sunday 11:00 A.M. to 6:00 P.M., Thursday through Saturday 11:00 A.M. until 8:00 P.M.; closed Monday, Tuesday, and legal holidays. Admission is $6.00 for adults, $5.00 for seniors, $4.00 for children (3 and over) and students.

Artist and pop-icon Andy Warhol was born in Pittsburgh. Opened in 1994, The Andy Warhol Museum is the largest single-artist museum in the United States. Housed in a funky historic industrial warehouse are 3,000 original works of art including paintings, drawings, prints, films, and a lot more. Public parking lots with attendants are located under the North Shore Expressway, 1 block north of the museum off Sandusky Street. There is additional parking behind the museum and in the area.

Amazing Pittsburgh Facts

With seven floors and more than 3,000 original works of art, the Andy Warhol Museum is the largest single-artist museum in the United States.

At the Warhol Museum children are especially drawn to the Silver Clouds gallery on the fifth floor, where silver, pillow-shaped balloons float around you. Hands-on activities are offered in the Weekend Factory on Saturdays and Sundays noon to 4:00 P.M.

 ## MATTRESS FACTORY (all ages)

500 Sampsonia Way; (412) 231–3169; www.mattrss.org. Open Tuesday to Saturday 10:00 A.M. to 5:00 P.M., Sunday 1:00 to 5:00 P.M. Suggested donation: Adults $4.00, students and seniors $3.00. Parking is available at 505 Jacksonia Street. Handicapped-accessible.

If your kids think art is stuffy, here's the antidote. Take them to the Mattress Factory, housed in an old mattress factory in the Mexican War Streets section, near the Andy Warhol Museum (also convenient to the National Aviary and the Children's Museum). This one-of-a-kind museum of contemporary art specializes in installations that physically surround you. For example, kids especially are mesmerized by the magical light effects in three permanent installations by artist James Turrell. A garden piece by Winifred Lutz allows kids (and adults) to crawl through tunnels, climb up stairs, even enjoy a picnic lunch right in the middle of an artwork. In an "apartment" designed by Alan Wexler, everything is movable.

A student guide pamphlet is available to help your family make the most of this experience with the playfulness of art. There are bathrooms both inside and in the garden. Completely handicapped-accessible.

The "Strip District"

Pittsburgh's "strip district" has nothing to do with exotic dancing. This is the nickname given to Pittsburgh's open-air marketplace. It's fun to take in the atmosphere on this half-mile strip along Penn Avenue and Smallman Street, starting at Eleventh Street. Enjoy the colorful produce, the smells of ethnic food, bakeries, restaurants, and other shops.

Near the strip district give your children a really extraordinary experience by participating in a children's workshop at the Society for Contemporary Crafts.

 ## SOCIETY FOR CONTEMPORARY CRAFTS (ages 4 to 12)

2100 Smallman Street; (412) 261–7003. Open Tuesday through Saturday 10:00 A.M. to 5:00 P.M. The Children's Studio is Free *and open during public hours.*

Here your family can appreciate and participate in crafts together. The exhibition gallery mounts four temporary craft exhibitions per year. Meanwhile, in the Children's Studio, parents and kids can learn first-hand the techniques used by the artists. The Children's Studio offers an opportunity to work on an artist-designed project that corresponds to the current exhibition. For example, during the 1999 exhibition, "Stop Asking/We Exist: 25 African-American Craft Artists," featured artist Bing Davis designed a jewelry-making project called "Artfull Adornment," involving found objects.

Craft projects are open to all ages from the youngest child who can barely hold a pencil to great-grandparents. Come as you are and stay until your masterpiece is complete.

THE SENATOR JOHN HEINZ PITTSBURGH REGIONAL HISTORY CENTER (all ages)

1212 Smallman Street; (412) 454–6000. Open daily 10:00 A.M. to 5:00 P.M. Admission: $6.00 for adults, $3.50 for children ages 3 to 18, and $4.50 for seniors (ages 65 and older) and students with ID.

Opened in April 1996, this museum features permanent exhibits spotlighting life in Western Pennsylvania from 1750 to the present. In the Great Hall children immediately notice a 1949 restored trolley, a Conestoga wagon, and the Pittsburgh city fire bell, cast after the great Fire of 1845.

The Children's Discovery Place tells the story of eight real children from the region (two are still living today) whose lives exemplify different aspects of history. For example, kids can learn about the everyday life of a child who worked in a steel mill, one who was an indentured servant, and one who lived a privileged life. Hands-on activities get the kids involved in these lives. For example, kids learn to pack pickles in the Heinz factory as one of these children did, beginning at age 14.

The building is handicapped-accessible, and there are baby-care facilities on the first and third floors. There is also a cafe and a museum shop.

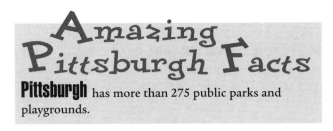

Amazing Pittsburgh Facts

Pittsburgh has more than 275 public parks and playgrounds.

South Side

On the south side of Pittsburgh, you'll have an excellent opportunity to see the city from the water or from one of two inclines.

Board the Gateway Clipper at Station Square, a five-minute stroll across the Smithfield Street Bridge from downtown Pittsburgh. Two contiguous rail-road buildings have been beautifully restored to create Station Square, a collection of sixty-five shops, eleven restaurants, and a hotel.

JUST DUCKY TOURS, INC. (all ages)

Station Square Dock; call (412) 928–2489 for information and reservations.

There's a great new way to tour the city of Pittsburgh—by DUCK! Not the kind of duck with feathers, but a World War II military amphibious vehicle, a bright green bus-boat that carries passengers on a tour of Pittsburgh, on land and water. The only requirement for passengers is that they quack. Hour-long tours depart from Station Square on Pittsburgh's South Side.

THE GATEWAY CLIPPER FLEET (all ages)

9 Station Square Dock; call (412) 355–7980 for information and a schedule of cruises.

The **Gateway Clipper** Fleet has a schedule of day and night cruises year-round, ranging from narrated sight-seeing trips to elegant dinner cruises with entertainment. Family Fun cruises are aimed at children 12 and under, such as the Goodship Lollipop Ride and seasonal cruises like Santa Family Fun, Halloween Monster Fun, and Bunny Fun. All the riverboats are climate controlled. The different vessels vary in facilities, but all have plenty of rest rooms, some with changing tables, others with wide counters. Some also have snack bars, and certain cruises include boxed lunches or pizza. Goodship Lollipop cruises feature Lolli the clown.

MONONGAHELA INCLINE (all ages)

Across the street from Station Square; (412) 442–2000. It runs Monday through Saturday 5:30 A.M. to 12:45 A.M. On Sunday and holidays it is open 8:45 A.M. to midnight. The fare is $1.00 each way.

The "Mon," the first passenger incline in the United States, is 635 feet long and rises to an elevation of about 368 feet at a 35-degree angle.

Inclined Planes of Pittsburgh

Two of Pittsburgh's famous inclines are located near Station Square: the Monongahela Incline and the Duquesne Incline.

So what is an "incline" anyway? It's a cable railway designed to carry passengers or freight up Pittsburgh's steep hills. Inclines were invented before electric streetcars and before automobiles. At one time the city had seventeen of these steam-driven engineering marvels. At present two survive, although now they are driven by electricity. Thousands of commuters use the inclines every day. (Both stations and inclines are now wheelchair-accessible.)

What's the difference between the two? Well, the Duquesne has red cars and the tracks are lit with red lights. The Monongahela has green and yellow lights on the tracks, and the cars are ivory with black trim. Both have overlooks from Mount Washington, with a great view of the city. Both have historical information in their upper stations.

DUSQUESNE INCLINE (all ages)

Located on Carson Street, directly across the river from Three Rivers Stadium. Call (412) 381–1665 for information. The Duquesne operates Monday through Saturday 5:30 A.M. to 12:45 A.M., Sunday 7:00 A.M. to 12:45 A.M. The fare is $1.00 each way. Free *parking is available at the lower station.*

The Duquesne Incline has been in operation since 1877. The interiors are made of hand-carved cherry panels, with oak and bird's-eye maple trim and amber glass transoms. You can rise up 400 feet at a 30-degree angle to the New Observation Deck at the upper station and take in the spectacular vista.

East Pittsburgh

Three miles east of downtown, you'll discover Pittsburgh's Oakland cultural district, where you can see the University of Pittsburgh, Carnegie-Mellon University, the Carnegie Museums of Art and Natural History, Schenley Park, and the Phipps Conservatory. Also in this area you can visit Kennywood Park, Sandcastle Waterpark, and the Pittsburgh Zoo. (Technically, Kennywood is in West Mifflin and Sandcastle is in West Hempstead, both of which are east of the city, so it gets a little confusing. In this guide we have listed them under West Mifflin and West Hempstead respectively.)

CARNEGIE MUSEUMS OF ART AND NATURAL HISTORY (all ages)

Located side by side on Forbes Avenue; (412) 622–3131; www.clph.org/moa/. Both museums are open Tuesday through Saturday 10:00 A.M. to 5:00 P.M., and Sunday 1:00 to 5:00 P.M.; closed on Monday, except in July and August. A combination admission to both museums for adults is $6.00, seniors $5.00, children and students $4.00. Handicapped-accessible.

The Carnegie Museum of Natural History has one of the world's finest dinosaur collections, a hall of gems and minerals, Egyptian artifacts (including mummies), and Polar World.

The dinosaur collection has full skeletons of ten different species of dinosaur, including the ever-popular *T. rex.* The Hillman Hall of Minerals and Gems includes some of the finest specimens of their kinds, plus a dazzling display of fluorescent minerals. Polar World explores the culture of the Inuit, including their keenly observed carvings. There are also Egyptian artifacts, African and North American wildlife, colorful displays of insects, butterflies, birds, and so much more.

***B*ig Dinobones!** Gideon is now two-and-a-half years old and we are entering the dinosaur phase for the third time. Judah and Seth both went through it at about this age.

I'll never forget the first time we took Judah to an exhibit of dinosaur bones. He was about three-and-a-half years old, and he looked up at the huge skeletons with his enormously wide eyes and shouted, "B-I-I-I-G dino-bones!"

The Discovery Room, for all ages, is open selected hours. There are also special programs for children, including the Natural Science Academy Summer Camp.

Founded in 1896 by Andrew Carnegie, the Carnegie Museum of Art was planned as a collection of "the old masters of tomorrow." At that time, that meant artists like Winslow Homer, James McNeill Whistler, and Camille Pisarro. Today the museum is known for its collections of American, French Impressionist, and Post-Impressionist works. It also includes European and American decorative arts, Asian and African art, and a new architectural department.

Schoolchildren will get a kick out of the Hall of Sculpture, patterned after a real Greek temple. Family, youth, and children's programs are available.

Since the Museum of Natural History and the Museum of Art are attached, one admission gets you into both, and there are often joint programs such as tours of both facilities. Also adjacent you'll find the Carnegie Music Hall and the Carnegie Library of Pittsburgh.

NATIONALITY ROOMS (ages 6 and up)

Fifth Avenue entrance Cathedral of Learning; (412) 624–6000. Reservations are recommended. Tour fees are nominal: adults, $2.00; seniors, $1.50; children over 8, 50 cents.

Within a few steps of the Stephen Foster Memorial towers the University of Pittsburgh's Cathedral of Learning. Compare New England Colonial architectural style with French Empire, Japanese, Indian, Austrian, Russian, Byzantine, Chinese Empire, first-century Israeli, or Irish Romanesque. Twenty-six different nations are represented in the Nationality Rooms Tours. Funded by gifts from Pittsburgh's ethnic communities, the Nationality Rooms are functioning classrooms in which your family can tour "around the world" with a university student guide who has been trained to adapt the tour to different ages and interests.

Younger children enjoy patting the laughing lion in the Chinese Room or identifying the fairy tales depicted in the German Room. The gift shop carries many unusual publications and an array of international gifts.

Also at the Cathedral of Learning:

HEINZ MEMORIAL CHAPEL (ages 8 and up)

Cathedral of Learning; (412) 624–4157. Open 9:00 A.M. to 4:00 P.M. on weekdays. Mass is celebrated at noon every day. Services are also offered on Sunday, when the chapel is open 1:30 to 5:30 P.M.

Stained-glass windows set a tone of Gothic other-worldliness.

STEPHEN FOSTER MEMORIAL/CENTER FOR AMERICAN MUSIC (ages 8 and up)

Forbes Avenue at Cathedral of Learning; (412) 624–4100. Open weekdays 9:00 A.M. to 4:30 P.M. Guided tours by reservation only. Admission to museum is Free.

A collection of memorabilia reflecting the life of the popular composer.

PHIPPS CONSERVATORY (all ages)

Schenley Park; (412) 622–6914; www.phipps.conservatory.com. Open year-round, Tuesday through Sunday 9:00 A.M. to 5:00 P.M. Admission: $6.00 for adults, $5.00 for seniors, $4.00 for students, $3.00 for children 2 to 12. Outdoor gardens are open dawn to dusk, **Free**.

Inside the Victorian glass structure of the Phipps Conservatory, you can see hundreds of orchids, palms, ferns, and other plants. The Japanese Courtyard Garden has an excellent collection of bonsai. In winter the indoor gardens soothe your cabin fever, and in warm weather you can enjoy both indoor and outdoor gardens and fountains.

FRICK ART AND HISTORY CENTER (ages 8 and up)

7227 Reynolds Street; (412) 371–0600. Open year-round, Tuesday through Saturday 10:00 A.M. to 5:30 P.M., Sunday noon to 6:00 P.M. Closed Monday. Admission to the museum is **Free**. *Admission to Clayton is $6.00 adults, $5.00 seniors, $4.00 for students.* **Free**, *secure parking.*

Another one of Pittsburgh's leading citizens was Henry Clay Frick, who lived at Clayton until 1905, when he moved to New York City (where his next house also became a favorite museum). The Frick Art and History Center is a six-acre site that includes Clayton, the Frick Art Museum, historic Car and Carriage Museum, Visitor Center, and cafe. The Victorian home has been meticulously restored, and about 95 percent of the furnishings are original. The new Car and Carriage Museum, opened in 1997, displays old-fashioned automobiles, sleighs, and carriages. Little ones will be interested in the Visitor Center, which was once the playhouse of Helen, the Fricks' daughter.

PITTSBURGH ZOO (all ages)

One Hill Road, in Highland Park (ten minutes from downtown Pittsburgh); (412) 665–3640; www.zoo.pgh.pa.us. Open daily except December 25. In winter the gates are open 9:00 A.M. to 4:00 P.M. If you're already inside the gate, you can stay until 5:00 P.M. In summer the gates open at 10:00 A.M. and close at 5:00 P.M., and you can stay inside until 6:00 P.M. Parking is $2.75 per vehicle. Admission is $6.50 for adults, $4.75 for seniors 60 and over, $4.75 for children 2 to 13.

Kids Kingdom, the Children's Zoos at the Pittsburgh Zoo, has been ranked one of the top three children's zoos in the country. Kids Kingdom includes exciting interactive exhibits such as walk-through deer and kangaroo yards, petting areas, and more. In the 40-foot flyway with over

200 bats, kids can see and hear the bats in flight. In the meerkat exhibit, kids can burrow through tunnels and pop up in bubble windows, right next to these animals you'll remember from Dis-

Out of the Mouths of Babes

We were looking at the photos we'd taken at the zoo. Seth was three and fascinated with all the animals.

I told him, "A gorilla is very strong." He said, "So is a boy-rilla."

ney's *The Lion King*. The sea lion pool features an underwater viewing window. Parents enjoy the fact that they can sit on the patio in Kids Kingdom while the kids learn to swing like spiders, slide like penguins, and enjoy the playground and live animals.

The animals here have natural enclosures. Highlights include the Siberian tigers in the Asian Forest; lions, leopards, rhinos, elephants, and gazelles of the African Savannah; and family groups of lowland gorillas, plus monkeys, gibbons, and orangutans of the Tropical Forest.

Coming in April 2000 will be a new aquarium, featuring the world's first rotating aquarium tank, as well as a touch tank and a lot more.

ALSO IN THE AREA

Pittsburgh is also a great sports town. Baseball fans can visit the remains of **Forbes Field,** including Mazeroski's Wall. The **Civic Arena** is home to the Pittsburgh Penguins (ice hockey); for tickets call (412) 642-1300. For other events at the Civic Arena, such as WWF Wrestling, call TicketMaster at (412) 323-1919. **Three Rivers Stadium** is where the Pirates (baseball) and Steelers (football) play. For credit-card ticket sales, call the Civic Arena at (412) 333-7328. There is no general information number for Three Rivers Stadium, but for the Pirates, call (412) 321-BUCS or (800) BUY-BUCS. For the Steelers, call (412) 323-0300 (the Steelers, however, are perpetually sold out).

While in Pittsburgh, you may wish to take in a performance at one of the many cultural venues: **Heinz Hall for the Performing Arts** (600 Penn Avenue, 412-392-4900); **Civic Light Opera** (Benedum Center, 719 Liberty Avenue, 412-281-2022); **The Playhouse** (222 Craft Avenue, 412-621-6695); **Pittsburgh Center for the Arts** (6300 Fifth Avenue, 412-361-0873); **Pittsburgh Opera** (711 Penn Avenue, 412-281-0912); or call TicketMaster at (412) 323-1919.

West Mifflin

Memories of a childhood in Pittsburgh usually include scrambling around a rocking Noah's Ark in Kennywood Park. Voted "Favorite Amusement Park" for eleven years in a row by the National Amusement Park Historical Association (NAPHA), Kennywood Park has also been called the "Roller Coaster Capital of the World." Kennywood's Thunderbolt was recently named NAPHA's favorite wood roller coaster, and its Steel Phantom NAPHA's third favorite steel coaster. And if all that isn't reason enough to visit the park, it has also been said that Kennywood's french fries are the best in the world.

 KENNYWOOD (all ages)

4800 Kennywood Boulevard; (412) 461–0500; www.kennywood.com. Open daily mid-May through Labor Day 11:00 A.M. to 10:00 P.M. Prices vary season-ally, but, in general, on weekdays you can get a Ride-All-Day ticket for $16.95, and on weekends for $19.95. Senior general admission is $3.95.

Now over a century young, Kennywood is only minutes away from downtown Pittsburgh, off the Swissdale exit (Exit 9) of Interstate 376 (Penn-Lincoln Parkway). Although some rides will get you wet, none require bathing suits.

A Pittsburgh landmark since 1898, today Kennywood is also a National Historic Landmark. The carousel pavilion and a restaurant are the original structures. Others were added over the years. One roller coaster, for example, the Jack Rabbit, with its "camel back" (double dip) looks just the way it did in 1921. "Pittsburgh's Lost Kennywood" re-creates Luna parks of the past. But Kennywood Park has continued to evolve, with rides like Steel Phantom, with a fastest speed of 84 mph and longest drop of 225 feet. The new Pitt Fall, added in 1997, is the world's tallest and fastest free-fall ride. Kennywood's new Exterminator combines a roller coaster with virtual reality to give you the ride of your life, in the dark, through underground tunnels and sewers where you'll encounter who knows what.

Amazing Pittsburgh Facts

Kennywood, now over 100 years young, is one of only two amusement parks that are National Historic Landmarks.

Kennywood makes your visit easy on your wallet in several ways. First, you're welcome to bring along a cooler and eat in the picnic grove. Another unique feature is the pricing schedule. Kennywood offers both a Ride-All-Day ticket that includes everything and a general admission for seniors. General admission can be a bargain for anyone who doesn't plan to go on many rides but still wishes to accompany the family. This ticket lets you into the park, but you have to pay for any rides separately. These two features allow families to save a little money and still have a great time together.

There are changing tables in all the bathrooms. In Kiddieland, there are kid-sized bathrooms and an area for nursing mothers.

West Homestead

 SANDCASTLE ACTION PARK (all ages)
1000 Sandcastle Drive, on Route 837 between the Homestead High Level Bridge and Glenwood Bridge; (412) 462–6666. Open daily in season, usually June through Labor Day weekend, 11:00 A.M. to 6:00 P.M. The park stays open until 7:00 P.M. in July and August. Admission: Whitewater Pass (includes all water activities—hot tubs, pools, Lazy River, and fifteen water slides) is $14.95 for adults and children three and older; Lagoon Pass (includes everything except water slides) is $8.50; senior citizen pool pass is $5.50.

Sandcastle Action Park, Kennywood's sister park in West Homestead, began life as an abandoned steel mill and was opened as a water park in July 1990. Sandcastle is a major riverside water park with a boardwalk, fifteen water slides, two pools, and a Lazy River. It also has two race-car tracks, video games, and miniature golf. Mon-Tsunami is a new 20,000 square-foot wave pool with huge roller waves as well as diamond waves.

Only the bravest water-sliders should attempt the Lightning Express twin body slides, 60 feet high and 250 feet long, each with a double dip, followed by a monster free fall. (AAAH!)

Another slide, Cliffhangers, uses a new concept in water-slide design: sky ponds. Each pond is at a different level above the ground. You and your inner tube can float in one pond before sliding down to the next.

If that doesn't sound like your speed, relax on the Lazy River, with its whirlpools, fountains, and gentle current. Wet Willie's Waterworks is recommended for younger children, and The World's Largest Hot Tub is perfect for stressed-out parents.

Parking and boat docking are **Free**. Special events and festivals are held in Sandcastle's Riverplex entertainment complex.

Springdale

Rachel Carson said, "Those who contemplate the beauty of the earth find reserves of strength that will endure as long as life lasts." The famous author of *Silent Spring* was born in 1907 in the farmhouse now known as the Rachel Carson Homestead, in Springdale, within minutes of Pittsburgh. As your family travels this region that is so much a part of our industrial development, a visit to Carson's home is a healthy reminder of the downside of "progress."

 ### RACHEL CARSON HOMESTEAD (ages 8 and up)

613 Marion Avenue, approximately 30 minutes from downtown Pittsburgh; (724) 274–5459; rachelcarson.org. Open April through November, Saturday 10:00 A.M. to 4:00 P.M. and Sunday 1:00 to 5:00 P.M. At other times you may call (4724) 274–5459 for an appointment. Admission: adults, $4.00; children 4 to 18, $2.50; seniors, $3.00.

You can tour the nineteenth-century house and find out about one woman who made a difference. Published in 1962, *Silent Spring* and Carson's other books pointed out for the first time the dangers of DDT and other pesticides. Her special interest in exposing children to nature was illustrated by her 1956 article "Help Your Child to Wonder." You'll also enjoy the nature trail that Rachel Carson walked and the gardens, especially the Butterfly Garden.

Special children's programs are offered. In May Rachel Carson's birthday is celebrated.

Tarentum

In Tarentum, only a few miles northeast of the Rachel Carson Homestead, you can find out what life was like for miners in this area.

 ### TOUR-ED MINE AND MUSEUM (ages 8 and up)

748 Bull Creek Road at Exit 14 of Route 28 North, located on the Allegheny Valley Expressway, opposite Woodlawn Golf Course; (724) 224–4720; nb.net/~tour-ed. Open Wednesday to Monday, Memorial Day to Labor Day, 1:00 to 4:00 P.M. Admission is $6.00 for adults, $3.00 for children.

You'll have to wear a miner's hard hat and mind your head as you board a mining car, modernized for comfort and electrically powered, to travel a half-mile underground at Tour-Ed Mine and Museum into a genuine coal mine. Your tour guide, a real miner, will help you learn about the history of coal mining. It's chilly down here, so bring your sweater. This is not for the claustrophobic.

Kids will enjoy the newest addition: a caboose. You can also see the company store, 1785 log home, and sawmill. You can even see a bedroom set up like the ones where the miners slept. There are covered picnic areas and snacks available.

Butler

The Butler County Historical Society administers several historic sites in the county, which are open seasonally. For information on any of these sites or to arrange a group or off-season tour, call the Historical Society at (724) 283-8116.

BUTLER COUNTY HERITAGE CENTER (ages 8 and up)

119 West New Castle Street; (724) 283-2505. Hours vary seasonally.

This center, opened in 1995, presents temporary exhibits on the history of this area. On permanent display, you'll find artifacts from Butler County's many industries, including a tin shop, a Bantam jeep, Spang oil tools, Franklin glasswork, and farm tools.

COOPER CABIN (ages 8 and up)

Off Route 356 on Cooper Road; (724) 283-8116. Hours vary seasonally.

On Halloween families gather around a bonfire at Cooper Cabin to hear ghost stories. On weekends from April to October the cabin offers demonstrations of horse-shoeing, basket weaving, quilting, spinning, and weaving, as well as an herb garden and outbuildings such as a spinning house, spring house, and tool shed.

LITTLE RED SCHOOL HOUSE MUSEUM (ages 6 and up)

200 East Jefferson Street; (724) 283-8116. Hours vary seasonally.

At the Little Red School House, you sit down in a real old-fashioned desk as your tour guide transforms into a teacher. The school house was built in 1838.

ALSO IN THE AREA

Senator Walter Lowrie (Shaw) House, 123 Diamond Street; (724) 283–8116. Hours vary seasonally.

Zelienople

Twenty-eight miles north of Pittsburgh on Route 19 is the historic town of Zelienople. The Zelienople Historical Society has restored the **Passavant House** and **Buhl House** (243 South Main Street and 221 South Main Street, respectively). Passavant House is primarily devoted to the furnishings and memorabilia of the Passavant family, who played an important role in the town's history. Buhl House displays a collection that tells the history of the entire community. Open May 1 to September 30, Wednesday and Saturday 1:00 to 4:00 P.M., otherwise by appointment. Call (412) 452–9457.

Harmony

The village of Harmony was founded in 1804 by members of a religious communal group, the Harmony Society. This group eventually built about 130 buildings including two outlying villages. At present, Harmony is known for its antiques shops, museums, restaurants, and parks.

THE HARMONY MUSEUM (ages 8 and up)

Mercer Street; (412) 452–7341. Tours are available June 1 to September 30, 1:00 to 4:00 P.M. daily except Monday. Open June to September, daily 1:00 to 4:00 P.M.; October to May, Monday, Wednesday, Friday, and Sunday 1:00 to 4:00 P.M., appointments strongly recommended for weekends. Closed holidays. Admission is $2.50 for adults, $1.00 for children.

The Harmony Museum offers walking tours of the historic district of Harmony, as well as the Ziegler Log House and the Wagner House. Limited handicapped accessibility. The museum displays Native American artifacts, as well as artifacts of the Harmonists and Mennonites.

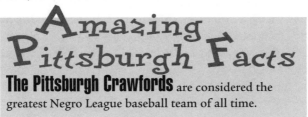

Amazing Pittsburgh Facts

The Pittsburgh Crawfords are considered the greatest Negro League baseball team of all time.

Portersville

MORAINE STATE PARK (all ages)

225 Pleasant Valley Road, off Route 422; (724) 368–8811. Open year-round 8:00 A.M. to sundown. Free, but there are rental fees for boats, cabins, etc. The beach is Free.

Moraine State Park offers a great variety of family-oriented nature programs. There are nature walks and canoe trips. Having recently reintroduced ospreys to Lake Arthur, the park offers educational programs about these and other waterfowl. You can rent motorboats, pontoons, or sailboats.

McCONNELL'S MILL STATE PARK (all ages)

Five miles west of Moraine State Park, off Route 422; (724) 368–8091 or (724) 368–8811. The gristmill, which is currently under restoration, is open for Free guided tours Memorial Day to Labor Day, 10:00 A.M. to 6:00 P.M. This scenic park features a covered bridge and a waterfall. For more information and park hours, call (724) 368–8091.

Also administered by Moraine State Park is McConnell's Mill State Park. It's definitely worth the walk to see the 400-foot Slippery Rock Creek Gorge, formed by the glaciers thousands of years ago. The huge boulders literally "slipped" down the walls of the gorge, creating a strange and wonderful landscape. You can also explore the 2,500 acres of park land, have a picnic, hike one of the trails, or take a Free guided tour. If you have your own boat, you can go kayaking or rafting.

JENNINGS ENVIRONMENTAL CENTER (all ages)

2951 Prospect Road; (724) 794–6011. The Education Center is open Monday through Friday, 8:00 A.M. to 4:00 P.M. or whenever educational programs are offered. Free admission. Some programs have fees. Call for information.

Jennings Environmental Center is the only state park environmental education center in western Pennsylvania, and one of only four in the state. This site is a true relict prairie ecosystem.

A what? A relict prairie ecosystem is a prairie formed by prehistoric glacial activity. Here, the glacier left only 4 to 6 inches of topsoil, with clay underneath. As a result, trees don't grow here, but grasses and wildflowers do. If you visit in late July or August, you can see spectacular wildflowers in bloom, such as the spiky purple blazing star. The prairie also supports unusual wildlife, such as the eastern massasauga rattlesnake, one of Pennsylvania's three species of poisonous snakes, and an endangered species in the state.

You can hike or picnic here from dawn to dusk, seven days a week. Public interpretive programs are offered on weekends. Please call for program schedules. In spring and summer special programs highlight the wildflowers in bloom. In March you can learn about maple sugaring, and in April Earth Day programs teach about biodiversity and related topics. Many other programs are also available.

Volant

Main Street in the quaint rural town of Volant offers more than fifty shops and restaurants featuring Victorian collectibles, arts and crafts, Christmas specialties, housewares, pottery, and special events such as a Quilt Show and Sale in July, an Autumn Pumpkin Festival, Old Fashioned Christmas, and more. Volant is located north of New Castle, on Route 208, ten minutes from routes I-79 and I-80. It is just minutes away from McConnell's Creek State Park and Living Treasures Animal Park. There's also a thriving Amish community in this area.

The shops are open daily except for New Year's Day, Easter, Thanksgiving, and Christmas. Hours are 10:00 A.M. to 5:00 P.M. Monday through Saturday and noon to 5:00 P.M. on Sunday. For more information call the Volant Merchants Association at (724) 533-2591.

New Castle

Bet you didn't know that New Castle, Pennsylvania, is the "Fireworks Capital of America." Two of the largest fireworks manufacturers, Pyrotecnico and Zambelli Internationale, are based in this city northwest of Pittsburgh.

So, if you happen to be in the area around the Fourth of July, check out the "**Fireworks Capital of America Fireworks Festival**" here. In the past the festivities have included a special children's ground fireworks display in which kids were able to see the fireworks close-up, and Locomotion, in which an antique locomotive came to life with fireworks, lights, and music. Fourth of July weekend in Lawrence County has recently been named one of the top 100 events in North America by the American Bus Association. Besides the Fireworks Festival, there's also "Back to the Fifties Weekend" at Cascade Park and the Ellwood City Arts, Crafts, and Food Festival at Ewing Park. All of these events feature fireworks, all are within a week of July 4th, and all are within a few miles of each other.

For details contact the Lawrence County Tourist Promotion Agency, Shenango Street Station, 138 West Washington Street, New Castle 16101; call (888) 284–7599 or (724) 654–8408.

 ### HARLANSBURG STATION'S MUSEUM OF TRANSPORTATION (all ages)

Routes 19 amd 108; (724) 652–9002. Open seasonally, so call for current hours. Generally, the museum is open weekends only in winter, Saturday 10:00 A.M. to 5:00 P.M. and Sunday noon to 5:00 P.M. In summer and fall, it is open Tuesday through Saturday 10:00 A.M. to 5:00 P.M. and Sunday noon to 5:00 P.M. Closed Monday, and January through February. Admission is $3.00 for adults, $2.00 for children under 12.

Family-owned, family-operated, and family-friendly, Harlansburg Station's Museum of Transportation looks just like an old railroad station, with four Pennsylvania Railroad cars in front. Inside one of the cars, you can see displays of railroad memorabilia such as uniforms, silver, linens, and more. As you enter the museum, a model conductor greets you. Inside the museum you're surrounded by planes, trains, cars, and trucks—all kinds of transportation. New this year is an exhibit devoted to trolleys and trolley memorabilia, and a Marathon Checker cab.

 ### HOYT INSTITUTE OF FINE ARTS (ages 8 and up)

124 East Leisure Avenue; (724) 652–2882. Open Tuesday to Saturday 9:00 A.M. to 4:00 P.M. Call for admission prices.

Two mansions once belonging to members of the Hoyt family now constitute the Hoyt Institute of Fine Arts. Self-guided tour brochures are available for both Hoyt West (the Alex Crawford Hoyt Mansion) and Hoyt East (the May Emma Hoyt Mansion). Art from the permanent collection is on display at Hoyt West, whereas temporary exhibitions are generally held in Hoyt East, as are art classes for children and adults. Summer art camps are offered for children ages 6 to 8 and 9 to 12. Partially handicapped-accessible.

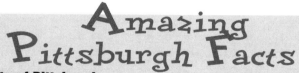

Amazing Pittsburgh Facts

The City of Pittsburgh contains more than 70 miles of riverfront land, one of the highest totals in the United States.

LIVING TREASURES ANIMAL PARK (all ages)

Route 422, 4 miles west of I–79 in Moraine; (412) 924–9571; www. ltanimalpark.com. Open weekends 10:00 A.M. to 6:00 P.M. in May, September, and October, and daily 10:00 A.M. to 8:00 P.M. Memorial Day through Labor Day. Admission is $6.50 for adults, $4.50 for children 2 to 12, and children under 2 are Free. Please note that there are two "Living Treasures Animal Park" locations: this one, in Moraine; and the other in Laurel Highlands on Route 711 south of Route 31. For the Laurel Highlands location, please call (724) 593–8300.

Get up close to more than one hundred species of friendly animals from all over the world at Living Treasures Animal Park.

New Brighton

MERRICK FREE ART GALLERY (ages 8 and up)

Fifth Avenue at Eleventh Street; (724) 846–1130. Open Tuesday through Saturday 10:00 A.M. to 4:30 P.M. and Sunday 1:00 to 4:30 P.M. Free admission.

The Merrick Free Art Gallery houses the collection of French, German, English, and American paintings of the eighteenth and nineteenth centuries that belonged to Edward Dempster Merrick. It has a display of artifacts belonging to the New Brighton Historical Society as well. The gallery also mounts many special exhibits such as its annual Victorian Christmas Toy Show.

Ambridge

OLD ECONOMY VILLAGE (ages 8 and up)

Fourteenth and Church Streets, 18 miles northwest of Pittsburgh on Route 65; (724) 266–4500. Open Tuesday through Saturday 9:00 A.M. to 5:00 P.M., Sunday noon to 5:00 P.M. Closed Monday and winter holidays. Admission: ages 6 to 12, $3.00; ages 12 to 59, $5.00; 60 and over, $4.50; family rate, $13.00.

Old Economy Village was built by the same Christian communal society who built Harmony (see page 161). Here you can visit seventeen restored buildings and gardens and learn about how this unusual community lived. The Harmonists expected the Second Coming in 1829, so they lived celibate lives, always stored one year's supply of grain, and hoarded gold. Your whole visit takes about an hour and a half, including the orientation film *Those Who Believed* and a tour of the exhibits, gardens, and buildings. The village had its own tailor, printer, shoe-maker, cabinetmaker, locksmith, and more, and the village store still posts the 1827 price list. Kids will enjoy using the hand pump to pour themselves a drink.

Many special events and tours are available, including events such as the Family Weekend in June, Erntefest (food festival) in October, and Candlelight Christmas. ADA rest rooms, diaper-changing areas.

 RACCOON CREEK STATE PARK AND WILDERNESS RESERVE (all ages)

Located in southern Beaver County, 25 miles west of Pittsburgh (take Route 22 or Route 30; access to the park is via Route 18); (412) 899–3611. Trails are open year-round from 8:00 A.M. to sunset. **Free** *admission.*

One of the largest and most beautiful state parks in Pennsylvania, Raccoon Creek State Park has about 7,000 acres and Raccoon Creek Lake, which itself is more than 100 acres.

Located within Raccoon Creek State Park, only steps east of the park entrance, is the 315-acre Wildflower Reserve, where you can choose between easy-walking trails and trails with gentle grades. Your best bet to see the most blooms is April or May, but something is blooming from late March through summer. If you're lucky, you might see deer, raccoons, wild turkeys, mink, birds, and other wildlife. Comfortable shoes are a must. On Soldier Days you can view historic reen-actments, military displays, and more.

Recreational facilities include boating, hiking, camping, swimming, and picnicking. Modern family cabins are available year-round, with electric heat, kitchens, and toilets.

While you're in Raccoon Creek State Park, you may wish to visit **Frankfort Mineral Springs,** about one-half mile south of the park entrance. From the 1790s to 1932, this was the site of a popular spa where many people were attracted to the purported medicinal proper-ties of the spring water. Call (412) 899–2200.

Avella

 MEADOWCROFT MUSEUM OF RURAL LIFE (ages 6 and up)

401 Meadowcroft Road; (724) 587–3412. Open weekends in June, July, and August; Saturday noon to 5:00 P.M., Sunday 1:00 to 5:00 P.M., otherwise open by appointment. Admissioin: $6.50 for adults, $3.50 for children 6 to 16; children

under 6 enter 𝐅𝐫𝐞𝐞. *The last complete tour starts at 3:00 P.M. Call for information about group reservations and many special workshops and events.*

Sixteen thousand years of history and prehistory in western Pennsylvania are brought to life at the Meadowcroft Museum of Rural Life. The grounds here include the archaeological site that contains the earliest evidence of human life in eastern North America. (This part of the site is not open to the public at this time, but displays explain about the work in progress.)

Tours are designed to engage the entire family. Everyone can sit down in a one-room schoolhouse and take part in a real school lesson, reading from *McGuffey's Reader*. Then try some of the playground games children played 150 years ago. Explore log houses, a covered bridge, a blacksmith's shop, and other exhibits.

Located off Route 50, less than an hour from Pittsburgh, the museum offers many hands-on educational programs for groups. Wear good walking shoes, because the paths between the buildings are natural. There is a snack bar and gift shop.

Washington

 ## THE PENNSYLVANIA TROLLEY MUSEUM (all ages)

One Museum Road; (724) 228–9256; www.pa-trolley.org. Open noon to 5:00 P.M. daily from Memorial Day to Labor Day; weekends 11:00 A.M. to 5:00 P.M. April 1 through December 30. Admission is $6.00 for adults, $5.00 for seniors 65 and over, and $3.50 for children 2 to 11.

Faith's kids could never resist a trolley. And here in Washington, you'll find the only museum where you can see, learn about, and actually ride historic electric-rail vehicles from Pittsburgh, Philadelphia, Johnstown, and other cities. Take several generations along for an opportunity for reminiscing and intergenerational storytelling.

First, go to the Visitor Education Center to buy your tickets and view an exhibit. Stop and browse through the exhibits or take in a film. During the winter holidays you can even find yourself at the controls of a model-train layout.

Rides leave from the Richfor Shelter across the picnic area and next to the car barn. You just won't believe how beautifully these streetcars have been restored. Your motorman and most of the staff are enthusiastic volunteers. You'll clatter on a 3-mile journey past a scenic section that was once an old coal-mining railroad. After you climb off the trolley, you may view about twenty-five trolley cars from the museum's collection, including the real "Streetcar Named Desire" from New Orleans. You can even peek in on the car shop where volunteers restore the cars. Bring along a picnic lunch if you like.

Just 30 miles southwest of Pittsburgh, near Exit 8 (Meadow Lands) off I-79, the Trolley Museum is convenient to Meadowcroft Village in Avella. Special events include: a Trolley Fair in June, with a trolley parade, antique vehicle display, and hand-car and caboose rides; the "Pumpkin Patch Trolley" in October and "Santa Trolley" in December.

 ## WASHINGTON COUNTY HISTORICAL SOCIETY'S LEMOYNE HOUSE (ages 8 and up)

49 East Maiden Street; call (412) 225–6740 for admission prices. Open February to mid-December, Wednesday to Friday noon to 4:00 P.M. and Sunday 2:00 to 4:00 P.M.

LeMoyne House is the headquarters of the Washington County Historical Society, including its collection of Civil War weapons and a time capsule prepared by President Ulysses S. Grant. The beautiful stone home, which also served as Dr. LeMoyne's medical office, still contains some of his old medical instruments and books. It was also a stop on the Underground Railroad.

Where to Eat

IN PITTSBURGH

Riverview Cafe, *Carnegie Science Center, One Allegheny Avenue, North Side; (412) 237–3417.* Casual atmosphere, city view on the Ohio River. Kid-friendly foods, booster seats.

Crewser's Restaurant, *1501 Smallman Street, Strip District; (412) 281–1099.* Nautical theme, located on the boardwalk in the strip.

Italian Spaghetti Warehouse, *2601 Smallman Street; (412) 261–6511.* Italian food, casual atmosphere, located on the strip.

Bobby Rubina's Place for Ribs, *10 Commerce Court Station Square; (412) 642–7427.*

Houlihan's Restaurant, *#15 Freight House Shops, South Side; (412) 232–0302.*

Where to Stay

IN PITTSBURGH

Best Western University Center Hotel, *3401 Boulevard of the Allies, Pittsburgh; (412) 683–6100 or (800) 245–4444.* Nearby: Oakland, downtown, stadiums, museums, university, Station Square, zoo, Kennywood.

Club House Inn Pittsburgh, *5311 Campbells Run Road, Pittsburgh; (412) 788–8400.* Nine miles from downtown, Carnegie Cultural Center, Three Rivers Stadium.

Doubletree Hotel Pittsburgh, *1000 Penn Avenue, Pittsburgh; (412) 281–3700 or (800) 222–TREE.* Full service luxury hotel in city of Pittsburgh. In heart of cultural district.

Green Tree Marriot, *101 Marriott Drive, Pittsburgh; (412) 922–8400 or (800) 525–5902.* Three miles from downtown.

Pittsburgh Hilton & Towers, *600 Commonwealth Place, Gateway Center, Pittsburgh; (412) 391–4600.* Adjacent to Point State Park. Walking distance to sports games and Carnegie Museum.

Northeastern Pennsylvania

With the Delaware and Susquehanna Rivers, the Pocono Mountains, wilderness areas, numerous lakes, and crystal clear rivers, Northeastern Pennsylvania has attracted vacationers since the 1800s. But Northeastern Pennsylvania is more than just a resort area. The discovery of one of the world's largest deposits of anthracite coal made the region a center for industry. Entrepreneurs, immigrant workers, and others came to the area to make money or find work. The country's first railroads were built to transport the coal to the cities. Other industries moved their operations here to take advantage of the cheap fuel.

Thanks to its history—both natural and industrial—Northeastern Pennsylvania offers a special mix to family vacationers today. Those looking for hiking, skiing, boating, and relaxing resorts will not be disappointed. But the region's industrial

Faith & Emily's
Favorite Northeastern Pennsylvania Attractions

1. Float trip on the Delaware River
2. Mountain biking in the Lehigh Gorge
3. Skytop Lodge
4. World's End State Park
5. Pocono Environmental Education Center
6. Steamtown National Historic Site
7. Lackawanna Coal Mine Tour
8. Quiet Valley Living Historical Farm
9. Woodloch Pines Inn and Resort
10. The Inn at Starlight Lake

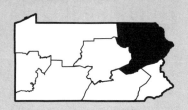

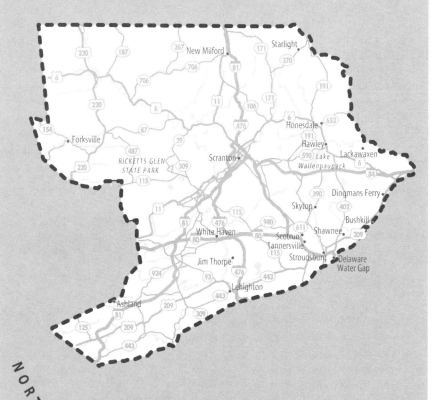

NORTHEASTERN PENNSYLVANIA

history adds some more unusual attractions, such as factories, railroad excursions, and coal-mine tours.

The Poconos may be the classic vacation destination—but there's good reason, especially where families are concerned. With so many resorts to choose from, every family can find one that fits its needs.

Despite overdevelopment in some areas, the unspoiled areas of the Poconos are absolutely beautiful—and very accessible. We're not talking huge snowcapped mountains; we're talking gentle hills; lovely trails, and babbling brooks that are easy for all members of the family to enjoy.

For example, the Poconos ski resorts are perfect for families. The vertical drops are steep enough to keep it interesting for mom and dad while gentle enough for kids to learn easily. Most of the resorts have great learn-to-ski programs for kids, starting as young as 3 years old.

One of the hottest things on the slopes in recent years is snowtubing. This is also very good news for families. Though parents may worry a bit the first time the kids take to the slopes on skis or snowboards, snowtubing—with its cushy, fit-the-whole-family inflatable rafts —is something everyone can do together.

Faith & Emily's
Favorite Events in Northeastern Pennsylvania

- **Wildflower Music Festival** in **Hawley–Lake Wallenpaupack** (July and August); (570) 253–1185.

- **Moscow Country Fair** (mid-August); (570) 842–9804.

- **Delaware River Sojourn** at **sites along the Delaware** (mid-June); (570) 685–4871.

- **Shawnee Mountain Lumberjack Festival** in **Shawnee-on-Delaware** (early October); (570) 421–7231.

- Rail Expo at Steamtown National Historic Site in **Scranton** (early September); (570) 340–5200 or (888) 693–9391.

- **Patch Town Day** at **Eckley Miner's Village** in **Weatherly** (mid-June); (570) 636–2070.

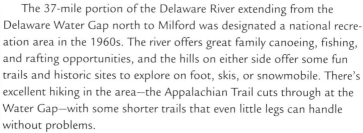

Delaware Water Gap and the Stroudsburg Area

For vacationers arriving in Pennsylvania from New Jersey, the Delaware Water Gap serves as a gateway to the Poconos. This natural land formation along the Kittatinny Ridge is a dramatic backdrop for a host of outdoor activities. The town of Delaware Water Gap is a good place to start exploring.

Stroudsburg and East Stroudsburg are the commerce centers of this part of the Poconos. You'll find restaurants and some lodgings in these towns, but most of the tourist attractions and resorts are located in the surrounding smaller towns.

  ### THE DELAWARE WATER GAP NATIONAL RECREATION AREA (all ages)

 Bushkill; (717) 588–2435; www.nationalparks.org/guide/parks/delaware-wat-1902.html. Open year-round. Visitor centers and hiking are Free*; day-use fee at beaches and some picnic areas.*

 The 37-mile portion of the Delaware River extending from the Delaware Water Gap north to Milford was designated a national recreation area in the 1960s. The river offers great family canoeing, fishing, and rafting opportunities, and the hills on either side offer some fun trails and historic sites to explore on foot, skis, or snowmobile. There's excellent hiking in the area—the Appalachian Trail cuts through at the Water Gap—with some shorter trails that even little legs can handle without problems.

Other attractions that kids enjoy are visiting Millbrook Village (actually, it's about 16 miles from the Gap on the New Jersey side), gazing at dramatic waterfalls located around the area, and swimming in the cool, clear river at Milford and Smithfield beaches. Best of all, the park is less than two hours from New York or Philadelphia.

The best places to view the Gap itself are three overlooks along Route 611 just south of Route 80. Route 209 going north offers a nice family drive along the river valley, with the Pocono Plateau rising to the west. (The Poconos are not a typical mountain range but rather a plateau.)

There's a visitor center at Kittatinny Point, just off I-80 on the New Jersey side of the river. It's open daily May through October and on weekends year-round. Another visitor center, located at Dingmans Falls, about 30 miles north of I–80 on Route 209, is open during the summer. To find out what's happening in the park during your visit and to get a ranger's recommendation on what to do and see, stop by one of the

Delaware River Canoe and Rafting Trips (ages 5 and up)

The Delaware is a wonderful, calm river for family rafting and canoeing. Although children 8 to 12 get the most out of this kind of trip, most liveries will accommodate younger children—even toddlers. Rafting is recommended over canoeing for children under 12, says David Jacobi of Adventure Sports in Marshall Creek. His organization is one of several that offer Delaware River rafting and canoe trips. Typical excursions range from a couple of hours to all day. Be sure to specify your family members' ages and abilities when talking with the liveries; they'll help you decide which excursion is best for you.

- **Adventure Sports in Marshalls Creek,** Route 209, Marshalls Creek; (800) 487–2628 or (570) 223–0505; www.adventuresport.com. Trips run seven days a week in summer. Fees: $23 for adults, $10 for children ages 13 through 17, and $5.00 for children ages 2 to 12.

- **Chamberlain's Canoes, Inc.,** River Road, Minisink Hills, PA 18341; (800) 422–6631 or (570) 421–0180.

- **Kittatinny Canoes, Inc.,** HC67, Box 360, Dingmans Ferry; (800) FLOATKC; www.kittatinny.com. $14 for tubing; $23 and up for canoeing and rafting.

- **Shawnee River Adventures,** River Road, Shawnee-on-Delaware, PA 18356; (800) SHAWNEE, or (570) 424–4000, ext. 1120. Mid-week specials: Tubing Tuesday, $10 per tube; Rafting Wednesday, $60 per raft; Canoeing Thursday, $30 per canoe. Regular rates: $14 per tube, $22 per person for rafts (four people) and canoes (two people). Open seven days a week April through October.

visitor centers. While you're there, pick up a Junior Naturalist Discovery Pack, a self-guiding booklet that helps children 6 to 12 explore the park. Kids who complete the pack are eligible to become a Junior Ranger.

WATER GAP TROLLEY (ages 2 and up)

Main Street, Delaware Water Gap; (570) 476–9766. Open April through October (weather permitting), 10:00 A.M. to 4:00 P.M. Admission: $5.00 for adults, $3.50 for children ages 2 to 12, children under 2 Free.

The Water Gap Trolley takes vacationers from the depot on Route 611 near the town's center (actually, it's right across from the town's only stoplight) into the National Recreation Area. The one-hour narrated tour covers the geological and cultural history of the region.

SHAWNEE PLACE PLAY AND WATER PARK (ages 2 and up)

Hollow Road, Shawnee-on-Delaware; (570) 421–7231. Open weekends from Memorial Day to June 15 and daily from June 16 to Labor Day, 10:00 A.M. to 5:00 P.M. Admission is $10.00 for adults and children, $5.00 spectators; children under 40 inches Free.

Kids will enjoy swimming and sliding at Shawnee Place Play and Water Park, located just north of Route 80 (take Exit 52 to Route 209 and follow signs). Especially geared for children under age 12, the park has two slides and two pools, both about 3 feet deep. There are three magic shows daily as well as fifteen unique play elements.

SHAWNEE MOUNTAIN (ages 4 and up)

Hollow Road, Shawnee-on-Delaware; (570) 421–7231; www.shawneemt.com. Open mid-December to mid-March, 9:00 A.M. to 10:00 P.M. weekdays, 8:00 A.M. to 10:00 P.M. weekends. Varying prices for lift tickets, rentals, and learn-to-ski programs.

Shawnee Mountain has twenty-three trails, a snowboarding area, snowtubing, and a vertical drop of 700 feet. In winter it also has an extensive ski program for kids. There's a Ski Wee program for 6- to 12-year-olds. Little ones (4 to 5 years) can join the Pre-Ski Wee group. More adventurous kids ages 10 to 15 will want to hook up with the Mountain Cruisers. Beginning to early intermediate snowboarders can join the Young Riders for 8- to 15-year-olds. Programs start at $40 a day for snowboarders, $55 a day for skiers. Three- and five-day packages are available. (Reservations required.) For nonskiing children 18 months and up, the Little Wigwam Children's Center is open daily for baby-sitting from 9:00 A.M. to 5:00 P.M. on weekdays and 8:00 A.M. to 5:00 P.M. on weekends ($4.00 an hour or $22 a day).

SHANNON INN AND PUB (all ages)

Exit 52 off I–80, East Stroudsburg; (800) 424–8052 or (570) 424–1951. A wide variety of ski and golf packages are available, custom-tailored to your needs, at reasonable prices.

Several of the attractions nearby recommend the Shannon Inn for families. With an indoor pool, on-site informal restaurant, and a kids-stay-free policy, this 120-room hotel has everything a family needs for a quality, budget-priced vacation. Through cooperative agreements with Shawnee and Camelback ski areas and other nearby sites, the Shannon Inn offers two-day ski and golf packages.

QUIET VALLEY LIVING HISTORICAL FARM (ages 3 and up)

Route 209, 3.5 miles south of Stroudsburg; (570) 992–6161; www. pastconnect.com/quietValley/. Open end of June through Labor Day, Tuesday through Saturday, 10:00 A.M. to 5:30 P.M.; Sunday 1:00 to 5:30 P.M. Admission: $7.00 for adults, $4.00 for children ages 3 to 12.

Take a trip back in time at the Quiet Valley Living Historical Farm. Here your family will spend time with the Zeppers, a German immigrant family that settled this land back in 1765.

After a brief welcoming presentation, leave the present day and step back into the 1800s. In the 1763 cellar kitchen you will learn how food was prepared and how nothing was wasted on the farm. The farmhand will introduce you to the animals, demonstrate the farm equipment, and let your kids jump in the hayloft. Special demonstrations of various crafts and skills necessary to early life are held throughout the summer.

In addition to regular tours during the summer months, the museum also has special holiday presentations, with a Farm Animal Frolic in May, a Harvest Festival in October, and an Old Time Christmas celebration in December. Call for more information and specific dates. The Farm Animal Frolic is especially recommended for small children, with baby bunnies, hatching chicks, piglets, lambs, and more, for children to touch and learn about.

Mount Pocono and Eastern Poconos (Tannersville, Scotrun, Skytop)

Mount Pocono is in the heart of Pocono resort country. There are lots of resorts and attractions—everything from petting zoos to cheesecake factories—to choose from within a few miles of Mount Pocono, but here are some of our top picks.

CAMELBACK SKI AREA AND CAMELBEACH WATERPARK (ages 4 and up)

Camelback Road, off Route 80 (exit 45), Tannersville; (570) 629–1661; www. skicamelback.com (winter), camelbeach.com (summer). Open for skiing late November through late March, weather permitting. Waterpark open late May through Labor Day. Call for specific dates. Lift tickets: adults, $24 and up; children (46 inches tall to 15 years) $20 and up. Children's ski instruction: $70 and up per

day (includes three hours of instruction and supervision from 9:00 A.M. to 3:30 P.M.). Summer recreation: $19.95 per person. For little ones too young for the slopes, baby-sitting is available for $3.00 per hour during the day for children 12 months to 4 years. Waterpark tickets: full ticket $22.95 per person; general admission $18.95 per person age 3 to 11 or age 65 and over.

The Camelback Ski Area is worth a stop in any season. In winter Camelback is one of the Pocono's largest ski resorts, with thirty-three trails, thirteen lifts, and a vertical drop of 800 feet. Since 1996, the organization has spent more than $7 million to improve the property. One of the newer additions is snowtubing, a great family activity. There's a full-scale ski program where children ages 4 to 12 can spend the day learning to ski or snowboard.

From May until the end of fall, Camelback transforms from a ski resort to Camelbeach Waterpark, with eight waterslides, an action river, swimming pool, kids' play area, miniature golf, an Alpine slide, and more. Ride the chair lift to the top of the mountain, enjoy the view of the Pocono Mountains, and take the Alpine Slide down. Buy a full ticket ($22.95 per person, discounted after Labor Day) and enjoy the waterpark attractions all day. There's also a summer day-camp program at the facility, and kids ages 5 to 12 can sign up for a day, a week, or the whole summer. A two-day vacationer package costs about $90.

 ## CAESAR'S BROOKDALE RESORT (all ages)

Route 611, Scotrun; (800) 233–4141; www.caesars.com. Open year-round. Rates start at $440 to $510 for a three-day, two-night package including meals.

Okay, I have to admit it: There's something a little comical about visiting a renowned couples resort with your toddler, but Caesar's really has something here. Though families don't have full use of all the couples-oriented facilities here (we were disappointed to know we weren't eligible for breakfast in bed), it is a great way to combine some time for yourselves *and* still have a family vacation. (After the kids are asleep, you can sneak into the bath and enjoy the Jacuzzi for two.) Kids 5 and older can join the Brookdale Kids Klub (no membership fee) and participate in a wide range of special activities just for kids, from face painting to special meals and magic shows.

We visited with our two youngest children, ages 2½ and 1½. The staff couldn't have been more accommodating, spreading out a tablecloth under the high chair at each meal, filling our sippy cups and bottles each day, and making us bagels for the road. At each meal we sat with a different family, which was fun for adults and children alike. While we ate, a clown, magician, or other entertainer made the rounds of the tables, creating animals from balloons or cracking jokes with the kids.

If you have small children, consider visiting in the off season (between foliage and winter), when the resort is quiet and empty. Our boys had a great time running around the roller rink at the recreation center and having the indoor pool to themselves—these activities would not have been near as much fun if they had to contend with big kids.

During the summer and winter seasons, there are lots of activities at the nearby ski resorts, National Recreation area, petting zoos, and other Poconos attractions.

One word of warning: The rooms are spacious but not easily baby-proofed. For example, the doors cannot be fully latched from the inside, so our boys were constantly opening them up and walking outside.

 ### SKYTOP LODGE (all ages)

Route 390, Skytop; (800) 345–7759; www.skytop.com. Open year-round. Rates run from $290 to $385 per room per night weekdays; $285 to $420 on weekends.

When we were children, our parents took us to several resorts within a couple hours of our home in New York. Although some resorts were by the ocean, others in the mountains, all had a few elements in common: a stately lodge, a rocking-chair porch, great trails for hiking and walking, and a casual but classy approach to everything.

Skytop Lodge was one of those places—and it has only gotten better in the intervening years. A spa has been added, guest rooms renovated, and twenty executive-style bedrooms added.

Rather than a resort that caters to kids, Skytop accommodates families the same way it accommodates all its guests: with individual attention and concern for detail. Families can check into Skytop for a weekend or a week and find plenty to do for everyone: hiking and cross-country ski trails from 1 mile to 10; guided nature walks and self-guided fitness trails; downhill skiing, mountain bikes, rowboats, canoes, and sporting clays available on site; a swimming lake and indoor and outdoor pools; a game room; and a gorgeous golf course.

Skytop offers Camp in the Clouds for children ages 3 to 12 every day in summer and weekends year-round. The program, which runs from 9:00 A.M. to 4:30 P.M., includes arts and crafts, nature walks, swimming, and other supervised activities. The cost is $18 per day per child.

Winter Camp in the Clouds is offered every Saturday January through March, 6:00 to 9:00 P.M. Free of charge. Parents can dine alone while kids ice skate, watch movies, and more, after a kid's dinner.

Skytop is a splurge; but if you can swing it, it's an excellent family vacation. Accommodations are on the American plan, which means all meals are included. The menu includes some excellent entrees for adults and some favorites for kids. There is a $16-per-day charge for children 17 and under who stay in their parents' room.

ALSO IN THE AREA

Pocono Cheesecake Factory, Route 611, Swiftwater; (570) 839-6844. Open daily 10:00 A.M. to 6:00 P.M. See cheesecakes made fresh daily.

Callie's Candy Kitchen and Pretzel Factory, Route 390, Mountainhome; (570) 595-2280 and (570) 595-3257. Open daily April through December, weekends only January, February, and March.

Located about 5 miles apart on Route 390, Callie's factories let you watch while candy and pretzels are made. Of course, then you'll want to buy some in the gift shop.

Bushkill

Route 209 from Route 80 up to Milford is a lovely drive along the Pennsylvania side of the Delaware River. Here are some suggested stops on the way.

 ### MARY STOLTZ DOLL MUSEUM (ages 3 and up)
Route 209 North and McCole Road; (570) 588–7566. Open daily 11:00 A.M. to 5:00 P.M. Admission is $2.50 for adults, $1.25 for children 3 to 12.

The Mary Stoltz Doll Museum is definitely a don't-touch place, but if you have a doll lover in the family, the collection of 125 dolls makes it well worth resisting the temptation. Kids especially like the impressive array of Barbie dolls.

 ### POCONO INDIAN MUSEUM (ages 6 and up)
Route 209 North; (570) 588–9338. Open daily (call ahead for hours). Admission charged.

This small museum traces the "human history" in the Delaware region from 10,500 B.C. to the American Revolution through artifacts, weapons, tools, and chronological commentary.

BUSHKILL FALLS (all ages)

Route 209; (570) 588–6682; www.visitbushkillfalls.com. Open April through October, 9:00 A.M. to dusk. Admission: $8.00 adults, seniors and groups $7.00, $2.00 for children ages 4 through 10; under 4 enter Free. Free *parking.*

The Peters family started charging admission to see these eight magnificent falls on their 300 acres back in 1905. The tourists haven't stopped coming since. Take a short nature walk back to the falls. Small children can usually manage the easy forty-five-minute to one-hour stroll. For the more energetic, there's a 2-mile hike that affords an even better view. A gift shop, food facilities, picnic area, and bathroom facilities are available to visitors. There are also paddleboat rides, fishing, miniature golf, an ice-cream parlor, and a new Native American exhibit.

FERNWOOD RESORT AND COUNTRY CLUB (all ages)

Route 209, Box 447 Bushkill; (570) 588–9500 or (800) 233–8103; www.resortsusa.com.

Undergoing major renovations this year, this Pocono resort will have newly updated rooms, a new indoor pool, and a restaurant that features a mall-like "food court"—ideal for families with diverse tastes!

Dingmans Ferry

POCONO ENVIRONMENTAL EDUCATION CENTER (ages 4 and up)

RD 2; (570) 828–2319; www.peec.org; peec@ptd.net.

For families interested in learning about the environment in a national park, there's no better deal than a weekend at the Pocono Environmental Education Center. The center conducts weekend and weeklong family vacation camps that include cross-country skiing, canoeing, hiking, "orienteering," natural history investigations, crafts, and field trips such as "The Waterfall Hunt." The thirty-eight-acre campus is located within the borders of the Delaware Water Gap National Recreation Area and includes classrooms, an indoor pool, a craft center, a dark room, a library, and a bookstore.

Accommodations are in one-room cabins that sleep between two and fifteen people. Meals are served at the dining hall. Sample rates for family programs are $94 per person for a three-day weekend including meals, lodging, and program activities (everything from candle making to birds-of-prey presentations). Children under 2 are $Free$, 4 and under are half price, and ages 5 to 8 are 25 percent off. PEEC provides linens and towels for an additional cost. For more information write to the center at Box 1010, Dingmans Ferry, PA 18328–9614.

ALSO IN THE AREA

Grey Towers. *Milford; (570) 296–9630.* Grey Towers will be closed for renovations until approximately fall 2001.

Promised Land State Park, *Route 390, 5 miles south of Route 84; (570) 676–3428.* Promised Land State Park is a 3,000-acre park surrounded by state forest land—creating a total of 11,000 acres of preserved wilderness. The area is home to a wide variety of wildlife, including one of eastern Pennsylvania's bigger populations of black bear. There are numerous housekeeping cabin resorts along Route 390, and camping is available in the park. There are environmental programs for children during summer. One primitive campground stays open year-round for cross-country skiers who can't bear to go home at the end of the day.

Hawley–Lake Wallenpaupack

Lake Wallenpaupack, the state's third largest man-made lake, is 15 miles long with 52 miles of shoreline. It was created in the 1920s by Pennsylvania Power & Light (PP&L) as part of a major hydroelectric project. At the PP&L Visitor's Center on Route 6 south of Hawley, exhibits outline the development of the project as well as available recreation on and around the lake. While there, ask about Shuman Point, Ledgedale natural areas, and Beech House Creek Wildlife Refuge, all maintained for public use by PP&L. They are great places for short nature hikes and spotting wildlife such as beavers, herons, hawks, and more.

Just north of the lake is the town of Hawley, a great town for antiquing. Kids will be more interested in the following area attractions.

 TANGLEWOOD SKI RESORT (ages 3 and up)
Route 507, Lake Wallenpaupack; (570) 226–SNOW. Open daily December through March.

If you're in the area during winter, check out nearby Tanglewood Ski Resort, which offers nine trails of downhill skiing, a snowboarding area, and several cross-country ski trails. A snowtubing park was added in

1997. There's also a Ski Wee children's program and nursery available for small children. The ski shop is one of the only ones in the area to rent cross-country as well as downhill equipment.

CLAWS'N'PAWS WILD ANIMAL PARK (ages 2 and up)

Off Route 590, near Hamlin; (570) 698–6154; www.clawsnpaws.com. Open daily May 1 through late October. Admission: $9.95, adults; $6.95, ages 2 through 11; $8.95, seniors; children under 2 are Free.

Claws 'n' Paws Wild Animal Park is a unique private zoo with 120 species of animals. There are two petting zoos—one with fawns and kids and other baby animals. Recent additions include giraffe feedings, and a parrot feeding area. During the reptile show kids can pet an alligator and a python. Other exhibits include bears, otters, primates of several types, many species of birds, a rare snow leopard, and a white tiger. The Dino Dig in the children's zoo lets kids dig for buried "bones." The easy-to-follow trails through the woods and the size of the facility help younger children from getting overwhelmed and overtired by the experience.

Lake Cruises

Along the lake there are numerous resorts and marinas geared to vacationers who want to spend time on the water.

- **Club Nautico of Lake Wallenpaupack.** *Shepards Marina on Route 507; (570–226–0580).* Rent a powerboat for the day. A wide variety of brand new and meticulously maintained powerboats and Waverunners are available, as is equipment for waterskiing, tubing, and other sports. If you don't have boating experience, ask for a list of skippers available for hire.

- **Pine Crest Yacht Club, Inc.,** *Route 507; (570) 857–1136. Open May through October.* Boat rentals from $26 per hour.

- **Pocono Action Sports,** *Route 507; (570) 857–1976.* Sailboats, rowboats, fishing, and waterskiing boats available.

- *Spirit of Paupack. Route 6 and Route 507; (570) 226–6266.* Open daily Memorial Day through October. Dinner, 7:30 to 9:00 P.M. Scenic tours, 9:00 A.M. to 5:00 P.M. daily; $5.00 for adults, $2.50 for children under 12. Dinner tours, 7:30 to 9:00 P.M., $34.50 for adults, $9.50 for children. For a sunset dinner cruise or a one-hour sight-seeing tour on the lake, the 48-foot *Spirit of Paupack* is a great way to see the lake.

TRIPLE "W" RIDING STABLES (ages 6 and up)

Beechnut Drive, off Owego Turnpike near Lake Wallenpaupack; (570) 226–2620. Open year-round (except hunting season).

Take a step beyond "follow-the-leader" riding at this 183-acre horse ranch featuring western riding experiences tailored to the individual. The staff at Triple W ensure a fun and rewarding ride for all members of the family by taking into consideration level of expertise and ambition. Overnight camping on horseback, hayrides, sleigh rides, and pony rides for children under 6 are also available. Riding rates for a family of four start at $27 per person per hour during the week, $29 per hour on weekends. The overnight camping trip is $150 per person.

If you're looking for overnight accommodations, stay at the Double "W" Bed and Breakfast, located on the same property, or bring your tent and camp on the ranch. For the bed and breakfast call toll-free (877) 540-RANCH.

WOODLOCH PINES INN AND RESORT (all ages)

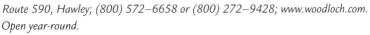

Route 590, Hawley; (800) 572–6658 or (800) 272–9428; www.woodloch.com. Open year-round.

If you follow 590 East from Hawley, you'll arrive at an excellent family resort, Woodloch Pines Inn and Resort. Named three times by *Better Homes & Gardens* magazine as one of America's favorite family vacation resorts and winner of the Pennsylvania Travel Council's 1999 "Spirit of Hospitality" award, Woodloch Pines was established as a small inn back in 1958. Since then, it has grown into a complex with 160 hotel rooms, a nightclub, several restaurants, game rooms, recreation complex, and more family activities and children's programs than you can cram into a seven-day stay.

The resort is located right on Lake Teedyuskung, sixty-five acres of crystal-clear waters with a sandy swimming beach and rowboats, paddleboats, canoes, and sailboats for exploring on your own. Woodloch Pines has the space and the layout that allow some families to be quiet and relax with one another while other groups applaud and cheer one another in games and contests.

Woodloch Pines rates include three meals a day and all activities and rentals. For families who prefer a more independent vacation, homes are available for rent at Woodloch Springs, a planned village centered around an award-winning golf course. Families staying at Woodloch Springs can participate in any daily activities at Woodloch Pines for no additional charge.

Woodloch Pines and Woodloch Springs are four-season resorts, with plenty to do and see no matter what the weather outside. Rates for the all-inclusive family resort at Woodloch Pines start at $185 to $215 per adult for a two-night stay during Thanksgiving week (the first child under 12 in the same room stays Free; charge for additional children varies according to age) and rise to $1,275 per adult for a week-long, midsummer stay in the best accommodations available.

At Woodloch Springs a family of four can rent a two-bedroom home for $150 a night or $1,000 per week from mid-October through April. During the peak summer season, a two-bedroom home is available for $340 per night or $2,241 per week. Three-, four-, and five-bedroom homes are also available. American plan (all meals included) is available at an additional cost.

ALSO IN THE AREA

Lacawac Wildlife Sanctuary (ages 6 and up), *Lacawax Road, Ledgedale; (570) 689–9494.* Open year-round. One-mile self-guided nature trail overlooking the Lake Wallenpaupack (pick up a trail guide at the parking lot) plus a host of special programs May through October.

Lukan's Farm Resort, *Long Ridge Road, Hawley; (570) 226–4576.* A quiet family resort with pool and other activities for kids.

Dorflinger-Suvdam Wildlife Preserve. *White Mills; (570) 253–1185.* Located off Route 6 between Hawley and Honesdale, this private preserve features hiking and cross-country ski trails and a great series of outdoor concerts in the summer months. The glass museum on the same property is interesting to adults and older children but not a great choice for toddlers and active kids.

Lackawaxen

Route 590 continues east from Woodloch Pines to the state line at Lackawaxen and the Delaware River. This tiny Pennsylvania town was the home of Zane Grey, author of such famous Western novels as *The Riders of the Purple Sage* and more than fifty others. Today the property is owned by the National Park Service as part of the Upper Delaware Scenic and Recreational River, which encompasses a 74-mile stretch of river from Sparrowbush, New York, to Hancock.

ZANE GREY MUSEUM (ages 8 and up)

River Road; (570) 685–4871; www.nps.gov/upde. Admission is $2.00 for adults, $1.00 for children 10 to 15; children under 10 are Free. Call ahead for museum hours.

This museum, operated by the National Park Service as part of the Upper Delaware Scenic and Recreational River, houses an impressive collection of memorabilia of Grey's life and his passion for the West. Little ones will be frustrated by the "don't touch" policy of the museum, but school-age and older kids interested in stories of the Wild West will enjoy the twenty-minute guided tour. If you luck out and get an individual tour, the guide may be able to gear his or her presentation to your family's interests.

Also at the museum is a gift shop (many of Grey's novels are on sale for some light vacation reading). The ranger on duty will be able to point out some of the highlights of the park, including Roebling's Delaware Aqueduct and the locks of the D&H Canal. Be sure to ask for the *Junior Ranger Program Activity Book.* Children who successfully complete six of the twelve activities in the pamphlet are awarded a certificate of achievement and a Junior Ranger patch.

ROEBLING'S DELAWARE AQUEDUCT (ages 6 and up)

Route 590; (570) 685–4871; www.nps.gov/upde. The bridge operates year-round.

Down the road about one-half mile from the Zane Grey museum is the Delaware Aqueduct, also known as the Roebling Bridge. Believed to be the oldest existing wire suspension bridge in the western hemisphere,

Flyfishing Both the Delaware and the Lackawaxen rivers are known as prime fly-fishing areas. Licensed guides will take you and your older kids out on the river for lessons. Check the list published by the park service.

it was designed and built in 1848 by John Augustus Roebling, the man who later designed the famous Brooklyn Bridge in New York City. Recently, the National Park Service restored the bridge to its original appearance. The Tollhouse contains historic photos from the canal era (1825 to 1898). It is open daily for a self-guided tour, weather permitting, Memorial Day to Labor Day, Wednesday through Sunday 10:00 A.M. to 5:00 P.M. and weekends in September and October. The bridge is open twenty-four hours a day for vehicular traffic.

Upper Delaware River Trips (ages 5 and up) The
Upper Delaware River is one of the last and longest free-flowing rivers in the northeastern United States. There are some rapids here, but most of the river is Class I, which means it is safe for beginning boaters and older children. (Always wear life jackets and exercise caution when on or near the water.)

There are several river accesses along the Upper Delaware, including one in Lackawaxen. If you don't have your own boat to launch here, contact one of the liveries that rent canoes, rafts, and tubes and conduct guided trips down the Delaware. The Park Service publishes a list of liveries and licensed guides. Most outfitters provide boats, life jackets, and drop-off and pick-up service at various river access points. They also have campsites available, although most are located on the New York side of the river. Remember, although the river is open to the public, the land on either side is privately owned. Please respect the rights and privacy of landowners.

Some of the bigger operations on the northern portion of the river include the following:

- **Kittatinny Canoes, Inc.** *HC67, Box 360, Dingmans Ferry; (800) FLOATKC; www.kittatinny.com.* $14 for tubing; $23 and up for canoeing and rafting.

- **Lander's River Trips & Campgrounds.** *Route 97 P.O. Box 376, Narrowsburg; (800) 252–3925; www.landersrivertrips.com.* $20 and up. Children must be 50 pounds. With landings in Hancock, Hankins, Callicoon, Skinners Falls, Narrowsburg, Ten Mile River, Minisink, Pond Eddy, Knights Eddy, and Matamoras, Lander's has the Upper Delaware covered. In addition to conducting rafting and canoe trips, the company rents equipment for self-guided expeditions. In 1997 the company updated its facilities, including campgrounds, motel (Ten Mile River Lodge in Ten Mile River, New York), and large grassy areas for playing near the river.

- **Wild and Scenic River Tours.** *166 Route 97, Barryville, New York; (800) 836–0366.*

Honesdale

Honesdale, located at the intersection of Routes 6 and 191, is in many ways the quintessential American small town. Its Main Street is lined with shops and stores that have been operated by the same families for years. Through a special Main Street program, many of the stores have been renovated to reflect the town's historic architecture. And the Victorian homes and big porches of north Main Street are classic examples of American design.

WAYNE COUNTY HISTORIC SOCIETY MUSEUM (ages 2 and up)

810 Main Street; (570) 253–3240. Open year-round; call for current hours. Admission is $3.00 for adults, $2.00 for children 12 to 18; children under 12 Free.

Here you can see a replica of the original Stourbridge Lion, the first commercial steam locomotive to run on an American rail in 1829. (The original is in the Smithsonian Institution in Washington, D.C.) Another exhibit traces the history of the D&H Canal, which connected Honesdale to the Hudson River, 108 miles away. There's also an impressive collection of Native American artifacts found in the Upper Delaware River Valley by a local archaeologist.

STOURBRIDGE RAIL EXCURSIONS (all ages)

303 Commercial Street; (570) 253–1960. Call for current schedule. Rates vary according to season and itinerary.

The Stourbridge Rail Excursions run on weekends in summer and for special occasions at other times. The excursions follow the Lackawaxen River to Hawley and Lackawaxen. Different themes include fall foliage tours, dinner-theater tours, the Great Train Robbery Run, the Halloween Fun Run, and the Santa Express.

The newly built Wayne County Visitors Center, at the same address, will soon house a number of railroad exhibits, and there's a gift shop featuring railroad souvenirs.

ALSO IN THE AREA

Carousel Water and Fun Park. *Route 652, Beach Lake; (570) 729–7532. Open May through October.* Go-carts, water slides, bumper boats, mini-golf, and batting cages are among the attractions here. Pay one price or pay by the ride.

Fun and Games. *Route 6 Plaza, Route 6; (570) 253–9111.* A pay-and-play center that can be just the ticket on rainy days.

Wayne County Fair. *Route 191.* The first week in August, the Wayne County Fairgrounds hosts a fairly traditional county fair. There are rides and food, but the best part is watching local 4-H kids with the animals they've raised and trained themselves.

Starlight and New Milford

Head north from Honesdale on Route 191 and you'll find yourself in northern Wayne County. The thick forests of this corner of the state add to the feeling of an escape from civilization.

INN AT STARLIGHT LAKE (all ages)

Lake Road, Starlight; (800) 248–2519; www.innatstarlightlake.com. Open year-round. Rates start at $125 to $165 for two people per night, including two meals. Children 7 to 12, $40 a day. Children under 7 in same room, Free *(meals a la carte).*

One of the best places to enjoy northern Wayne County is the Inn at Starlight Lake, which has been attracting vacationers since 1909. Guests can stay in the inn itself, but families will generally prefer the cottages. Each cottage is a little different: Some have fireplaces, others have sleeping lofts for kids. All have private bathrooms.

The inn, as the name suggests, is located right on Starlight Lake, a pretty little body of water that's great for swimming and exploring by rowboat or small sailboat (no powerboats allowed). There is a tennis court, shuffleboard, and a library and game room for evenings and rainy days. In winter visit nearby Mount Tone and Elk Mountain for downhill and cross-country skiing.

The inn is also the first stop on a four-day self-guided inn-to-inn bike tour of Wayne and Susquehanna counties. For families with older children, this is a great combination of an active vacation and lovely accommodations.

OLD MILLE VILLAGE MUSEUM (ages 5 and up)

Off Route 81, New Milford; (570) 465–3448. Open mostly weekends in summer; call for current hours. Admission is $4.00 for adults, $1.00 for children 9 to 12, Free *for children under 9.*

Follow the signs from the Interstate to this group of historic buildings and artifacts depicting life in the area in the 1800s. During summer artisans demonstrate different crafts, from blacksmithing to quilting. There are also special events and festivals throughout the season, including an Annual Arts and Crafts Day, an antique doll show, Old Time Country Music Contest, and more.

Scranton

Until the opening of the Steamtown National Historic Site in downtown Scranton in 1995, this industrial city was hardly thought of as a vacation destination. Visitors, however, are often pleasantly surprised that Scranton has a lot to offer—especially to family travelers.

STEAMTOWN NATIONAL HISTORIC SITE (all ages)
Entrance off Lackawanna Avenue, just west of Steamtown Mall; (570) 340–5200 or (888) 693–9391; www.nps.gov/stea. Open daily year-round. Admission: $7.00, adults; $6.00, seniors; $2.00, children 6 to 12; children 5 and under, **Free***.*

Railroad buffs of all ages won't want to miss Steamtown. Occupying fifty-two acres of a working railroad yard in downtown Scranton, Steamtown traces the history of railroading in the region and throughout the country. The new structure, opened in 1995, includes a visitor center, a theater, technology and history museums, a renovated roundhouse, and a museum store.

Watch the eighteen-minute film *Steel and Steam* to learn about the history of American steam railroading. At the history museum meet the people (actually lifelike statues) who worked, used, and depended on the railroad. Visit the roundhouse to see several examples from the Steamtown collection of locomotives and railroad cars. Learn about locomotive design and railroad communications at the technology museum.

From Steamtown you can arrange to take a two-hour train excursion to the nearby town of Moscow ($10.00 for adults, $8.00 for seniors, $5.00 for children) or a thirty-minute loop to the Historic Scranton Iron Furnaces (included in general admission). According to one park ranger, children are "glued to the window or fast asleep during these trips. Either way, it's great for parents!" Call the park for current information and train schedules.

The visitor center and most of the railroad yard and outdoor exhibits are **Free**. Admission is required for entry to the museums and the theater. If you plan to take a train ride to Moscow, you'll save money with a combination ticket.

The Steamtown site is handicapped-accessible, and there are bathrooms with changing tables. The Moscow excursion is accessible, but prior reservations are required. There are chemical toilets on the train, and snacks are available during a brief stop at Moscow.

After touring Steamtown, walk up the long ramp to the Steamtown Mall. (On rainy days, or when little ones are tired, it may be better to drive to the mall and park in the lot there.) There's a food court with fast food for every taste. The mall now operates a seasonal shuttle along the boardwalk between Steamtown and the food court. If you prefer a more leisurely dining experience, head downstairs, where there are two restaurants to choose from.

LACKAWANNA TROLLEY MUSEUM (all Ages)

300 Cliff Street on property of Steamtown; call (800) 22–WELCOME or (570) 963–6363 for information.

Brand new in late 1999, the Lackawanna Trolley Museum shares a parking lot with Steamtown, making one-stop shopping for kids who love the rails. This new museum tells the story of electric traction and trolley systems in Northeastern Pennsylvania. Trolley excursions depart regularly from the same platform as the Steamtown trains, and the trolleys operate seven days a week, year-round. The Children's Gallery teaches "painless geography" through models set on maps of the area. Kids can generate their own electricity, run a trolley system, and build their own model anthracite communities.

A Paulsen Family Adventure On a rainy weekend in November, Faith and I took Eli (one and a half years old) and Gideon (two and a half) to Steamtown National Historic Site in Scranton. It is tailor-made for train-loving toddlers who need a chance to run around. The boys loved the roundhouse and climbing up on the trains. They loved the train sounds and the photographs of trains in the museum.

On our way out to the car, the excursion train was pulling into the station. The boys were so excited to see the big engine coming closer and closer. We picked them up so they could see better. They waved at the passengers and at the engineer. In reply, the engineer blew the loud train whistle. Both boys immediately burst out in tears. It was probably not the reaction the engineer expected!

RADISSON LACKAWANNA STATION HOTEL (all ages)

700 Lackawanna Avenue; (570) 342–8300; www.radison.com/scranton.pa. Family package at $109 a night includes breakfast for four; children under 18, Free.

Sticking with the railroad motif, why not stay in a glorious old railway station? The Lackawanna Station Hotel, a National Register building now operated by the Radisson chain of hotels, is just a few blocks from Steamtown. The station's waiting area has been transformed into a palatial lobby with two restaurants and complete hotel facilities—including a game room that's a hit with kids.

HOUDINI MUSEUM (ages 3 and up)

1433 North Main Avenue; (570) 342–5555 or (570) 342–8527; www. houdini.org. Open daily Memorial Day through September 15; other times by appointment. Admission is $10.00 for adults, $8.00 for children under 10.

The Houdini Museum is a must-see for budding magicians. The museum takes visitors back to the days of vaudeville, when traveling performers like Houdini frequently visited the Scranton area. There are continuous guided tours, a film, and non-stop magic shows, along with Houdini memorabilia and exhibits about Scranton's vaudeville past. A wonderful magic show is performed by nationally-known magicians Dorothy Pietrich and Bravo the Great. Lots of laughs, live animals, and audience participation.

The Halloween "Spook-tacular" Theater of Illusion takes place from Columbus Day through Halloween. Appropriate for all ages, this magic show features classic illusions with nothing too scary for little ones.

LACKAWANNA COAL MINE (ages 3 and up)

McDade Park; (800) 238–7245 or (570) 963–MINE; visitnepa.org. Open daily April through November. Admission: $6.00, adults; $4.00, children ages 3 to 12; children under 3 are Free.

Coal is a major part of this region's history. One of the best places to gain an understanding of the life of a coal miner is on the Lackawanna Coal Mine Tour at McDade Park in Scranton. Here visitors ride 250 feet down into a real underground coal mine. Former miners and sons of miners tell the story of what a typical workday was like for the men and boys (as young as 7 years old!) of the mines. According to Barbara Colangelo, most children's favorite part of the tour is when the guide turns out the lights and the group stands in total darkness for a long couple of seconds. "They think the total darkness is awesome," she says. "Children who get scared of the dark should be prepared!"

The tour is partially handicapped-accessible, as long as the person can move from a wheelchair to the car. It's chilly and damp down below (55 degrees, year-round), so be sure to bring along a sweatshirt.

McDade Park

The Lackawanna Coal Mine may be the main attraction, but there's lots more to do in McDade Park. Next door to the mine is the Anthracite Heritage Museum, which traces the history of coal and its influence on the people of this area, including immigrant workers in the coal mines. Call (570) 963–4804 for more information.

McDade Park is also home to a summer theater festival, a fall balloon festival, and other special events. In addition, it's a great place for a family picnic and outdoor play. For more information and a schedule of upcoming events, call (570) 963–6764.

MONTAGE MOUNTAIN (ages 2 and up)

1000 Montage Mountain Road; (800) GOT–SNOW or (570) 969–7669; www.skimontage.com. Water park: $20 per family. Skiing: $30 on weekdays, $38 on weekends. The summer park is open from mid-June to Labor Day, weekdays noon to 5:00 P.M. and weekends 11:00 A.M. to 5:00 P.M.

Another center of family-oriented activity is Montage Mountain, located on the opposite side of Scranton. During winter, Montage is a ski resort with a 1,000-foot vertical drop and twenty slopes to choose from. In off-season Montage becomes a performing-arts center and family fun spot with special concerts, water slides, batting cages, chairlift rides, children's activity park, playground, and more.

ALSO IN THE AREA

Lackawanna County Stadium (ages 5 and up). *Montage Mountain Road, (570) 969–BALL.* Home to the Red Barons, an AAA farm club for the Philadelphia Phillies. Call for game information and schedules for the upcoming season.

Everhart Museum (all ages). *Nay Aug Park, 1901 Mulberry Street, Scranton; (570) 346–7186. Open year-round. Admission is $5.00 for adults, $3.00 for students, $2.00 for children; children under 5 are* ℱ𝓇ℯℯ.

Permanent exhibits include a dinosaur hall, rocks and mineral display, and bird gallery as well as examples of American and European painting, prints, and more. The Everhart often attracts high-quality traveling exhibits, so be sure to call ahead and see what will be there during your stay. The museum has recently added a Children's Gallery.

Annual Armed Forces Air Show. *Wilkes-Barre/Scranton International Airport, Avoca; call toll-free (877) 2–FLYAVP for information, dates, and admission prices.* If your family enjoys air shows, schedule a visit to the Scranton area for mid-August, to coincide with the Annual Armed Forces Air Show, billed as the premier air show in the Northeast. Precision formation flying, parachuters, aerial ballet, tactical demonstrations, and other in-the-air performances complement a full array of land-based exhibits of aircraft.

Eckley Miners' Village. *RR 2, Box 236, Weatherly; (570) 636–2070.* Open daily year-round. Admission: $3.50 for adults, $3.00 for seniors, $1.50 for children 6 to 12, $8.50 for families.

Just 9 miles east of Route 81, Eckley Miners' Village offers the chance to visit an authentic nineteenth-century "patch" town. The town was originally built in 1854 by the mining firm of Sharpe, Leisenring and Co. for its workers, mostly new immigrants to the States. The town, which was restored in the late 1960s for the filming of the movie *The Molly Maguires,* is now a historic site, administered by the Pennsylvania Historical and Museum Commission. Throughout the summer season the village holds various special events, including Patch Town Days, a Living History Weekend, and Family Sunday, which features a community picnic typical of the 1800s.

The Lehigh Gorge and Surrounding Area (White Haven, Jim Thorpe, Lehighton)

The Lehigh River cuts through the section of the Pocono Plateau south of Wilkes-Barre and creates a gorge that has become a mecca for recreation enthusiasts. A bike path along the river is a dramatic but easy ride (especially going north to south), and the river itself offers challenging white water for boating. There's also great skiing in the area, as well as some terrific resorts for families.

For a family that wants to combine outdoor activities like biking, hiking, and swimming with more urbane pursuits such as museums, shops, and restaurants, the town of Jim Thorpe has a winning combination.

THE MOUNTAIN LAUREL RESORT (all ages)

White Haven; (800) 458–5921 or (570) 443–8411; www.mountainlaurel.com. Open year-round. Rates start at $75 per person midweek and $85 on weekends, including breakfast and dinner. Children up to 12 years old stay and eat Free *(one child per adult).*

Nominated as one of the top family resorts in America by *Family Circle* magazine and *People* magazine, this resort offers a wide range of features just for families. Daily in summer and on weekends year-round, there are day camps for kids—one for children 3 to 5 and another for kids 6 and up. For the littlest ones a nursery operates from 9:00 A.M. to 9:00 P.M. to give parents a chance to spend time together or with older children.

On-site there are indoor and outdoor swimming pools, an 18-hole golf course, tennis courts, miniature golf, a petting farm, and numerous trails for hiking, biking, and cross-country skiing.

MAUCH CHUNK LAKE PARK (all ages)

625 Lentz Trail, Jim Thorpe; (717) 325–3669. Open year-round.

In the late 1800s and early 1900s, tourists flocked to Mauch Chunk (now Jim Thorpe) to ride the famous Switchback Railroad. This 18-mile figure-eight of track was more like a roller coaster than a train ride—at some points on the trip, cars reached speeds of 60 miles per hour. Now, a century later, the Switchback is again attracting tourists. Although the railroad has not operated in many years, its railbed has been transformed into one of the best-known mountain-bike trails on the East Coast.

Much of the Switchback trail is located within or near Mauch Chunk Lake Park, a county park that offers more than a vacation's worth of activities. The park features nice campsites, a sandy beach on a beautiful lake, excellent programs at the environmental center, and 18 miles of biking, hiking, or cross-country skiing trails. On weekends during the month of October—peak foliage time—the park offers hayrides along the Switchback Trail.

Other special attractions of the park include handicapped access to the lake, a handicapped-accessible fishing pier, bathrooms with changing tables, and a nice playground for kids. Fees are charged for many of the park's activities, including swimming, hayrides, equipment rentals, and camping.

MAUCH CHUNK MUSEUM AND CULTURAL CENTER (ages 4 and up)

41 West Broadway, Jim Thorpe; (570) 325–9190. Open Thursday through Sunday, April through December. Call ahead for current hours. Admission: $3.00 for adults; children up to 12 are Free.

Stop here to learn about the history of the Switchback Railroad and the town that grew up around it. There's also a display about the life of Jim Thorpe, the Native American Olympic athlete for whom the town was renamed in the 1950s. Although Thorpe was never a resident of the town, his widow heard of the area's efforts to revitalize its economy and offered her husband's memorabilia in exchange for naming the town in his honor.

The museum sponsors a shuttle bus ($2.00 per person) that circles the town, transporting visitors to the various sites.

THE OLD JAIL MUSEUM (ages 6 and up)

128 West Broadway, Jim Thorpe; (570) 325–5259. Open Memorial Day through October. Call ahead for current hours. Admission: $4.00 for adults, $2.50 for children 6 to 12, $3.50 for seniors and students.

Asked what kids like best about his museum, Thomas McBride answers, "It's a real jail and it's spooky. Real 'bad guys' were here!" Indeed, this building served as the Carbon County jail from 1871 to January 1995. It was also the site of the hanging of the Molly Maguires. Purchased by Thomas and Betty Lou McBride in 1995, it has now been preserved as a museum. Tour guides take visitors through the kitchen, cell blocks, even down to the dungeon, where prisoners were kept in solitary confinement. Yes, it's a bit spooky, but there are lessons to be learned here. Older kids especially seem fascinated. Look for the "mysterious handprint" left by a prisoner in 1871. No matter how many times the room is repainted, the ghostly handprint always bleeds through!

BLUE MOUNTAIN SPORTS AND WEAR (ages 8 and up)

Route 209, Jim Thorpe; (800) 599–4421); www.bikejimthorpe.com. Open daily.

If mountain biking or other outdoor sports are your pleasure, stop in at the Blue Mountain Bike Shop for information about the excellent trails in the area. The store offers top-quality bike rentals and shuttle service to various trailheads. Tell the experienced staff your skill level and how much time you want to spend, and they'll guide you to the right trail. Bike rentals run from $8.00 to $10.00 per hour or $20.00 to

$40.00 per day, including helmet, water bottle, and map. Shuttle service is $10.00 per person, $15.00 if you have your own equipment. In addition to bike rentals, the store has camping equipment, kayaks, rowboats, canoes, cross-country skis, and snowshoes for rent.

 ## POCONO WHITEWATER ADVENTURES (ages 5 and up)

Route 903, Jim Thorpe; (800) WHITEWATER or (570) 325–8430; www. whitewaterrafting.com. Rates for family-style float trip: $33.00 for adults, $21.95 for children 5 to 16.

Another option for outdoor enthusiasts is a rafting trip down the Lehigh River. Pocono Whitewater Adventures offers "Family-Style Floatrips" for kids from "five to eighty-five," including riverside barbecue. One child per two paying adults rides **Free**.

RAIL TOURS, INC. (ages 4 and up)

P.O. Box 285, Jim Thorpe; (888) 546–8467 or (570) 325–4606. Admission: $6.00 to $14.00 for adults, $3.00 to $7.00 for children 2 through 11.

The Visitor's Center in the old Jersey Central Railroad Station is the starting point for a number of special train-ride excursions. The schedule changes throughout the season, but rides take place on most weekends from April to October and the first two weekends of December.

 ## ASA PACKER MANSION (ages 8 and up)

Packer Hill, Jim Thorpe; (888) JIM–THORPE or (570) 325–3673. Open daily Memorial Day through October 31. Call ahead for hours. Admission charged.

Although not a place to take your wound-up preschooler, older kids will enjoy ogling over the opulence of the furnishings in this Victorian mansion.

OLD MAUCH CHUNK H. O. SCALE MODEL TRAIN DISPLAY (all ages)

41 Susquehanna Street, Jim Thorpe; (570) 386–2297). Open year-round. Hours vary. Admission charged.

Across the street from the Visitor's Center, in the Hooven Mercantile Co. building, head up to the second floor to see the Scale Model Railroad Display. With 1,000 feet of track, 60 cars, 200 miniature buildings, and 100 bridges, it sure is an impressive display.

THE INN AT JIM THORPE (all ages)

24 Broadway, Jim Thorpe; (570) 325–2599; www.innjt.com. Rooms from $65 to $115, suites from $150 to $250.

With a restaurant on-site and kid-friendly policies, this is a great place to stay right in Jim Thorpe. You can walk to all the sights. Suites have dining areas, whirlpools, VCRs, refrigerators, microwaves, and coffeemakers—things that make a family vacation much easier!

ALSO IN THE AREA

Pocono Museum Unlimited (ages 2 and up), *Route 443, Lehighton; (570) 386–3117. Open year-round. Call ahead for days and hours. Admission is $4.00 for adults, $2.00 children 5 to 12; children under 5 are* **Free**. If you enjoyed the model train display in Jim Thorpe, then head south to see the even larger display at the Pocono Museum Unlimited, located on Route 443 just west of Lehighton. The display measures 117 feet by 32 feet and features sixteen operating trains and 2,006 feet of track in a complete miniature environment, with waterfalls, drive-in movie theater, zoo, amusement park, 40-foot lake, and more.

JEM Classic Car Museum (ages 2 and up), *Route 443; (570) 386–3554. Open weekdays year-round. Call ahead for hours. Admission: $4.00 for adults, $2.50 for children 5 to 12.* To continue a transportation tour, from trains to cars, travel on Route 443 west to Andreas and the JEM Classic Car Museum, an 18,000-square-foot display floor that features an impressive collection of antique automobiles. The collection belongs to John E. Morgan, who began buying vintage cars more than thirty years ago. Recently, Morgan has branched out to large-scale model airplanes and a display of American and foreign dolls.

Big Boulder and Jack Frost Ski Resorts, *Lake Harmony; (570) 722–0100 or (800) 468–2442; www.big2resorts.com.* Big Boulder and its neighbor, Jack Frost, offer a great vacation deal for families. For $87 a night per person (based on double occupancy midweek), families can try skiing (downhill and cross-country), snowtubing, snowboarding, and paintball and stay in a vacation home on the property. Even better, kids under 5 stay **Free**. Both resorts also offer babysitting, ski lessons, and nightlife. Jack Frost has just opened TRAXX, a 15-mile course through the woods with divisions for motocross, ATV and BMX bikes. This course is available for people 10 and up. Bring your own equipment, but you can rent bicycles only. Also new at Jack Frost is night-time snowtubing on Saturday nights.

Ashland

PIONEER TUNNEL COAL MINE & STEAM TRAIN (all ages)

Nineteenth and Oak Streets; (570) 875–3850; www.easternpa.com/ pioneertunnel. Open April through November. Call ahead for specific times. Mine tour: $6.00 for adults, $3.50 for children under 12. Steam train: $3.50 for adults, $2.00 for children under 12.

If you didn't visit the Lackawanna Coal Mine in Scranton—or if you and your kids enjoyed it so much you're ready for another mine tour—then head to Ashland and the Pioneer Tunnel Coal Mine. Like the Scranton mine, this is an actual coal mine. When the coal company shut it down, some local volunteers and former miners transformed it into a fascinating study of a coal miner's life. Visitors enter the mine in open mine cars, just as the miners did when they started their workdays.

After the thirty-five-minute mine tour, take a ride on a narrow-gauge steam locomotive, the Henry Clay. Along the 1.5-mile round-trip, you'll see two other examples of coal mining: a strip mine and a bootleg coal mine, where men snuck past guards to get coal to sell or to heat their own homes.

ALSO IN THE AREA

Museum of Anthracite Mining. *Seventeenth and Pine Streets, Ashland; (717) 636–2070.*

Red Rock

RICKETTS GLEN STATE PARK (ages 2 and up)

Route 487; (570) 477–5675 or (888) PA–PARKS; www.dcnr.state.pa.us. Open year-round. **Free**.

Ricketts Glen State Park may well be the most beautiful and least well known of Pennsylvania's many state parks. The park, which spills into Luzerne, Sullivan, and Columbia Counties, covers 13,050 acres with lakes, waterfalls (twenty-two in all!), hiking and cross-country skiing trails, and many opportunities for fishing, boating, camping, horseback riding, and more.

A Paulsen Family Adventure

A Paulsen Family Adventure The cabins in Pennsylvania's State parks are a great, inexpensive family vacation option. The cabins have beds, a family room with sofas, a bathroom, and a kitchen. But be sure to bring along bed linens, towels, and anything you might need to cook a meal. And I do mean anything.

When a friend of mine and I took Eli (eight months old) for a weekend at Ricketts Glen State Park, I thought I had remembered everything: sleeping bags, blankets, ingredients for dinner, pots and pans for cooking, even pancake mix for the morning. But at dinner, I discovered I forgot a can opener. So much for the soup I brought. When I went to take a shower, I discovered I forgot to bring a towel. Luckily, my friend had brought two. At breakfast, I discovered I forgot maple syrup. So much for the pancakes.

We had a great time on our weekend anyway. We put Eli in the backpack and hiked through the woods in the snow. That night, we saw the comet Hale-Bopp in the dark night sky. Who needs soup anyway?

The Glens Natural Area, a registered National Natural Landmark, is the centerpiece of the park. Here, where two branches of Kitchen Creek create deep gorges, there are rare stands of virgin hemlock and other trees, some more than 500 years old. Much of the hiking in the park covers pretty steep territory, but with the help of a park ranger, you can choose trails that may be easier for children. For example, the Evergreen Trail, just half a mile long, takes hikers through giant hemlocks and pine trees and to a view of several waterfalls. There are 120 tent and trailer campsites available year-round at the park. In summer there are flush toilets and hot showers. In winter, only pit toilets are available.

If camping sounds a bit too rustic, consider staying at one of the ten comfortable family cabins in the park. Each has a living area, kitchen, bath, and two or three bedrooms. Advance reservations are required for the cabins.

Hunting is permitted in parts of the park. If you visit during the hunting season (primarily in late fall), check in with park rangers to find out what safety precautions are appropriate.

Pennsylvania State Parks

With 116 parks adding up to more than 277,000 acres, Pennsylvania has the largest state park system east of the Mississippi—and one of the best travel bargains anywhere. From the majesty of old growth forests to the drama of waterfalls, from the solitude of fishing to the camaraderie of a multi-generational family vacation, these parks offer something for just about everyone. And, admission is Free.

But while many families are aware of the recreational offerings of the state parks, many don't know about the cozy cabins and excellent campgrounds that offer an escape from ordinary life. Located in the woods, on the edge of a lake, by a babbling brook, or at the edge of an inspiring vista, these accommodations are the stuff vacation dreams are made on—at prices that make wishes come true.

Cabin rentals start as low as $19 per night for a tiny rustic cabin for two or $39 per night for a modern cabin with living room, bathroom, kitchen, and bunk beds for six. You'll have to reserve a weekday for the best rates, but even on weekends, the cabins are still a bargain. In summer, the cabins are available by the week, starting at $124 for the little rustic cabin and just over $300 for the modern ones. Bring your own food, linens, and cooking utensils and you've got a terrific vacation.

Campsites start at about $10 per night, even less for a primitive site. Some sites are equipped with electric and water hook-ups and are ideal for family travelers with a camper.

The Pennsylvania State Park system has introduced new reservation procedures that make reserving a cabin, campsite, or pavilion much easier than before.

By calling the new toll-free number (888–PAPARKS), you'll be able to make reservations up to eleven months in advance at any of the state parks in Pennsylvania. If one park has no available cabins for the dates you select, the operator will locate another that does. You can also check the website at www.dcnr.state.pa.us.

Your best bet is to call the individual parks if you have specific questions. For general park information, call (800) 63PARKS. But for cabin, campsite, or pavilion reservations, the number to call is (888) PAPARKS.

Forksville

WORLD'S END STATE PARK (ages 6 and up)

Route 154; (570) 924–3287 or (888) PA–PARKS; www.dcnr.state.pa.us. Open year-round. 𝐅𝐫𝐞𝐞.

Despite its small size (less than 1,000 acres), it's easy to feel as if you're at the edge of the world in this remote valley. If you're looking for a good place to introduce your children to wilderness camping, this is the spot. There are seventy tent and trailer camp sites and nineteen cabins, equipped with refrigerator, range, fireplace, table, chairs, and beds. (There's a central shower facility.)

The park includes numerous hiking trails including the Loyalsock Trail, a 59.3-mile hike, part of which runs through the park. Most of the trails are pretty steep, so this park is a better choice for older kids and more experienced hikers.

Festivals of Forksville Sullivan County Chamber of Commerce (570–946–4160) or Endless Mountains Visitors Bureau (570–836–5431).

Forksville might as well be called Festiville, with all the annual events planned for the fairgrounds and other locations around town. The fun starts in January with the annual Endless Mountains 50 Sled Dog Race. The 50-mile race, which is run in the state game lands near Forksville, attracts six-dog racing teams from as far away as Canada and Alaska.

In February the Forksville fairgrounds is the site of the Forksville Sleigh Ride and Rally. Here, horses pull the sleighs. In addition to divisions for men, women, and children, there's a timed obstacle-course race and a "Currier & Ives" class, where contestants are judged on the "postcard" quality of their sleighs. July brings the Sullivan County Rodeo and Truck Pull, and, at the end of summer, the Sullivan County Fair is held at the Forksville Fairgrounds. In October it's time for the Flaming Foliage Festival, with demonstrations by quilters, wood-carvers, and apple-butter and apple-cider makers. There are wagon rides, draft horses, and lots of activities for children.

Where to Eat

IN THE DELAWARE WATER GAP AND STROUDSBURG AREA

Brandli's Pizzeria & Italian Restaurant, *6A Foxmoor Village, East Strouds-burg; (570) 223–1600.*

Brownie's, *Main and Oak Streets, Delaware Water Gap; (570) 424–1154.*

Brownie's in the Burg, *700 Main Street, Stroudsburg; (570) 421–2200.*

The Sarah Street Grill, *550 Quaker Alley, Stroudsburg; (570) 424–9120.*

IN THE MOUNT POCONO AND EASTERN POCONOS AREA

Memorytown, *Grange Road, Mt. Pocono; (570) 839–1680.* Shops, snack-bar, restaurant, and amusement area all in one.

Smuggler's Cove, *Route 611, Tan-nersville; (570) 629–2277.*

IN THE HAWLEY-LAKE WALLENPAUPACK AREA

Ehrhardt's Lakeside Restaurant, *Route 507, 1 mile south of Route 6, Hawley; (570) 226–2124.* Dining with a view.

Falls Port Inn & Restaurant, *Main Street, Hawley; (570) 226–2600.* Children's menu, Sunday brunch, historic building.

IN THE HONESDALE AREA

Beach Lake Cafe. *Route 652, Beach Lake. Open year-round.* The most popular place around for weekend breakfasts, this little coffee shop serves up omelettes and pancakes. Get there early on Saturdays to avoid a wait.

IN SCRANTON AREA

Cooper's Seafood House, *701 North Washington Avenue, Scranton; (570) 346–6883.*

Pat McMullen's Restaurant, *217 East Market Street, Scranton; (570) 342–3486.*

The Mall at Steamtown, *Lackawanna Avenue, Scranton; (570) 343–3400.* Food court upstairs and two sit-down restaurants downstairs.

Where to Stay

IN THE DELAWARE WATER GAP AND STROUDSBURG AREA

Ramada Inn, *Delaware Water Gap; (570) 476–0000.*

Sheraton Four Points, *1220 West Main Street, Stroudsburg; (570) 424–1930 or (800) 777–5453; www.quikpage.com/P/ pocono.*

Shawnee Inn & Golf Resort, *River Road, Shawnee-on-Delaware; (570) 424–4000 or (800) SHAWNEE; www.shawneeinn.com.*

IN MOUNT POCONO AND EASTERN POCONOS

The Britannia Country Inn. *Upper Swiftwater Road, Swiftwater; (570) 839–7243.* Open year-round. Rates start at $35 to $70 per adult, $15 to $20 for children 4 to 13. Children under 3 stay **free.** If you can't bear to leave the pooch at home for your family vacation, consider a cottage at the Brittania Inn. Located on twelve acres with an outdoor pool, the inn serves up a taste of England in the Poconos. Modified American Plan (MAP) rates and ski packages available. And dogs are welcome ($20 per stay)!

Hampton Court Inn, *Route 611, Mt. Pocono; (570) 839–2119.*

Pocono Super 8 Motel, *Route 611, Mt. Pocono; (570) 839–7728.*

Mount Airy Lodge, *Route 611, Mt. Pocono; (570) 839–8811 or (800) 441–4410; www.mountairylodge.com.*

IN THE SCRANTON AREA

Best Western University Inn, *320 Franklin Avenue, Scranton; (570) 246–7061.* Near Steamtown National Historic Site.

Courtyard by Marriott, *16 Glenmaura National Boulevard, Moosic; (570) 969–2100.* Indoor pool, restaurant on site.

Holiday Inn Scranton-East, *200 Tigue Street, Dunmore; (570) 343–4771.* Indoor pool, newly renovated rooms.

IN THE HONESDALE AREA

Beach Lake, located on Route 652, makes a great home base for exploring the Upper Delaware Valley and Honesdale areas.

Central House. *Off Route 652; (570) 729–4411 or (570) 729–8341.* Open year-round. Rates: $45 per room/per night in the off-season; $60 in summer. Central House, with its on-the-lake location, family-style meals, and on-site swimming pool and volleyball court, is a nice spot for a value-priced family vacation.

Pine Grove Cabins. *Off Route 652; (570) 729–8522.* Open May through October. Rates: $60 per cabin/per night. For families who prefer to cook their own meals, the Pine Grove Cabins can't be beat. Owners Jerry and Barbara Zimmerman keep this bungalow colony immaculate. The cabins are tiny, but there's a kitchen, a small living room, a bathroom with shower, and two bedrooms crammed into each one. The property is right on the lake, with a sandy beach for swimming, paddleboats and rowboats for guest use. Special week-long packages available.

For More Information

Carbon County Visitor Center. *Broadway, Jim Thorpe; (888) JIM–THORPE.* Open year-round. Stop by to pick up brochures, ask questions, and check out the historic displays.

Endless Mountains Visitors Bureau, *RR 6, Box 132A, Tunkhannock PA 18657; (800) 769–8999 or (570) 836–5431; emvb@epic.net.*

Luzerne County Tourist Promotion Agency, *200 North River Street, Wilkes-Barre 18711; (570) 825–1635.*

Pennsylvania's Northeast Territory Visitors Bureau, *201 Hangar Road, Suite 203, Avoca 18641; (800) 22WEL-COME or (570) 457–1320; www. visitnepa.org.*

Pocono Mountains Vacation Bureau, *1004 Main Street, Stroudsburg, 18360; (800) 762–6667 or (570) 424–6050; www. poconos.org.*

Schuylkill County Visitors' Bureau, *91 South Progress Street, Pottsville 17901; (800) 765–7282 or (570) 622–7700.*

Upper Delaware Council, *Bridge Street, Narrowsburg, New York; (570) 252–3022.* An organization of businesses and individuals along the New York and Pennsylvania shores of the river. Contact them for more information about the area.

Central Pennsylvania

The center of Pennsylvania holds a wonderful array of cultural, historical, and recreational opportunities for families. Two cities, Williamsport and State College, give the area great museums, cultural events, and a wide variety of amenities, such as accommodations, shopping, and restaurants. Either one makes a good base for exploring the surrounding areas.

Dotted around the region are charming small towns, wonderful state parks, farms, and other rural attractions. Campgrounds are plentiful, and little bed and breakfasts often welcome families. The local county tourism organizations and chambers of commerce are great resources for planning your trip. Here are our recommendations.

Faith & Emily's Favorite Central Pennsylvania Attractions

1. Peter J. McGovern Little League Baseball Museum
2. Knoebels Amusement Park and Campground
3. Mountain Dale Farm
4. Shaver's Creek Environmental Center
5. Bellefonte Museum of Centre County
6. Children's Discovery Workshop
7. Walnut Acres Organic Farms
8. Happy Valley Friendly Farm
9. Historic Williamsport Trolley
10. Walking Tour of the Victorian Downtown in Lewisburg

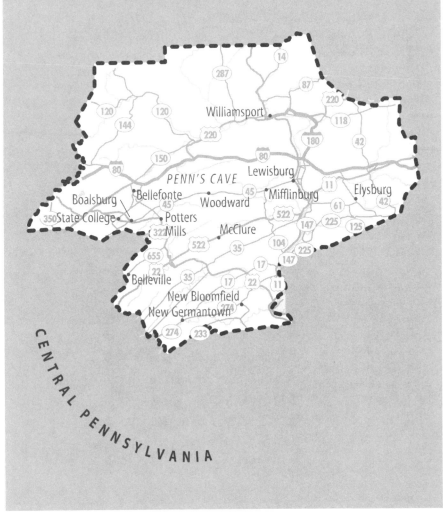

287

14

120   120   Williamsport   87   220

144   118

220   190   42

80

150

80   PENN'S CAVE   Lewisburg

Boalsburg   Bellefonte   45   Mifflinburg   11   Elysburg

State College   45   Woodward   61   42

350   Potters   522   147   225   125

32 Mills   McClure   104

522   35   225

655   17   147

22   17   11

Belleville   35   22

New Bloomfield

New Germantown   274

274   233

CENTRAL PENNSYLVANIA

Williamsport

If you've got a child in Little League, then Williamsport—the home of the Peter J. McGovern Little League Baseball Museum—is a required stop on your vacation in Central Pennsylvania. Once you get to the city, you'll find that the museum is a great destination, but there's more to Williamsport than baseball.

PETER J. MCGOVERN LITTLE LEAGUE BASEBALL MUSEUM (ages 5 and up)

Route 15 South; (570) 326–3607. Open Monday through Saturday 9:00 A.M. to 5:00 P.M.; Sunday noon to 5:00 P.M. Adults, $5.00; children 5 to 12, $1.50.

The Peter J. McGovern Little League Baseball Museum traces the history of Little League from its founding in 1939 to the present, when more than two and a half million children in eighty countries participate in the program. There are interactive displays and batting and pitching cages with instant replay monitors so that kids can see themselves in action. You can watch highlights of the Little League World Series—a truly international sporting event that takes place here each August. The Hall of Excellence includes tributes to such famous former Little Leaguers as Tom Seaver, Kareem Abdul-Jabbar, columnist George Will, and former New Jersey Senator Bill Bradley.

*F*aith & *E*mily's
Favorite Events in Central Pennsylvania

- Mifflinburg Buggy Days in Mifflinburg (end of May); (570) 966–1355.
- Belleville Auction in Belleville (Wednesdays); (570) 248–6713.
- Central Pennsylvania Festival of the Arts in State College (July); (814) 237–3682.
- Ag Progress Days in State College (mid-August); (814) 865–2081.
- Big Spring Festival in Bellefonte (mid-May); (800) 355–1705.

CHILDREN'S DISCOVERY WORKSHOP (ages 3 to 11)

343 West Fourth Street at Elmira Street; (570) 322–5437; williamsportymca. com. Open September through May Tuesday through Friday and Sunday 10:00 A.M. to 5:00 P.M., Saturday 11:00 A.M. to 5:00 P.M.; June through August Tuesday through Friday and Sunday 9:00 A.M. to 4:00 P.M., Saturday 10:00 A.M. to 4:00 P.M. Admission: $3.50 per person; children under 2 are **Free**.

Located inside the Williamsport YMCA, the Children's Discovery Workshop is a hands-on museum for children ages 3 to 11. The interactive exhibits are designed to inspire children's imaginations, explorations, and discoveries. Features include a toddler area, bricks to build a castle, a pretend ice-cream parlor, and changing exhibits. One of the most popular new features is the 129-foot-long "FUNnel," which children can crawl through.

If playing works up a family-sized appetite, head across the street to the Hepburn Diner, known locally for its home cooking.

LYCOMING COUNTY HISTORICAL SOCIETY MUSEUM (ages 5 and up)

858 West Fourth Street; (570) 326–3326. Open Tuesday through Saturday year-round, Sunday from May to October. Adults, $3.50; children 12 and under, $1.50.

Model-train enthusiasts will want to stop here to see the Larue Shempp Model Train exhibition, with more than 300 toy trains and two working layouts—reputed to be one of the finest displays of its kind in the country. There's a frontier room, which re-creates the furnishings from the county's first European settlement in 1769; a general store from the turn of the century; a one-room schoolhouse; a working gristmill; and a collection of farming, blacksmithing, and milling tools from the 1700s to 1900s.

HISTORIC WILLIAMSPORT TROLLEYS (all ages)

Downtown Williamsport; (800) CITYBUS or (570) 326–2500; www.citybus. com. Open Tuesday, Thursday, and Saturday during June, July, and August. Tours are $2.00 per person.

One of two great ways to tour the sights of Williamsport, the Historic Williamsport Trolleys are run by the City Bus company of the Williamsport Bureau of Transportation. The two trolleys, the *Herdic* and the *Weightman*, are actually replicas of historic streetcars (the *Weightman* is wheelchair-accessible). Each makes a ninety-minute narrated trip around the historic areas of Williamsport. The route takes you past Millionaire's Row (6 blocks of magnificent mansions), the field where the first Little League game was played, and other sights of the city. Riders can get on and off at one of the downtown stops and each of the two outlying stops. On Tuesday and Thursday you can get off the trolley and onto the *Hiawatha* for a cruise—the other great way to tour the sights of this city.

HIAWATHA CRUISES (all ages)

Susquehanna State Park; (570) 326–2500 or (800) 248–9287. In season only (570) 326–1221; www.williamsport.org. Cruises operate Tuesday through Sunday, May through mid-October. Public cruises: Adults, $7.00; children 3 to 12, $3.00. Family Night Cruises: Adults, $5.00; children 3 to 12, $2.00. First come, first served after tickets go on sale day of sale 10:30 A.M.

The other way to tour the town is aboard the *Hiawatha*, a paddle-wheeler that plies the Susquehanna River. The hour-long public cruise includes a narration that relates the history of the area, from the time when the Susquehannock Indians lived along these shores through the European settlements and boom years of the lumber industry. On Tuesday nights in June, July, and August, come aboard for a special cruise just for families, ninety minutes long, including an ice-cream sundae. Sunday brunch cruises, for $15 per person, will sail you to the Antlers Country Club for brunch, then take you back by Historic Williamsport Trolley. A similar dinner cruise, offered one Friday per month, is frequently sold out.

CLYDE PEELING'S REPTILAND (ages 4 and up)

Route 15, south of Williamsport; (570) 538–1869; reptiland.com. Open daily 9:00 A.M. to 7:00 P.M. May through September. October to April, open daily 10:00 A.M. to 5:00 P.M. Adults, $7.00; children 4 to 11, $5.00; children under 4 are **Free***.*

Don't miss Clyde Peeling's Reptiland, an accredited zoo with a collection of sixty different species of reptiles and amphibians. Poison dart frogs, a giant toad, a gaboon viper, a green tree python, a king cobra, alligators (including the 800-pound "Ivan"), giant tortoises, turtles, iguanas—they're all here in a newly opened reptile and amphibian facility. There are educational programs five times during the day that give visitors a chance to see and touch the animals up close.

Elysburg

KNOEBELS AMUSEMENT PARK AND CAMPGROUND
(ages 2 and up)

Route 487, about 12 miles south of Bloomsburg; (800) ITS–4FUN or (570) 672–2572; www.knoebels.com. Open weekends in April, May, and September; daily in June, July, and August. Admission **Free** *to park; camping, $22.50 a night; cabins, $69.*

If you've ever wondered what happened to the traditional amusement parks you remember from your own childhood, head to Knoebel's (pronounced with a hard "k"). This park got its start at the turn of the century, when Henry Hartman Knoebel charged 25 cents to water, feed, and brush the horses that brought groups to swim on his property. After a few years he added picnic tables and sold ice cream and other snacks to the visitors. A pool, overnight cottages, and a carousel were added in 1926. By the 1940s Knoebels had graduated to an amusement resort.

At present Knoebels offers forty-six rides (including two world-class wooden roller coasters, the Phoenix and the Twister), a huge swimming pool, and many rides especially for the younger set. There are several restaurants, snack bars, and picnic areas as well as a collection of shops and regularly scheduled entertainment. All of this is nestled among natural streams and shady hemlock trees that keep the temperatures here a good 10 degrees lower than elsewhere in the area.

If this sounds like too much for a day trip, stay the night—or longer—at one of 500 campsites and log cabins. A campsite runs about $140 for a full week. Cabins sleep six, have electricity, and cost $69 a night. Call (570) 672-9555 for campground information.

Lewisburg

A pretty Victorian town that is home to Bucknell University, Lewisburg is a good place to stop and stretch the legs or grab some lunch. Pick up a walking-tour brochure from the Union County Tourist Agency at 418 Market Street (570-524-2815). There are some great historic homes in town that are open for tours. Although not geared for small children, older ones enjoy the tours.

Because it is home to Bucknell University, this is a good place to find a place to stay or have a bite to eat. The Union County Tourist Agency can point you in the right direction.

SLIFER HOUSE MUSEUM (ages 6 and up)

1 River Road; (570) 524–2245. Open April 15 through December 31, Tuesday through Sunday 1:00 to 4:00 P.M.; January 1 through April 14, Tuesday through Friday, 1:00 to 4:00 P.M. or by appointment. Admission: adults, $4.00; seniors, $3.50; children 10 to 16, $2.00; children under 10 are Free.

House tours aren't on most kids' Top 10 list, but the Slifer house has several exhibits that children 6 and older enjoy. An artifact quiz is designed to stimulate minds, both yound and old. Among the favorites are the children's bedroom and old toys, a Regina music box, and the doctor's office, with antique medical tools. In summer there's an outdoor concert series, followed by Free ice cream. A sure hit with kids. Slifer House also hosts family activities such as Civil War encampments, storytelling, and workshops. Recent workshop topics have included gingerbread house making and origami.

PACKWOOD HOUSE MUSEUM (ages 6 and up)

15 North Water Street; (570) 524–0323. Open Tuesday through Saturday, 10:00 A.M. to 5:00 P.M. Admission: adults, $4.00; seniors, $3.25; children and students, $1.75; children under 6, Free.

Christmas is a special time for children at the Packwood. Even younger children love seeing the decorations and lights. The rest of the year, the museum is more geared for school-age children. There is an impressive collection of antique furniture glass, ceramics, textiles, and more at the Packwood.

Mifflinburg

In addition to the sights listed below, Mifflinburg serves as the headquarters for no fewer than four Pennsylvania state parks: McCalls Dam State Park (known for its fishing); R. B. Winter State Park (with lake swimming, environmental education, and camping); Ravensburg State Park (fishing, hiking, and camping); and Sand Bridge State Park (known for snowmobiling trails). For information on any one of these parks, call (570) 966–1455 or (800) 63-PARKS.

MIFFLINBURG BUGGY MUSEUM (ages 3 and up)

523 Green Street; (570) 966–1355; www.lycoming.org/buggy. Open May through October, Thursday through Sunday 1:00 to 5:00 P.M.; weekends in October. Admission charged. Free *parking.*

If you've been admiring the buggies that the Amish and some Mennonite families use to get around, stop at the Mifflinburg Buggy Museum to see them up close. Through the late nineteenth century, Mifflinburg earned the nickname "Buggy Town" by producing roughly 5,000 horse-drawn vehicles a year, more per capita than any other town in Pennsylvania. Over an eighty-year period, the town was home to seventy-five separate buggy makers. Only one of these factories remains, the W.A. Heiss Coachworks, now part of the Buggy Museum. The Mifflinburg Buggy Museum is believed to be the only museum in the United States housed in an original carriage factory with original contents.

Visitors can take a guided tour of the original factory, complete with tools and supplies; the Repository (showroom) with vehicles on display; and the family home. Each May the Museum hosts the annual Mifflinburg Buggy Day Festival featuring craft vendors, antiques dealers, live entertainment, food, activities for children, demonstrations, and buggy rides.

CHRISTKINDL MARKET (ages 2 and up)

Downtown Mifflinburg; (570) 966–1666.

Another Mifflinburg traditional celebration is Christkindl Market, held the Thursday through Sunday after Thanksgiving each year. The festival re-creates a traditional German Christmas, with authentic food, seasonal music, and handmade gifts for sale. There's also a Santa's Workshop with crafts and games just for kids.

ALSO IN THE AREA

Walnut Acres Organic Farms (all ages), *Route 104, just south of the town of Penns Creek; (800) 433–3998; www.walnutacres.com. Open year-round, Monday through Saturday 9:00 A.M. to 5:00 P.M. and Sunday noon to 5:00 P.M. Admission is* **Free**. Just a few miles south of Mifflinburg, Walnut Acres Organic Farms has been growing fruits, grains, and vegetables without pesticides for over fifty years. The farm is also home to a thriving mail-order business and a farm store. Visitors are welcome to take a self-guided tour of the property. Most of the trails are 1 mile or less, suitable to little legs or even strollers. On weekdays tours are given of the plant, where fresh fruits and vegetables are canned and packaged. Walnut Acres' number one product is their peanut butter. Parent supervision is required on plant tours. Hold those toddlers' hands, please! A self-service deli is open 10:00 A.M. to 3:00 P.M.

McClure

MOUNTAIN DALE FARM (all ages)

Rural Route 2; (570) 658–3536; www.pafarmstay.com. Open year-round. $43 and up per night.

If your family wants to experience farm life firsthand, then a vacation at Ken and Sally Hassinger's Mountain Dale Farm is just the ticket. This 175-acre farm is surrounded by state forest and game land, making it a complete getaway from civilization. But you don't have to rough it completely. The farm offers accommodations in a variety of cabins and efficiencies. There is a 200-year-old restored log house that has four bedrooms and sleeps up to fourteen people (yours for a family of four for less than $99 a night!). Efficiency cabins start at $70 a night for four people, and the more rustic and secluded forest cabins go for just $43 a night for four people. Children under 12 are half-price, and those under 2 years old stay 𝐅𝐫𝐞𝐞. Meals are provided at an extra cost upon request, but most visitors enjoy cooking in their own kitchens or in the common kitchen.

Kids love helping out with the barn chores and getting to know the farm animals. Other activities include boating, fishing, swimming, or ice skating on three ponds; cross-country skiing or hiking in the woods; or just relaxing on the front porch of your cabin. Come before Christmas and choose your own tree from the Christmas tree farm.

New Bloomfield

LITTLE BUFFALO STATE PARK (all ages)

Off Route 34; (570) 567–9255; www.dcnr.state.pa.us/stateparks/parks/ buffalo.htm. Open year-round. 𝐅𝐫𝐞𝐞 *for most activities.*

In Perry County 830-acre Little Buffalo State Park has both historic and natural attractions. There's an eighty-eight-acre lake, a swimming pool (fee charged), hiking trails, fishing, and picnic areas. But there are also a covered bridge, a working gristmill from the 1800s, and an old tavern, all of which have been restored (or are in the process). In winter there are 7 miles of cross-country trails, a sledding and tobogganing area, and a skating area on the lake (the rest of the lake is open for ice fishing in winter). There is no camping in the park, but the park ranger can furnish names of other campgrounds in the area.

BOX HUCKLEBERRY NATURAL AREA (all ages)

Route 34; (570) 536–3191. Open year-round. 𝐅𝐫𝐞𝐞.

Just a few miles south of Little Buffalo State Park on Route 34 is the Box Huckleberry Natural Area, a special reserve for a box huckleberry plant estimated to be 1,300 years old. A short interpretive nature trail around the area is a favorite of small children. This is a good place to teach your kids about the importance of preserving our natural resources. Trail maps and a written history of the plant are available on-site.

New Germantown

TUSCARORA STATE FOREST (all ages)

Route 274, southwest of New Germantown; (570) 536–3191; www.dcnr. state.pa.us/forestry/forests.tuscar. Open year-round. Admission 𝐅𝐫𝐞𝐞.

Traveling southwest on Route 274 from New Germantown, you'll come upon the entrance to the Tuscarora State Forest—90,512 acres of amazing vistas, undisturbed areas, trout streams, state parks, hiking, snowmobiling, and more. The forest roads are well maintained, making a great route for a mild "off-road" driving experience. The Bureau of Forestry has developed a brochure that will guide you on a 26-mile auto tour of the forest. The dirt roads are in good shape, so you shouldn't need four-wheel drive to navigate the route in good weather.

APaulsen Family Adventure The first rule of traveling with children should be: If possible, get a hotel with a pool.

Most kids love the water. At the Holiday Inn in State College, Eli (eighteen months) learned how to jump from the edge of the pool into our arms. He thought this was great fun and jumped and jumped until his lips turned blue.

Eli was totally wound up from a day of sightseeing and visiting with his grandparents. He wanted to run around, but the confines of a small hotel room, the car, or a restaurant didn't allow this. The pool let him get his ya-yas out.

Which leads to the third benefit of a pool: it wears kids out. After playing in the pool, we put him in his pajamas and put him in his portacrib. He was out like a light in a matter of minutes. No mean feat for a kid who was bouncing off the walls earlier in the day.

Highlights in and around the state forest include: Hemlocks Natural Area, a 131-acre area of virgin hemlock forest with 3 miles of hiking trails; the Iron Horse Trail, a rails-to-trails project that provides 10 miles of hiking with only moderate climbing necessary; the Tuscarora Trail, a 22-mile side trail of the Appalachian Trail; Fowler Hollow State Park, with eighteen campsites and fishing in the creek; and Colonel Denning State Park, with fifty-two trailer and tent sites, excellent hiking, and an extensive environmental education program during summer months. For more information about the State Forest and natural areas, contact the Bureau of Forestry, RD 1, Box 42-A, Blain 17006. For more information about the state parks within the forest, call (570) 776–5272 or (800) PA–PARKS.

Belleville

Everyone loves a farmer's market: rows of fresh vegetables, home-baked goods, handmade crafts, and the chance to meet the people who produce them. The town of Belleville may have the ultimate farmer's market.

THE BELLEVILLE AUCTION (all ages)

Route 655; (570) 248–6713. Open year-round Wednesday 6:00 A.M. to 6:00 P.M. **Free** *admission.*

The Belleville Auction, an Amish farmer's market, takes place every Wednesday from six in the morning to six at night. The ten-acre market has livestock yards, auction barns, and 400 flea-market stalls. It's a popular event, so be prepared to walk a ways from your car to the auction areas. For more information about the area, call the Juniata Valley Area Chamber of Commerce at (570) 248–6713.

ALSO IN THE AREA

Mifflin County Trout Hatchery (ages 4 and up), *Route 655, between Belleville and Reedsville; open Wednesday and Saturday.* While you're in the area, check out the Mifflin County Trout Hatchery, where children can fish for trout and pay only for what they catch. Fishing poles and bait are provided.

State College

A visit to a college campus is a great way to inspire a child's educational dreams. The home of Penn State University, one of the country's best public universities, State College has much to offer families.

Bolstered by the university population, State College is a thriving town with many hotels, shops, and restaurants. Many of the area's attractions are within an easy drive, making the town an ideal base for your explorations.

 CENTRAL PENNSYLVANIA FESTIVAL OF THE ARTS (all ages)
Downtown State College; (814) 237–3682. Five days in July. Free *admission.*
State College is the site of the Central Pennsylvania Festival of the Arts, a five-day celebration that takes place in July each year. The first day of the festival is traditionally Children and Youth Day, featuring the creations of local children ages 8 through 18 and a wonderful procession through town in which children wear masks and carry their works of art. Life-sized puppets also take part in the procession. Storytelling, marionette performances, concerts, and more round out this not-to-be-missed event. Organizers have made special attempts to include people with special needs, including visual impairments.

 FROST ENTOMOLOGICAL MUSEUM (ages 5 and up)
Headhouse 3, halfway between Shortlidge and Bigelar Roads; (814) 863–2865. Open Monday through Friday 9:30 A.M. to 4:30 P.M. Free*. Pick up a parking permit at an information booth on campus.*
The Insect Zoo features a functional beehive plus a variety of insects and other arthropods such as scorpions, tarantulas, and cockroaches. Kids will get a kick out of it; parents may or may not.

 EARTH AND MINERAL SCIENCES MUSEUM (ages 5 and up)
122 Spiedle Building, Pollock Road; (814) 865–6427; e-mail: sicree@geosc.psu. edu. Open year-round Monday through Friday 9:00 A.M. to 5:00 P.M. Free*.*
The halls of the Spiedle Building are lined with crystals, gems, carvings, and fossils. Kids especially like the ultraviolet light room that highlights minerals invisible under normal incandescent lights. The shrunken head collection also gets an enthusiastic reception from most kids.

GREENBERG INDOOR SPORTS COMPLEX (ages 2 and up)

Pollock and McKean Streets; (814) 865–4102.; www.psu.edu/deptice_pavilion. Open to the public for part of most days. Call ahead for current hours. Admission: $3.50 for adults, $3.00 for persons 18 and under. Skate rental: $1.50.

After checking out the museums, you might want to take a spin around the indoor ice-skating rinks at the Greenberg Indoor Sports Complex. The complex offers two rinks with superior surfaces.

BEAVER STADIUM (ages 5 and up)

University Drive and Curtin Road; (814) 863–1000 or (800) 833–5533. Various prices.

Of course, for many people the most famous aspect of Penn State is its football team. The Nittany Lions play in the Big Ten College Football League and sports fans come from around the country to see a game at Beaver Stadium. Call for current schedules and tickets.

BRYCE JORDAN CENTER (ages 5 and up)

University Drive and Curtin Road; (814) 865–5555 or (800) 863–3336.

Men's and women's basketball as well as a variety of special events take place across the street from Beaver Stadium at the Bryce Jordan Center. Call for schedules and tickets.

COLLEGE OF AGRICULTURAL SCIENCES (all ages)

Agriculture Administration Building, University Park; (814) 865–4433. Open 9:00 A.M. to 4:00 P.M. **Free**.

Near Beaver Stadium, check out the animals at the agricultural facilities of the College of Agricultural Sciences. See white-tailed deer, sheep, cattle, horses, and pigs. There's also an exhibit of flowering plants and vegetables.

Throughout the year special events are scheduled for the nearby Ag Arena. Check the marquee outside to see what's scheduled or call ahead. Children especially enjoy the shows of horses or dairy cattle. Around Christmas, the Festival of Trees features more than one hundred different trees, decorated by area businesses and organizations.

AG PROGRESS DAYS and the JEROME K. PASTO AGRICULTURAL MUSEUM (all ages)

Russell E. Larson Agricultural Research Center, Route 45; (814) 865–2081; www.cas.psu.edu/docs/AGIS/APD.html. **Free** *admission.*

Penn State's Ag Progress Days is one of the largest agricultural shows in the country. It takes place in mid-August each year and features live animal exhibitions, a petting zoo, computer-based games, demonstrations of the latest farming technologies, and displays of antique farm equipment. The Family and Youth Building has special programs just for kids.

On the same site as the Larson Agricultural Research Center, the Jerome K. Pasto Agricultural Museum traces the history of farming in America with displays of old tools and appliances from the days before electricity. It's open April 15 to October 15. Call ahead for scheduling information (814–865–8301). Admission is **Free**, but donations are encouraged.

MILLBROOK MARSH NATURE CENTER (all ages)

Puddintown Road, State College; (814) 863–2000. Open year-round. Call ahead for current hours. **Free** *admission.*

A brand-new cooperative venture of many local educational organizations, this is the site for several nature programs conducted by the Shaver's Creek Environmental Center (see below). The mission of the center is to educate and inspire people about the natural world and to instill a passion for the environment through science, history, culture, and art. Call for updated information and a schedule of events.

STONE VALLEY RECREATION AREA (all ages)

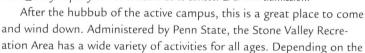

State Route 1029, off Route 26 South; (814) 863–1164; www.psu.edu/dept/ stone_valley. Open year-round. Sunrise to sunset. **Free** *admission.*

After the hubbub of the active campus, this is a great place to come and wind down. Administered by Penn State, the Stone Valley Recreation Area has a wide variety of activities for all ages. Depending on the season you can enjoy boating (canoes, rowboats, or sailboats—all of which are available for rent), fishing (trout and bass), hayrides, hiking, ice skating (rentals available), sledding, ice fishing, or cross-country skiing (lessons available). There are eleven handicapped-accessible cabins for overnight accommodations. The one-room cabins are equipped with bunk beds, refrigerator, electric range top, electricity, and gas heat. There are central bathroom and shower facilities nearby. Bring your own linens and cooking and eating utensils. Call for rates and reservations.

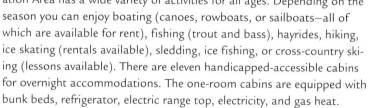

SHAVER'S CREEK ENVIRONMENTAL CENTER (all ages)

State Route 1029, off Route 26 South; (814) 863–2000. Open year-round. Call ahead for current hours. Admission: $2.50 per person; children under 3 are **Free**.

At the Environmental Center, learn about the local wildlife and how injured eagles, hawks, and owls are rehabilitated in the Raptor Center. There's a bookstore with a good selection of books for children; you'll also find other wildlife accessories there. Special gardens attract butterflies, bees, and hummingbirds. Shaver's Creek is the site of a wonderful day camp program for children 6 and up. For children 6 to 11, the Discovery and Explorer Camps run from Tuesday through Friday and end up with an overnight at the camp. Parents are invited to join their children for the overnight. Rates are $95 per child for nonmembers, $75 for members.

Children 12 and up can choose from several different camp experiences, including Adventure Camp (with an emphasis on caving, rock climbing, and mountain biking) and Raptor Camp (in which campers work with rehabilitated birds of prey).

Boalsburg

Looking for a special way to spend the upcoming three-day weekend? The town of Boalsburg has several claims to fame that make it a good destination any time of year. For Memorial Day weekend how about visiting the place where the holiday got its start? Boalsburg has been commemorating this day since 1864. Today there are community picnics and parades to enjoy.

In July Boalsburg is the site of the **Peoples' Choice Festival of Pennsylvania Arts and Crafts.** The weekend of activities includes **Free** museum tours for children, a petting zoo, and a stuffed-animal vet.

Columbus Day weekend coming up? What better place to get in touch with the discoverer of the New World than at the **Christopher Columbus Family Chapel,** part of the Boal Mansion and Museum. And, for Veterans' Day, learn the history of our nation's veterans at the Pennsylvania Military Museum across Route 322.

BOAL MANSION AND MUSEUM (ages 6 and up)

300 Old Boalsburg Road; (814) 466–6210; www.vicon.net/~boalmus. Open Tuesday through Sunday 1:30 to 5:00 P.M. spring through fall; 10:00 A.M. to

5:00 P.M. in summer; Sundays noon to 5:00 P.M.; closed Monday. Admission is $10.00 for adults, $6.00 for children 7 to 11, children under 7 enter Free.

This historic house has an added attraction: original objects belonging to Christopher Columbus. Originally part of the Columbus family castle in Spain, the chapel contains heirlooms that date back to the 1400s. The *Wall Street Journal* called the collection "a strong tangible link to Columbus in the New World." Kids especially enjoy looking at the antique weapons and dresses and hearing stories about nine generations of the Boal family, across 210 years in the same house, continuing today.

PENNSYLVANIA MILITARY MUSEUM (ages 5 and up)
Route 45 and Business Route 322; (814) 466–6263. From April through October, open Tuesday through Saturday, 9:00 A.M. to 5:00 P.M.; Sunday noon to 5:00 P.M. Closed Mondays except for Memorial Day, July 4th, and Labor Day. From November through March, call ahead for hours. Admission: $3.50 for adults; $1.50 for children 6 to 12; children under 6 are Free.

Starting with Ben Franklin's first military unit, the museum traces the history of the military—and Pennsylvanians' involvement—all the way through the Vietnam conflict. A tour of this museum is highlighted by a 100-foot-long re-creation of a front-line trench from World War I. The museum building is surrounded by a sixty-five-acre park that includes equipment, monuments, and memorials. There are daily living-history demonstrations and many special celebrations during the year. On Memorial Day each year, the museum is the site of a Civil War encampment.

TUSSEY MOUNTAIN SKI RESORT (ages 3 and up)
301 Bear Meadows Road; (800) 733–2754 or (814) 466–6810. Open year-round. Lift tickets: $10 to $34 for adults, $7 to $23 for juniors (7 to 10 years old); children under 6 ski Free *with an adult.*

Heading east from State College on Route 322 is Tussey Mountain Ski Resort, a great place for family skiing and snowboarding. At the Kid's Mountain Learning Center, children ages 3 to 6 can ski in a specially designed learning area. They can even join a Paw Prints group and enjoy instructed play and an introduction to skiing. The Mountain Lion group, for children 6 to 10 years old, is aimed at building children's skiing skills. Both classes run two hours and are scheduled twice a day on weekdays and three times a day on weekends. The Paw Prints session costs $10, $15 with rentals. Mountain Lions runs $15, $20 with rentals.

Tussey Mountain has recently added Avalanche Canyon, a snowtubing area. A five-run ticket costs $6.00.

Eastern Centre County

Just east of State College are several small towns with worthwhile attractions for families. Here are a few of the best.

HAPPY VALLEY FRIENDLY FARM (all ages)

Route 322, 12 miles east of State College, Potters Mills; (814) 364–1902. Open April through October; Tuesday through Saturday 10:00 A.M. to 5:00 P.M., Sunday noon to 5:00 P.M., closed Monday. Admission is $5.75 for adults, $5.00 for children 1 through 12.

Especially good for toddlers, this hands-on farm provides a safe place where children can feed and touch chicks, lambs, and other farm animals. But even older kids and adults will enjoy this agricultural experience for the whole family. More than 250 animals are housed here, including many exotic species. There's a working goat dairy and a fudge factory: Watch the goats being milked; then eat the ice cream and fudge made from the milk. Hayrides are available throughout the season, and you can pick your own pumpkin in the fall. There's a shady picnic area, so bring your lunch and enjoy the day. If you don't want to bring your lunch, in the small town of Potter's Mills, Homans General Store makes sandwiches, and Utah House serves lunch.

PENN'S CAVE (ages 4 and up)

Route 192, 5 miles east of Centre Hall; (814) 364–1479. Open 9:00 A.M. to 5:00 P.M. February 15 to December 31 (weekends only in December). Admission is $9.00 for adults and $4.25 for children 2 to 12.

Kids love caves. Penn's Cave has been attracting visitors for centuries, since the Seneca Indians discovered it. It has been a tourist attraction since the late 1800s, when a hotel was built on the site.

Penn's Cave is the country's only water-filled cave, and tours are given by motorboat. Along the hour-long ride you'll see amazing stalactites and stalagmites in a series of "rooms." Colored lights illuminate formations with names like the Statue of Liberty, Chinese Dragon, and Niagara Falls. If you're lucky, you'll spot some of the bats that live in the cave.

No matter what the temperature outside, it's always 52 degrees inside the cave, so bring a jacket in summertime. Some children are initially scared by the dark and the idea of being underground. Most become more comfortable as they become involved in spotting the formations and enjoying the colored lights. According to tour guides the temperament of the child is more of a factor than age.

But there's more to Penn's Cave than the cave. There's also 1,000

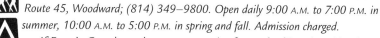

Cave Exploration Woodward Cave and Penn's Cave may get most of the attention, but Central Pennsylvania actually has hundreds of fascinating caves and caverns. If you're interested in doing some cave exploring that's a bit off the beaten path, contact the Nittany Grotto, headquartered in State College. This group of enthusiastic cave explorers encourages safe and responsible cave exploring. Its members are pleased to arrange special family trips on request. In order to take advantage of this service, families may be asked to join the group at a cost of $10.00 a year. For more information contact Keith Wheeland at (814) 238–2057 or check out the organization's website at www.clubs.psu.edu/nittanygrotto.

acres with an operating farm and a wildlife sanctuary with elk, mountain lions, deer, wolves, and mustangs. Professional guides take you through the park in four-wheel-drive vehicles, pointing out animals and telling about their habits. Tours last about one and a half hours. The sanctuary is open daily March through November. Call ahead for rates and reservations.

In September Penn's Cave is also the site of the Nittany Antique Machinery annual show. Model trains, tractor parades, demonstrations of antique machinery, toy tractors, and a children's pedal pull are among the attractions.

WOODWARD CAVE AND CAMPGROUND (ages 4 and up)

Route 45, Woodward; (814) 349–9800. Open daily 9:00 A.M. to 7:00 P.M. in summer, 10:00 A.M. to 5:00 P.M. in spring and fall. Admission charged.

If Penn's Cave has whet your appetite for spelunking, head back to Route 45 and continue east to Woodward Cave and Campground, one of the largest caverns in Pennsylvania. A sixty-minute tour takes you through the five rooms of the cavern, each filled with rock formations. The Hanging Forest features a large collection of stalactites. In the Hall of Statues, see one of the largest stalagmites in the United States: the

Tower of Babel. If you're planning to camp in the area, inquire about the nineteen-acre campground with sites for tents as well as RVs. Cabin rentals are also available.

A Paulsen Family Adventure

We weren't sure how eighteen-month-old Eli would react to being in a small boat, let alone how he would like being in a cave. But at Penn's Cave, the country's only water-filled cave, we got to try both.

There was just one other family and a couple on the tour with us. The other children were about eight and ten—the perfect age for looking for bats and spooking each other. Eli, on the other hand, wasn't so sure about this darkness stuff. He whimpered a bit as the driver pushed off from the dock.

He squirmed out of my lap and into my husband's, then back to mine, as if searching for a place where he might feel safe. I wondered to myself if they've ever had to turn a boat back when a child got scared of the dark.

Once the light show started, Eli started to calm down. He wasn't exactly enjoying himself, but he wasn't complaining either.

At the end of the cave, the driver gave us the option to pull out onto the lake that borders the Penn's Cave Wildlife Sanctuary. Even though it was drizzling, the group gave unanimous approval. As we pulled into the daylight, Eli perked up. At the sight of a group of very ordinary ducks, his eyes lit up, he pointed and started making quacking sounds. He smiled and laughed.

Even though we were outside maybe five minutes, that glimpse of the the ducks and the daylight was all he needed to reassure him as we headed back into the cave. On the way back, he stayed interested, turning around to see what the guide was talking about. I guess the dark isn't so intimidating once you know it's not forever.

Bellefonte

About 12 miles north of State College on Route 26, Bellefonte is the county seat for Centre County. This lovely Victorian town celebrated its bicentennial in 1996, and things are hopping still. A new museum, a restored theater, and several festivals have been added to the list of attractions for families.

With a historic district of more than 300 buildings, taking a walking tour through this town is like taking a walk back in time. Pick up a copy of *Historical Walking Tour of Bellefonte,* a brochure you'll find at the train station on High Street. The town is especially beautiful when decked out for a Victorian Christmas each December (call 814-353-8074 for more information).

BELLEFONTE MUSEUM OF CENTRE COUNTY (ages 5 and up)

Allegheny Street; (814) 353–1473. Open year-round. Admission charged. Call for schedule and rates.

An innovative new museum, the Bellefonte launched well before it recently found a home in one of the town's historic buildings. The goal of the museum is to promote appreciation of the area's heritage, especially among children. The hard-working volunteer staff visits schools and has set up exhibits around town.

In the fall of 1997, the museum moved into the historic Linn House, donated to the town by the Omega Bank next door. The exhibits change at least three times per year and are designed for both children and adults.

This museum is not only great fun for kids, it's a fount of information and inspiring ideas for parents and others who might want to start something similar in their own communities.

BELLEFONTE HISTORICAL RAILROAD (all ages)

Train Station, High Street; (814) 355–0311. Various excursions throughout the year, mostly on weekends. Call for schedules and prices.

When you're tired of walking, climb aboard one of the rail excursions offered by the Bellefonte Historical Railroad. The train station is located across the High Street Bridge. On weekends from Memorial Day to Labor Day, the railroad offers trips to Curtin Village (see below), Sayers Dam (a nice place for a picnic), the town of Lemont, or the gliderport at Julian. In fall the route takes you to Bald Eagle Ridge, aflame with autumn leaves. The Santa Claus Express in December features a visit from you-know-who. Other excursions are offered throughout the year.

EAGLE IRON WORKS AND CURTIN VILLAGE (ages 4 and up)

Route 150, 2 miles north of Route 80; (814) 355–1982. Open weekends in May, September, and October; daily during summer; it is also open in mid-December for Christmas at Curtin. Call for current hours and rates.

Heading north on Route 150 from Bellefonte, stop off at Eagle Iron Works and Curtin Village, a historic site that gives a glimpse of life in the

1800s. There's a restored iron furnace, the iron master's mansion, and a worker's log cabin. Throughout the year the museum holds special events, including craft shows, Civil War encampments, and antique tool demonstrations.

GARMAN OPERA HOUSE (ages 4 and up)

Across the street from the County Court House; (814) 355–7884. Call for schedule and ticket prices.

Recently restored, this former vaudeville house now offers live theater, concerts, and other events, including performances for families and children.

*B*ellefonte Festivals

The Victorian Christmas is the biggest festival in Bellefonte's schedule, but there are several more that are worth checking out. In mid-May come for the Big Spring Festival, which celebrates the spring that supplies the town with water. For more information and this year's schedule, call (800) 355–1705.

In June the streets of Bellefonte fill with antique and vintage automobiles as the town re-creates a Historic Cruise, that lapping-the-block ritual favored by teens in the 1950s. For more information contact Historic Bellefonte at (814) 355–3692. August brings the annual Bellefonte Arts and Crafts fair, with area craftspeople exhibiting and selling their creations and with special events for children. Once again, Historic Bellefonte organizes this annual event.

Where to Eat

IN THE WILLIAMSPORT AREA

Manhattan Bagel, *1790 East Third Street; (717) 322–4500; e-mail: yrgyo3@prodigy.com.*

Bonanza Steak House, *1503 East Third Street; (717) 326–7114.*

Hoss's Steak and Sea House, *1954 East Third Street; (717) 326–0838.*

Vinnie's Italian Eatery, *44 West Fourth Street; (717) 326–1998.*

Chi-Chi's Mexican Restaurant, *2502 East Third Street; (717) 321–9208.*

Heavenly Pasteria, *135 West Third Street; (717) 321–9035.*

Olive Garden, *1825 East Third Street; (717) 321–9250.*

Peter Herdic House, *407 West Fourth Street; (717) 322–0165.*

Red Lobster, *1951 East Third Street; (717) 323–0423.*

IN STATE COLLEGE

Backstage at Michael's, *240 South Pugh Street; (814) 238–8454.* Breakfast and family dinner daily.

Chili's Grill & Bar, *139 South Allen Street; (814) 234–5922.* Mexican fare.

The Corner Room, *corner of College and Allen Streets; (814) 234–3051.*

The Tavern Restaurant, *220 East College Street; (814) 238–6116.*

Whistle Stop Restaurant, *Pennsylvania Avenue; (814) 364–2544.*

Where to Stay

IN THE WILLIAMSPORT AREA

Genetti Hotel. *200 West Fourth Street, Williamsport; (717) 326–6600 or (800) 321–1388.* Located in downtown Williamsport, this full-service historic hotel offers suites as well as standard guest rooms. An on-site pool and restaurant make it a good choice for families.

Holiday Inn & T.G.I.Friday's Complex. *1840 East Third Street, Williamsport; (717) 326–1981 or (800) 36–WILPA; www. holiday-wilpa.com.* This newly renovated hotel complex offers some great features for families—an outdoor pool, Free Disney channel, on-site restaurants—plus kids stay and eat Free. In summer a "Pool-side King Room" may be the best choice for families. Features include a king-sized bed plus pull-out sofa just steps from the pool.

Sheraton Inn. *100 Pine Street, Williamsport; (800) 325–3535 or (717) 327–8231.* The Sheraton has two clinchers that make this hotel a hit with kids: an indoor pool and Nintendo-equipped televisions. And the hotel's kids-eat-Free policy at the on-site restaurant makes it a hit with parents, too.

IN THE LEWISBURG AREA

B/W Country Cupboard Inn. *Route 15 North, Lewisburg; (717) 524–5500.* Hotel, restaurant, and gift shop all in one complex.

Days Inn–Lewisburg. *Route 15, Lewisburg; (717) 523–1171.* Perkins Family restaurant on premises.

IN THE STATE COLLEGE AREA

Many of the major hotel/motel and restaurant chains have facilities in and near State College. Here are a few to check out:

Best Western State College Inn. *1663 South Atherton Street, Business Route 322, State College 16801; (814) 237–8005 or (800) 635–1177.* Breakfast is included, and there is a twenty-four-hour restaurant on premises.

Courtyard by Marriott. *1730 University Drive, State College 16801; (814) 238–1881.* An indoor pool, suites, and an on-site restaurant make this a good choice for families.

Days Inn Penn State. *240 South Pugh Street, State College 16801; (814) 238–8454 or (800) 258–DAYS.* Just blocks from campus, the Days Inn has on-site parking, a restaurant/Sports Bar, and an indoor pool. Continental breakfast is included.

Holiday Inn State College. *1450 South Atherton, State College 16801; (814) 238–3001 or (800) HOLIDAY.* Two out-door swimming pools make this an especially good choice in the summer.

The Nittany Lion Inn. *200 West Park Avenue, State College 16803; (814) 231–7500 or (800) 233–7505.* Colonial-style inn on the Penn State campus.

Bellefonte/State College KOA Campground. *2481 Jacksonville Road, Bellefonte 16823; (814) 355–7912 or (800) KOA–8127.* Full-service camp-ground with cabin rentals available.

For More Information

Bellefonte Tourism Commission, c/o *Chamber of Commerce, Train Station, Bellefonte, PA 16823; (814) 355–2917; www.bellefonte.com.* Call ahead for rec-ommendations on accommodations, train schedules, and other events in the area.

Centre County Lion Country Visi-tors and Convention Bureau, *1402 South Atherton Street, State College 16801; (814) 231–1400 or (800) 358–5466.* Pick up a **Free** visitor's guide and campus map at one of the many infor-mation booths on campus or at the Lion Country Convention and Visitors Bureau. Call ahead for lists of restau-rants, hotels, bed and breakfasts, events, and attractions.

Columbia-Montour Tourist Promo-tion Agency, *121 Papermill Road, Bloomsburg, PA 17815; (800) 847–4810 or (570) 784–8279.* Call for more infor-mation about accommodations, restaurants, and the twenty-four cov-ered bridges in the area.

Lycoming County Tourist Promotion Agency, *454 Pine Street, Williamsport, PA 17701; (800) 358–9900 or (570) 326–1971; www.williamsport.org.* Call or write for more information about things to do and see in Williamsport, as well as a list of restaurants, motels, and other accommodations.

Perry County Tourist and Recre-ation Bureau, *Courthouse Center Square, P.O. Box 447, New Bloomfield 19068; (717) 582–2131.* Call ahead for lists of campgrounds, restaurants, and other accommodations in the area.

Susquehanna Valley Visitors Bureau, *219D Hafer Road, Lewisburg, PA 17837; (800) 525–7320 or (570) 524–7234.* Call for more information about attractions, accommodations, and upcoming events in Northumber-land, Snyder, and Union counties.

Pennsylvania's Northern Tier

According to 1990 U.S. Census data, Pennsylvania has the largest rural population in the country. That means there are more people living in towns of fewer than 2,500 people here than in any other state in the country. Although all of the regions covered in this book have many towns that meet that description, along Pennsylvania's Northern Tier, it's hard to find towns that don't. There are large stretches of this region that remain wilderness—and provide wonderful opportunities for camping, boating, hiking, skiing, and more.

Scenic Route 6 traverses the northern tier of Pennsylvania, passing some of the region's best-loved sights and towns. Pine Creek Gorge, billed as Pennsylvania's Grand Canyon, is a spectacular achievement of nature. Allegheny National Forest is one of only fifteen national forests in the eastern United States and harbors some of the last remaining virgin stands of northern hardwoods left in the East.

Faith & Emily's
Favorite Attractions in Pennsylvania's Northern Tier

1. Pine Creek Gorge
2. Ole Bull State Park
3. Crook Farm and Country Fair
4. Knox, Kane, & Kinzua Railroad
5. expERIEence Children's Museum
6. Appledore Cruises
7. Heart's Content National Natural Landmark
8. Cook Forest Sawmill for the Arts
9. Presque Isle State Park

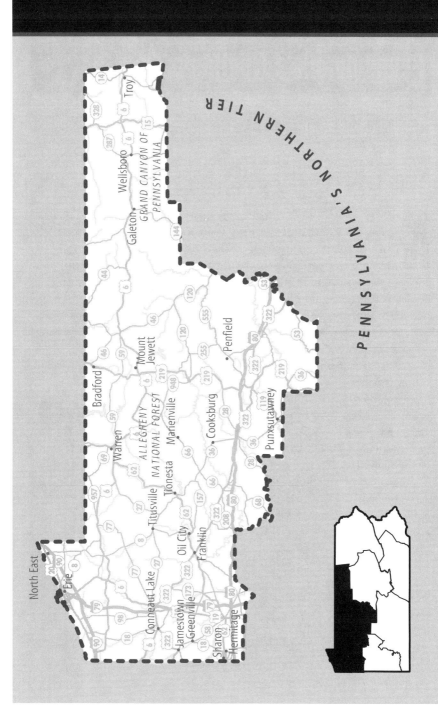

PENNSYLVANIA'S NORTHERN TIER

This is a big area. Our advice would be to keep your ambitions within limits. Pick a state park, a town, or a sight that interests you most, and build your vacation around it. Try to see more than a portion of this region, and you'll spend more time in the car than enjoying its many offerings. You can always come back to see more at another time.

Troy

We start our tour of Pennsylvania's northern tier in the town of Troy, located on Route 6 just west of the Susquehanna River.

BRADFORD COUNTY HERITAGE MUSEUM (all ages)

Route 14 North, one-half mile from Troy; (570) 297–3410; www.pavisnet. com/troy/farmmuseum. Open April through October, Friday to Monday and holidays 10:00 A.M. to 4:00 P.M. Admission is $3.50 for adults, $1.50 for students; children under 6 are Free.

Young and old alike will enjoy the farm museum, recently established by the Bradford County Heritage Association on the Troy Fairgrounds. A local resident and dairy farmer Wilmer Wilcox's impressive collection of farm antiques is on display. The displays work together to tell the story of rural farm life in Bradford County. There's a kitchen and antique clothing, as well as a doctor's office and an old country store. The association has recently begun work to restore the oldest house in Troy Township, built in 1822, adjacent to the current museum. Formerly an inn on the stagecoach route, it will now house period furniture, glassware, and antique toys and clothing. Portions of this house are currently on display.

Faith & Emily's
Favorite Events in Pennsylvania's Northern Tier

- **Fabulous 1890s weekend** in **Mansfield** (end of September); (570) 662–3442.
- **Teddy Bear Weekend** in **Cooksburg** (end of July); (570) 744–9670.
- **Bobsled Festival** in **Wellsboro** (February); (570) 724–1926.
- **We Love Erie Days** in **Erie** (August); (570) 454–7191.

During the Fall Carriage, Wagon, and Sleigh Festival in mid-September, children 6 and older enjoy the flax demonstration, blacksmithing, carpentry, tinsmithing, and stories of how chores were done in the past—from butter making with a dog-treadle butter churn to laundry with washboards and wringers. Throughout the season the heritage gardens display heirloom varieties of vegetables, plants used to make dyes, herbs, and perennials.

The museum is open daily during the Troy Fair, a typical country fair with farm animals, agricultural displays, and amusements, which has usually been held each year for more than one hundred years, toward the end of July. For more information about the Troy Fair, call (570) 297–3648.

Wellsboro Area

Located on scenic Route 6 in Tioga County, Wellsboro is an ideal base for adventures in Pine Creek Gorge, Pennsylvania's Grand Canyon. Forty-seven miles long with a maximum cliff height of 1,450 feet, this majestic canyon is surrounded by four state parks and hundreds of thousands of wilderness acres to explore by boat, foot, horseback, snowmobile, cross-country skis, mountain bike, and more.

Festivals Sponsored by Greater Mansfield Chamber of Commerce

Home to Mansfield University, part of the Pennsylvania state university system, the town of Mansfield hosts a series of events and festivals throughout the year. Call (570) 662–3442 for more information. The town and university team up to host two great festivals in September: the Northern Appalachian Storytelling Festival and the Fabulous 1890s weekend. The first attracts storytellers and enthusiasts from across the country. The second commemorates the first night football game, in which Mansfield University played Wyoming Seminary on September 28, 1892. The entire Mansfield community comes out to celebrate with a motorless parade, a balloon rally, a football reenactment, and fireworks.

COLTON POINT STATE PARK (ages 8 and up)
Five miles south of Route 6 at Ansonia; (570) 724–3061; www.dcnr.state.pa.us/stateparks/parks/leon.htm. Open year-round.

Perhaps the easiest way to get a glimpse of the Pine Creek Gorge is to head south from Route 6 at Ansonia. There's a sign there that directs you to the park. The drive follows the rim, with short trails that lead to views over the canyon. Although there are guard rails at official overlooks, make sure children don't run ahead or rough-house near the edge.

In addition to great views, Colton Point offers family camping, hiking trails, snowmobiling, and picnic areas. Most of the trails involve steep terrain and are recommended for experienced hikers aged 8 and up.

LEONARD HARRISON STATE PARK (ages 8 and up)

Route 660, 10 miles west of Wellsboro; (570) 724–3061; www.dcnr.state.pa.us/ stateparks/parks/leon.htm. Open year-round.

Leonard Harrison State Park is on the east rim of the canyon. Stop at the visitor center to learn about the history of the canyon. Camping is available, and there are hiking trails of varying length and difficulty. Experienced family hikers (ages 8 and up) won't want to miss the Turkey Path, a steep, 1-mile journey that takes you from the rim of the canyon down to Pine Creek.

PINE CREEK TRAIL (all ages)

Trailheads at Route 6 in Ansonia and at Route 414 in Blackwell. Open year-round. Bathrooms at trailheads. Call (570) 724–3061.

In an ongoing Rails to Trails project, 22 miles of the abandoned ConRail Railway along Pine Creek have been converted into a trail for hiking, biking, horseback riding, and other nonmotorized transportation. The relatively flat, groomed trail is wonderful for family hiking. The trail is handicapped-accessible and perfect for all-terrain strollers. Steve Farrell, park manager for Leonard Harrison State Park, recommends the less strenuous Ansonia access for families.

PINE CREEK OUTFITTERS (ages 6 and up)

RR4, Box 130B, Wellsboro 16901; (570) 724–3003; www.pinecrk.com.

Whether you're looking for trail maps, equipment rentals, shuttles to trailheads, camping permits, guide service, you-name-it, the folks at Pine Creek Outfitters are the ones to talk to. If they can't provide it themselves, they'll point you in the right direction. For families with young children, they particularly recommend their Upper Pine half-day trip, which navigates a calm section of the creek. There is no minimum age on this trip; others have a minimum age of 12. Pine Creek also leads guided bike tours through the canyon as well. When you're planning your trip, send for the current edition of the *Outdoor Adventure Guide for Pennsylvania's Grand Canyon,* published by Pine Creek Outfitters.

TIOGA TRAIL RIDES (ages 8 and up)

RD 106, Route 105; (570) 724–6592; www.pavisnet.com/ttr/. Rates start at $13 per hour on weekdays, $17 per hour on weekends.

Tioga Trail Rides offers western riding on day rides or overnight trips. Children without experience must be at least 12 years old; younger children are allowed on shorter rides if they can control their horses and have an inseam of at least 21 inches (gotta be able to reach the stirrups!). Overnight trips start at $102 per person for groups of two to four people. Sunset and supper rides are also available. During winter Tioga Trail Rides offers bobsled rides.

A Paulsen Family Adventure

Pine Creek Canyon is a sight to behold almost any time of the year. But if you're not a hunter, it's probably not a good idea to visit the Monday after Thankgiving, the first day of deer season in Pennsylvania.

We made that mistake when Eli was just six months old. We were returning home from the holiday with my husband's family in Ohio. It seemed a shame to let a little thing like the first day of hunting season get in the way of doing some research for this book.

Although there were few hunters in the Colton Point State Park, we could hear the rifles in the distance. We wanted to check out each of the overlooks but we didn't want to spend much time out in the open. "Wow, that's beautiful," I said. "Now let's get back in the car!"

MOUNTAIN TRAIL HORSE CENTER (ages 8 and up)

Wellsboro; (570) 376–5561; www.mountaintrail.com; e-mail: maier@epix.net. Open spring, summer, and fall. Wagon rides through canyon (weekday rates): $12.50 for adults; $6.25 for children 4 to 12; children under 4, Free.

Mountain Trail Horse Center offers a wide variety of horseback rides designed as wilderness adventure. Covered-wagon rides are good for families of varying ages and abilities. There's no age minimum on the rides through the gorge. During the twice-yearly Family Vacation Horseback Adventures, the minimum age for overnight trips is dropped to 8 (from the usual 12). The two-day, one-night Family Vacation starts at about $188 per person. Longer trips are available. Rates go down per person with groups of more than four people.

STORMS HORSE DRAWN RIDES (all ages)

RD 4, Box 1031, Little Marsh; (570) 376–3481. Open spring through fall. Rates start at $15 per person for a 1½-hour ride.

Scenic views, a comfortable horse-drawn wagon, home cooking over a campfire—this is a backcountry adventure with style!

TIOGA CENTRAL RAILROAD (all ages)

P.O. Box 269, Wellsboro; (570) 724–0990. Various rates.

Wellsboro Festivals Wellsboro has several top-notch festivals and fairs throughout the year. Check out the Bobsled Festival and Winter Weekend in February, the Pennsylvania State Laurel Festival in June, and the Canyon Country Blue Grass Festival in July.

Take the 24-mile round-trip excursion from the station near Wellsboro to the north end of Hammond Lake, near the New York State border. The trip takes about an hour and twenty minutes and runs three times a day on weekends.

ALSO IN THE AREA

Hills Creek State Park. *East of Wellsboro; (570) 724–4246; www.dcnr.state.pa.us/stateparks/parks/hillscreek.htm.* 110 campsites, cabins available, 137-acre lake.

Little Pine State Park. *Waterville; (570) 753–8209.* 104 campsites; ninety-four-acre lake; hiking, biking, and cross-country ski trails; nature programs and swimming in summer.

Galeton Area

Home of the Pennsylvania Lumber Museum and headquarters for four state parks, Galeton has a full roster of events and activities for families.

PENNSYLVANIA LUMBER MUSEUM (ages 6 and up)

P.O. Box 239, Route 6, 12 miles west of Galeton; (814) 435–2652. Open daily April through November. Admission is $3.50 for adults, $3.00 for seniors, $1.50 for youth (6 to 12); children under 6 are Free.

From Wellsboro head west on Route 6 to the Galeton area to enjoy a visit to the Pennsylvania Lumber Museum. Antique tools and other logging artifacts tell the story of this area's logging history. Tour a real logging camp and sawmill. A restored Barnhart Log Loader has been added to the display. The museum is the site for several unusual special events throughout the year, including the Bark Peeler's Convention the weekend closest to July 4th.

LYMAN RUN STATE PARK (all ages)

RR 1, Box 136, Galeton; (814) 435–5010. Open year-round.

Lyman Run acts as the headquarters for three other state parks in the area: Cherry Springs, Patterson, and Prouty Place. Lyman Run offers trout fishing, ice fishing, swimming, and camping. Cherry Springs has picnic areas, hiking trails, hunting, snowmobile trails, and a campground. It's also the site of the Woodsmen's Carnival in early August. Patterson State Park offers picnicking, hiking, and camping. Prouty Place State Park is known for its picnic areas, cold-water fishing, hiking, and camping.

OLE BULL STATE PARK (all ages)

Off Route 144, Cross Fork; (814) 435–5000 or (888) PA–PARKS for reservations. Open year-round.

About 20 miles south of Galeton is the Lodge at Ole Bull State Park, voted by *Condé Nast Traveler* magazine as Pennsylvania's top getaway. The lodge is actually a three-bedroom log cabin built by the Civilian Conservation Corps in the 1930s. It sleeps ten comfortably and is well-equipped with everything you need for a woodsy adventure. It even has a playground out back for the kids. The first floor is handicapped-accessible. It rents for about $400 per week, but book your reservations early (up to eleven months in advance). This is the kind of place where people come back each year. (Best bets: February and March, says Mary Herrold, park manager. You can book the lodge for as few as two nights and as many as fourteen, and the cross-country skiing is great.)

Even if you're not lucky enough to book a week at the lodge, Ole Bull is still a great place for a family adventure. There are eighty-one tent and trailer sites along Kettle Creek, some with electrical hookups. Swimming, hiking, fishing, and biking, also are all available in the secluded 125-acre park. During summer weekends there's a full schedule of environmental education programs.

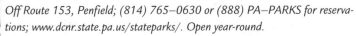

Penfield

PARKER DAM STATE PARK and S. B. ELLIOT STATE PARKS (all ages)

Off Route 153, Penfield; (814) 765–0630 or (888) PA–PARKS for reservations; www.dcnr.state.pa.us/stateparks/. Open year-round.

There are some great family programs available at Parker Dam State Park and S. B. Elliot State Park. Parker Dam offers a variety of naturalist programs for families, starting with maple sugar weekends in March all the way through apple cider Sundays in October. During summer there are bat programs, evening campfire talks on the weekends, and even a guided trip to see the elk herd. In summer you can swim in the twenty-acre lake.

The camping here is Class A, which means hot showers are available. There are also rustic log-frame and stone cabins available for rent year-round. There's no running water in the cabins, but there's a separate building with showers. A big fireplace supplies the heat, and you can cook with an electric stove and refrigerator.

S. B. Elliot State Park offers a quieter setting on top of a hill. There are six cabins here and some class B campsites, but no flush toilets or showers.

Bradford

PENN-BRAD OIL MUSEUM (ages 6 and up)

Route 219; (814) 362–5984. Open daily Memorial Day through Labor Day. Admission charged. Call ahead for current hours.

Just as eastern Pennsylvania has coal, the northwestern part of the state is oil country. This museum traces the state's involvement in oil drilling and includes a working example of the 1890s-style wooden oil rig that once dotted the countryside.

Sights of St. Marys

Sights of St. Marys From Bradford head south on 219 into Elk County, home of one of the two free-roaming elk herds east of the Mississippi—and the only one in Pennsylvania. The 1995 annual elk population survey counted 255 in the herd. One of the best places to spot the herd is near the airport in St. Marys. The herd also frequents the area around the town of Benezette, near Elk State Forest on Route 555. Early morning or late afternoon are the best times to see them.

Another unusual sight in St. Marys is the Queen of the Herd at the Ayrshire Dairy Farm on Old Kersey Road. Ask anyone in town how to get there; it's definitely an area landmark. Standing 15 feet tall, 20 feet long, 5 feet wide, and weighing in at 1,200 pounds, this fiberglass cow has stood here on the Uhl family farm for more than thirty years. The same family has owned this 500-acre dairy farm since 1919, and, if schedules allow, they'll be happy to show you around a bit.

CROOK FARM AND COUNTRY FAIR (all ages)

Route 219, third exit north of Bradford; (814) 368–9370. Open Tuesday through Friday afternoons during May through September and various times throughout the year. Call ahead for hours and admission prices.

The Crook Farm is a collection of restored buildings from the 1800s, including a farmhouse, a one-room schoolhouse, a blacksmith's shop, a carpenter's shack, a barn, and a candle-making shop. At the end of August, join the celebration at the Crook Farm Country Fair with crafts, food, entertainment, and special events for children.

ZIPPO/CASE FAMILY STORE AND MUSEUM (ages 6 and up)

1932 Zippo Drive, off Route 219; (888) 442–1932. Open Monday through Saturday year-round. Call for hours. Admission is Free.

Here's something you don't see every day: a collection of antique and rare Zippo lighters and cases. For the uninitiated Zippo Manufacturing has been making "windproof" lighters with a lifetime guarantee since 1932. The company also makes steel tape measures (a favorite among children, in our experience), knives, money clips, pens, and key holders. Zippo products are popular among collectors, with swap meets and collector's clubs around the world.

In 1996 the museum was expanded into a 15,000-square-foot facility with more than 2,000 Zippo products on display. New exhibits include the Zippo/Case Audio Kinetic Rolling Ball Machine and a 14-

foot flag made entirely of Zippo lighters. Definitely not just another roadside attraction.

ALSO IN THE AREA

Holgate Toy Store and Museum (all ages). *Wetmore Avenue, Kane; (814) 837–7600.* Open daily year-round. Come see toys being made at the toy factory. Kids love the trolley cars based on Mr. Rogers's Village of Make-Believe.

Allegheny Arms and Armor Museum (ages 5 and up). *Route 46, Smethport; (814) 362–2642.* Call for hours and admission prices. Handicapped-accessible. Kids love this military museum with its changing displays of helicopters, tanks, vehicles, armor, and more.

Warren

ALLEGHENY NATIONAL FOREST (all ages)

P.O. Box 847, 222 Liberty Street; (814) 726–5150. www.penn.com/~anf. Open year-round.

With more than a half-million acres, there's room for many a family adventure within the boundaries of Allegheny National Forest, the only national forest in Pennsylvania.

You will find a working forest when you visit the Allegheny. Congress mandates that national forests be managed for a variety of uses, using techniques that ensure future generations will be able to enjoy the benefits of these lands. Recreation, wood production, and wildlife habitat improvements are just some of the many activities going on in Allegheny National Forest.

Several towns act as good bases for explorations of the forest, including Warren, Marienville, Bradford, Ridgway, Tionesta, and Kane. Warren serves as the headquarters for the park, but there are information centers in Marienville, Ridgway, and Marshburg. Before planning your trip be sure to get a copy of the **Free** Outdoor Recreation Map of the Allegheny National Forest Region, available at tourist information centers or by calling ahead. It displays the small roads of the forest much more clearly than most road maps.

The forest has just about everything a family adventurer looks for: camping (developed and backwoods), fishing, hiking, ATV trails, horseback riding, snowmobiling, cross-country skiing, and hunting. There are nearly 200 miles of trails, 700 miles of streams, two Wild and Scenic

A Paulsen Family Adventure

What do you do with a baby on a trip to a place like Allegheny National Forest? Well, lots of things. My husband and I have realized that, although having a child changes many aspects of our lives and our travel habits, there are still a lot of outdoor activities and adventures we can include Eli in.

Hiking: We started hiking with Eli soon after he was born. We put him in a front pack facing out. He insisted on this fairly early on, even if it meant we had to hold his head up for him. Most of the time, he would fall asleep fairly quickly. But at the Hearts Content section of the Allegheny National Forest, he stayed awake for a 2-mile hike through the old growth forest. He seemed aware that it was a rare treat to see trees hundreds of years old.

Cross-country Skiing: By the time Eli was nine months old, he graduated from the front pack to the back pack. We bought a top-of-the-line model with all sorts of straps and supports. Snapped into the pack, Eli accompanies us not only on hikes, but also cross country ski trips. We make sure he's dressed very warmly, and we don't stay out as long as we did without him, but he loves getting outside, even on a winter's day. As Martin heads down a gentle slope, Eli says "WEEEE" and claps his hands in the air.

Driving long distances: Lots of people dread taking their kids on long car trips, but (knock on wood) so far so good. Our secret: get on the road early; I mean really early. We usually take off on a long trip by 4:30 in the morning. We just move Eli from his crib to the car seat. Although he wakes up for a bit, he's usually back to sleep within a half hour and stays asleep until 6:30 or 7:00. Entertain him for an hour, and we've done half of a six-hour drive before stopping for breakfast.

Rivers, and several lakes and reservoirs within the forest.

But if you only have a few hours to explore the park, head to Heart's Content, a National Natural Landmark that harbors one of the last stands of old-growth forest in the eastern United States. The turnoff from Route 62 is easy to miss (it's just before the bridge to Tidioute). Stop at the Tidioute Overlook, where an easy path leads to two vistas over the river gorge. Look carefully; it's not unusual to see a bald eagle circling over the river. At Heart's Content, there's a 1-mile interpretive trail. White pines and hemlocks that are hundreds of years old reach high into the sky.

Although no motorized vehicles are allowed in the old-growth forest, there are several excellent scenic drives through other parts of the forest. Route 62 follows the Allegheny River from Tionesta to Warren; the

Allegheny Reservoir Scenic Drive circles the large lake formed by the Kinzua Dam, and the Longhouse Scenic Drive starts at the Kinzua Dam and includes other area highlights.

Marienville

KNOX, KANE, & KINZUA RAILROAD (all ages)

P.O. Box 422, Route 66; (814) 927–8881 or (800) 280–2267. Various schedules May through October. Rides cost $20 for adults; $13 for children 3 through 12.

One way to enjoy the beauty of the forest without expending too much energy is a ride on the Knox, Kane, & Kinzua Railroad. But just because you aren't hiking or biking doesn't mean you're not going to have an adventure on this 96-mile ride from Marienville to Kinzua Bridge and back. Spanning 2,053 feet and standing 301 feet high, the Kinzua Bridge is reputed to be the second highest railroad viaduct in the United States.

Mount Jewett

KINZUA BRIDGE STATE PARK (all ages)

Off Route 6, Ormsby Road, Mount Jewett; (814) 965–2646. Open year-round.

Even if you can't take the Knox, Kane, & Kinzua Railroad, stop at the state park and take a look at the bridge. It's an engineering feat that will take your breath away. The brave can walk across the bridge. Others can just gawk from the overlook.

Tionesta

FLYING W RANCH (all ages)

Tionesta; (814) 463–7663. Trail rides cost $15 per person per hour. (Children must be 4 feet, 6 inches tall.) Dinner rides cost $49.50 per person. Overnight pack trips cost $175 per person. Two bedroom cottage rates are $80 per night. Camping is $15 per night.

Another highlight of the Allegheny National Forest is the Flying W Ranch, west of Marienville in Tionesta. This 500-acre working ranch sits within the boundaries of the national forest and offers countless opportunities for adventure. Spend an hour or a week here taking western riding lessons, canoeing on the Allegheny River, hiking, fishing, and more. In July come for the professional Allegheny Mountain Championship Rodeo. For a real adventure go on one of the overnight horseback trips into the national forest.

Accommodations range from bunkhouses to cabins, or you can bring your RV and hook up at the campground. In summer the ranch offers a western riding camp for children ages 9 through 16.

Cooksburg

Not only does this area harbor one of the largest stands of virgin hemlock and pine forests in the East, it is also home to a thriving arts center. The combination is unbeatable for a family vacation.

COOK FOREST SAWMILL CENTER FOR THE ARTS (ages 6 and up)

Breezemont Drive; (814) 927–6655 (May through September); (814) 744–9670 (October through April); www.sawmillcenter.org. Open summer and fall. Admission Free. *Ticket prices for performances and fees for classes vary.*

Cook Forest Center for the Arts has a full schedule of art exhibits, demonstrations, classes, and festivals for all ages from May through September and at various times throughout the year. In summer there's a children's program for ages 6 to 12 that meets for two hours a day, five days a week. Each day, the children make a different craft and learn about the arts or even recycling and the environment. There's a young people's drama workshop for a week each summer. Seven different festivals take place here during the season. One of the most popular is the Teddy Bear Weekend at the end of July.

COOK FOREST STATE PARK (all ages)

Exit 8, 9, or 13 off I–80 (P.O. Box 120); (814) 744–8407; www.dcnr.state.pa.us

Named one of the nation's Top 50 parks, Cook Forest contains one of the last remaining old-growth forests of 200- to 350-year-old white pine and hemlocks that reach 200 feet into the sky. At the Log Cabin Inn Visitor's Center, check out the Historical Room, which displays logging and rafting tools as well as models and other artifacts of the logging industry.

There are 27 miles of trails that are wonderful for hiking, cross-country skiing, and more. Many of the trails are less than a mile in length—a distance that's just right for little hikers. During the summer season nature programs are offered on Friday and Saturday nights, and guided walks are conducted regularly. The easy flowing Clarion River is a great way to introduce yourself and your family to tubing or canoeing.

The twenty-four rustic cabins in the forest are a popular vacation option. The cabins are grouped in two areas. There are eleven small, one-room cabins in the Indian area, located by the park office and near the accessible fishing pier. Flush toilet and shower facilities are nearby. The thirteen River cabins are located on a hillside overlooking the Clarion River. Twelve of these are some of the largest models built by the CCC, with a living room, kitchen, and two bedrooms. Recently the park has completed work on two cabins to make the doors and kitchen appliances accessible to people in wheelchairs. Another bonus of these larger cabins: cold running water. But you'll still have to use the composting toilets.

PINE CREST CABINS (all ages)

Cook Forest; (814) 752–2200. Horseback riding: $13 to $25. Camping: $15 and up per night. Cabins: $75 per night or $400 per week. Horseback riding about $13 for a one-hour tour; $22 for two hours. Camping starts at $12 a night for a primitive site; more if you want water or electric at the site.

For families who want to combine horseback riding with their vacation, one of the best choices is the Pine Crest Cabins. Don't let the name fool you: There is a campground on the property as well as stables. There are also canoes, go-carts, bumper boats, and long-putt golf—all on a seventy-five-acre family-oriented resort. More than half of the land has been preserved in its natural state and provides great hiking territory for families. Log cabins sleep eight to ten people and have indoor and outdoor fireplaces and two or three bedrooms.

DOUBLE DIAMOND DEER RANCH (all ages)

Route 36 South of Cook Forest; (814) 752–6334; www.users.penn.com/~dddr. Call for current hours and admission prices.

If you want to see your wildlife up a little closer, check out the Double Diamond Deer Ranch, near the entrance to the State Park on Route 36 South. Here a herd of twenty deer have been raised since birth. The deer are tame, so they'll come right up and greet you, eat from your hand, and enjoy a good scratch behind the ears. Fawns are born each spring, and during June through August they are bottle-fed. Children are welcome to hold the bottles. A new Wildlife Education Center, opening in May 2000, will offer a chance to learn about the animals you've seen in the woods.

Punxsutawney

On Groundhog Day each year, the world focuses its attention on the little town of Punxsutawney and on a groundhog named Phil. If he climbs out of his burrow on Gobbler's Knob and sees his shadow, the story goes, winter will be sticking around for a while longer. Phil's an old hand at this prediction stuff: He (or his ancestors) has been doing it every year since February 2, 1887.

PUNXSUTAWNEY GROUNDHOG ZOO (all ages)

124 West Mahoning Street; (800) 752–PHIL; www.groundhog.org or www.penn.com/punxsycc. Open year-round. Admission **Free**.

You don't have to wait until February to get a glimpse of Phil. He can be found living with his family at the Punxsutawney Groundhog Zoo at the Civic Complex in town. Each summer the town celebrates its favorite son with a week-long Groundhog Festival in July. Parades, dances, contests, flea markets, and lots of food are all part of the festivities.

This is also the site of the Punxsutawney Chamber of Commerce, your source of information on accommodations, restaurants, attractions, and, of course, all things groundhog.

PUNXSUTAWNEY HISTORICAL AND GENEALOGICAL MUSEUM (ages 6 and up)

401 West Mahoning Street; (814) 938–2555; www.users.penn.com/~mweimer. Call for hours and admission charges.

Lest you think that groundhogs are all there is to Punxsutawney, check out the Punxsutawney Historical and Genealogical Museum. Of course, a good bit of the museum is devoted to groundhog history and lore, but there are other treasures from the town's past as well.

Franklin

Franklin is a great area for biking, hiking, and camping. Here are a couple of outfitters to help you plan your trip:

- **Outer Limits (ages 8 and up).** *Route 322 East, Franklin; (814) 432–8432 or (800) 707–6520. Various rates.* Outer Limits offers customized outdoor adventures for families and other groups. From hiking, biking, and backpacking to canoeing and fishing, the guides provide everything you need, including equipment, meals, and transportation. All tour guides are certified in First Aid and CPR.

- **Country Peddlers Recreational Rentals and Sales (ages 8 and up).** *Route 322 East, Franklin; (814) 432–8055.* Touring bikes, $3.00/hour; in-line skates, $5.00/hour. Canoe excursions, from $20.00/canoe for three-hour trip. Located on the Allegheny River at the trailheads for two excellent family adventure trails: the Samuel Justus Recreational Trail (5.8 miles) and the Allegheny River Trail (14 miles). Country Peddlers rents the bikes, skates, or canoes you need to enjoy this beautiful area.

ALSO IN THE AREA

Dandy's Frontier Family Fun Park (ages 2 and up) *Route 322; Cranberry, (814) 677–5278. Open Friday 4:00 to 11:00 P.M., Saturday 11:00 A.M. to 11:00 P.M. and Sunday 11:00 A.M. to 7:00 P.M. during the school year; open daily 11:00 A.M. to 11:00 P.M. during summer. Admission* **Free.** From the easygoing tyke train to the exhilarating Rodeo Raceway, this family fun park has something for everyone in the family. There's an indoor play area and video arcade for rainy day amusement.

Oil City and Titusville

To get a better picture of the history of oil in this area, head to Oil City and Titusville.

OIL CREEK & TITUSVILLE RAILROAD (all ages)

7 Elm Street, Oil City; (814) 676–1733. Open mid-June through October. Adults, $9.00; children 3 to 17, $5.00.

In Oil City you can board the Oil Creek & Titusville Railroad through "the valley that changed the world." The two-and-a-half-hour narrated trip describes the world's first oil boom.

OIL CREEK STATE PARK (all ages)

Off Route 8, between Oil City and Titusville; (814) 676–5915; www.dcnr.pa.state.us. Open year-round.

The 9.5-mile paved bicycle trail through Oil Creek Gorge is the main attraction here. Bike rentals are available from the concession at the Old Egbert Oil Office. Hikers and, in winter, cross-country skiers are also welcome to use the trail.

DRAKE WELL MUSEUM (ages 6 and up)

Off Route 8, south of Titusville; (814) 827–2797. Open year-round. Adults, $5.00; children 6 to 12, $2.00.

Heading up Route 8 toward Titusville, stop at the Drake Well Museum, where Edwin Drake drilled the first oil well in 1859. Here you'll find displays recounting the history of oil in the area, as well as operating oil equipment. Kids will love the fire engine displays as well as blowing the whistle on a running steam engine. Look for a new exhibit on transportation in the near future. Trails in adjacent Oil Creek State Park provide great hiking, and there's a picnic pavilion.

CASEY'S CABOOSE STOP (all ages)

221 South Monroe Street, Titusville; (814) 827–6597. Rates are $65 and up per night.

Got a train lover in your family? Stay at this twenty-one-caboose motel, where cabooses have been converted into accommodations complete with cable TV, heat, air conditioning, telephones, and computer data ports. Pretty cool.

OTTO CUPLER TORPEDO COMPANY (ages 8 and up)

Dotyville Road, East Titusville; (814) 827–2921. Open June through October. Call ahead for schedules and admission prices.

Don't miss the Otto Cupler Torpedo Company and Nitroglycerin Museum. Weekends from June to October, there is a daily Nitroglycerin Special Effects Show that demonstrates the role nitroglycerin played in the area's oil fields starting in the 1870s. This company is the only oil well–shooting organization still in operation.

Greenville

There are a couple of museums worth a look-see in Greenville.

THE CANAL MUSEUM (ages 6 and up)
Lock 22 Alan Avenue; (412) 588–7540. Call for hours and admission.
This museum traces the history of the Erie Extension Canal. You can see a full-sized replica of a packet boat and a working model of a canal lock.

GREENVILLE RAILROAD PARK AND MUSEUM (all ages)
314 Main Street; (412) 588–4009. Call for hours and admission.
Here your kids can climb aboard the largest switch engine ever built. There are also railroad cars, a 1914 Empire automobile, and the world's first parachute on display.

GREENVILLE FARMERS' CURB MARKET (all ages)
Corner of Penn Avenue and Main Street. Open Wednesday and Saturday, 7:00 A.M. to 2:00 P.M.
If you're in town on a Wednesday or Saturday, check out this outdoor market that features the produce of farmers within a 20-mile radius of town.

BRUCKER GREAT BLUE HERON SANCTUARY (all ages)
Route 18, south of Greenville. Open year-round. Admission **Free**.
More than 400 of these majestic birds nest at this wildlife reserve—the largest colony of herons in the state.

Sharon and Hermitage

Chocolate lovers will want to stop by two unusual factories in the towns of Sharon and Hermitage, both south of Greenville on Route 62. These towns are also known for their shopping malls and they make great home bases for explorations of this area.

DAFFIN'S CANDIES (all ages)
496 East State Street, Sharon; (412) 342–2892. Store is open daily year-round. Factory tours are available Monday through Friday 9:00 A.M. to 3:00 P.M.

Daffin's Candies Chocolate Kingdom is a sight to behold. The display area is filled with giant rabbits, turtles, elephants, and more—all made of chocolate. The rabbit alone required 700 pounds of chocolate to create! If you make arrangements in advance, you can tour the chocolate factory, located on Route 60, south of Sharon.

PHILADELPHIA CANDIES (all ages)

1546 State Street, Hermitage; (412) 981–6341. Open daily year-round. Admission is **Free**.

In Hermitage tour the 30,000-square-foot facility at Philadelphia Candies, a company that's been making fine chocolates and other confections since 1919. The retail store is located right at the factory, so you can bring home a sample for all your friends back home (if the candies make it that far!).

AVENUE OF FLAGS (all ages)

2619 State Street, Hermitage; (412) 345–3818. Open daily year-round. Admission is **Free**.

Before you leave Hermitage take a walk down the Avenue of Flags. The street is lined with 444 flags, making it the world's largest display of American flags.

Conneaut Lake Area

You'll find lots of family fun around Pennsylvania's largest lake.

CONNEAUT LAKE PARK (all ages)

12382 Center Street; Conneaut Lake; (814) 382–5115. Open daily early summer to late fall. Admission is **Free**.

For more than one hundred years, families have come to Conneaut Lake Park to enjoy the lake, ride the rides, and just plain have fun. There is a 167-room historic hotel, a 105-site modern campground with camping cabins, and a full range of rides and amusements. The classic Blue Streak wooden roller coaster is sure to thrill, and the Waterpark is a hit with most kids. When you've had enough of the rides, relax on the lake beach or take a ride on the stern-wheeler *Barbara J*.

Admission to the park is **Free**—you pay only for the rides you want.

PYMATUNING STATE PARK (ages 5 and up)

Route 58, Jamestown; (412) 932–3141. Open year-round.

With the 27-square-mile Conneaut Lake as its centerpiece, the park offers boating, hiking, fishing, camping, and winter sports.

PYMATUNING DEER PARK (all ages)

Route 58, Jamestown; (412) 932–3200. Open weekends in May; daily Memorial Day through Labor Day. Call for current admission prices.

This small zoo offers train and pony rides as well as an opportunity to pet and feed the animals. Small children especially seem to enjoy this stop. The park has recently expanded, adding more animals including lions, tigers, bears (oh my!), wallabies, kangaroos, and camels in addition to the favorite farm animals.

Erie

Erie is the area's largest population center, the state's only Great Lake port, and the home of Governor Tom Ridge. The city celebrated its bicentennial in 1995, and things have been booming ever since. With a newly opened Bayfront Highway, several new or refurbished museums and historical sights, and a vibrant arts program, Erie has never been better.

PRESQUE ISLE STATE PARK (all ages)

Peninsula Drive (P.O. Box 8510); (814) 833–7424. Open year-round. **Free** *admission.*

Presque Isle State Park is one of the most remarkable aspects of Erie. This narrow spit of sand (*presque isle* literally means "almost an island") juts out into Lake Erie, providing an unusual environment for wildlife and a beautiful retreat for humans. To plan your day at the park, stop at the interpretive center, where there is a wonderful nature gift shop and bookstore as well as exhibits about local wildlife.

Choose the calm waters of Presque Isle Bay for boating or the almost oceanlike waves of Lake Erie for swimming. Water enthusiasts can rent canoes, rowboats, or motorboats to explore the waters on their own, whereas landlubbers can enjoy 13 miles of hiking trails. Bring your binoculars; Presque Isle is touted as one of the best bird-watching sites in the country; more than 300 species live in or pass by the park.

B.O.A.T. (Best of All Tours, Inc.) runs the forty-nine-passenger *Lady Kate* from the Perry Monuments at Presque Isle. Starting in 1997, the company has added a thirty-six-passenger water taxi, Presque Isle Express, that runs between Presque Isle and Dobbins Landing in Downtown Erie. It's a great way to pack in a full day of Erie sights and fun.

Although busiest in summer, there's something to do year-round at the park. In winter hiking trails turn to cross-country ski trails, and Presque Isle Bay provides great ice fishing.

 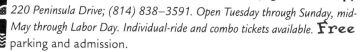

WALDAMEER PARK AND WATER WORLD (ages 3 and up)

220 Peninsula Drive; (814) 838–3591. Open Tuesday through Sunday, mid-May through Labor Day. Individual-ride and combo tickets available. **Free** parking and admission.

Right outside the entrance of Presque Isle State Park is Waldameer Park and Water World. If you don't spot it, your kids definitely will. There are eleven adult water slides and five for children, three "tad pool" areas, and a heated pool. The amusement park has sixteen major rides and ten rides for children, including the fantastic log flume ride, Thunder River. Use of tubes and life jackets is **Free**, and there is a variety of gift shops, snack bars, and midway games at the park. Or you can bring your own picnic. Puppet shows and musical shows are offered throughout the day. A new world-class roller coaster is slated for opening in 2001.

ERIE MARITIME MUSEUM (ages 6 and up)

150 East Front Street; (814) 871–4596. Open seven days a week year-round. Open Monday through Saturday, 9:00 A.M. to 5:00 P.M., Sunday noon to 5:00 P.M. Last tickets sold at 4:00 P.M. Admission: adults, $6.00; seniors $5.00; family ticket $15.00; youth 6 to 12, $4.00; children under 6 are **Free**. *Call ahead for hours.*

The maritime attractions of downtown Erie have recently been united in the brand new Erie Maritime Museum, opened in May 1998. This state-of-the-art facility features exhibits about the ecology of the Great Lakes; Lake Erie; Pennsylvania's North Coast maritime history's *Wolverine* and interactive Fighting Sailing Deck; several video displays about the *Niagara*, the Battle of Lake Erie, Reconstruction of the *Niagara*, and live fire exhibit. In addition, when it is in port, tour O. H. Perry's flagship.

You can take a look at the *Wolverine*—at least what's left of it. The ship, originally christened the USS *Michigan*, was the first iron-hulled ship ever built. Now the bow is all that remains of this impressive part of maritime history.

When it's in port, you can tour the flagship *Niagara,* a brig built to fight the naval battles of the War of 1812. To avoid disappointing children with their hearts set on seeing this boat, call ahead.

BICENTENNIAL OBSERVATION TOWER (ages 3 and up)

Dobbins Landing; (814) 455–6055 or (814) 455–7557; www.eriepa.com/ tower. Open year-round. Call for current hours and days. Admission: adults $2.00; children 6 to 12, $1.00; children under 6 are **Free**. *Admission is* **Free** *for all ages on Tuesdays.*

This 185-foot-tall tower gives an amazing view over Presque Isle, downtown Erie, and Lake Erie. Take the 210 stairs to the top observation deck or take the elevator. If you take the stairs, follow the sixteen stations that point out historic, geographic, and other landmarks.

APPLEDORE CRUISES (ages 3 and up)

17 State Street at Dobbins Landing; (814) 459–8339; www.bbyc.com; e-mail: baybreeze@bbyc.com. Summer only. Two-hour cruise: adults, $25; children 12 and under, $11.

Enjoy a hands-on sailing adventure on the beautiful 85-foot schooner *Appledore*—truly an unforgettable experience for all members of the family.

ERIE ART MUSEUM (ages 8 and up)

411 State Street, Discovery Square; (814) 459–5477. Open Tuesday through Saturday year-round. Admission: adults, $1.50; children under 12, 50 cents. Admission is **Free** *on Wednesday.*

Currently located in the historic Erie Customs House, the Erie Art Museum will get expanded and updated gallery space upon completion of the Discovery Square project. Call for information about regularly scheduled children's programs.

expERIEnce CHILDREN'S MUSEUM (all ages)

420 French Street; Discovery Square; (814) 453–3743. Open year-round Tuesday through Saturday 10:00 A.M. to 4:00 P.M., Sunday 1:00 to 4:00 P.M. Closed Monday year-round and Tuesday during school year. Admission: ages 2 and up, $3.50.

For small children the highlight of Erie is the newly opened expERIEnce Children's Museum, housed in an old livery stable. The museum is aimed at kids ages 2 to 12, but those under age 8 seem to enjoy it the most. According to one of the museum's curators, "This is a hands-on museum, which means that kids can come in and break things, and after they leave, we fix them."

There's a Gallery of Science on one floor and a Gallery of the Human Experience on the other. You can also see a simulation of a cave, in which children learn about cave painting, cave exploration, and fossils. At the Wegman's Corner Store, children can shop in a re-creation of a supermarket, complete with scanners, shopping carts, and very real-looking groceries. Youngsters may want to pick out a funny outfit from the costume closet and put on a show on a real stage.

ERIE HISTORICAL MUSEUM AND PLANETARIUM (all ages)

356 West Sixth Street; (814) 871–5790. Open Tuesday through Sunday afternoons year-round. Call for current hours. Museum admission: adults, $2.00; children 2 to 12, $1.00. Planetarium admission: adults, $2.00; children 2 to 12, $1.00. Children under 2 are admitted **Free** *to both exhibits.*

Kids of all ages love planetarium shows. Even toddlers will point out the moon and the stars! Call ahead for schedule of shows.

ERIE ZOO (all ages)

423 West 38th Street; (814) 864–4091. Open year-round. Call for admission prices and hours.

More than 300 animals representing nearly one hundred different species live in this fifteen-acre park. There's a children's zoo where kids can feed and pet baby animals, and there's a train ride around the zoo.

ALSO IN THE AREA

Wooden Nickel Buffalo Farm (all ages), *5970 Koman Road, Edinboro; (814) 734–BUFF; www.Edinboro.com/buffalo. Open year-round.* **Free** *admission.* A herd of more than fifty buffalo roam on this fifty-acre ranch outside Erie. It's quite a sight to see. Who knows, you might get inspired to get into buffalo farming yourself. The Wooden Nickel says it is "thinning the herd": You can buy a 2½-year-old breeding bull for $3,000.

North East

About 20 miles east of Erie on Route 20 is the historic village of North East. Take a walking tour of the historic district (brochures are available at local stores and museums).

HORNBY SCHOOL MUSEUM (ages 4 and up)

11573 Station Road; (814) 725–5680. Open Sunday 1:00 to 5:00 P.M. or by appointment. Donations accepted.

If you call ahead and make arrangements, your children can experience what it was like to learn in a one-room schoolhouse built in the 1870s. Even the books and slates are original equipment.

LAKE SHORE RAILWAY HISTORICAL SOCIETY MUSEUM (ages 2 and up)

Corner of Wall and Robinson Streets; (814) 825–2724 or 725–1191. Open Wednesday through Sunday afternoons from Memorial Day to Labor Day. Call for exact hours and admission.

Another historical sight of interest to children is the Lake Shore Railway Historical Society Museum. Here, you can see a variety of train equipment, including a pullman car, a caboose, and a dining car. Located on a busy stretch of railroad track, the site practically guarantees that your children will get to see several modern trains pass by during your visit.

Where to Eat

IN THE COOKSBURG AREA

Americo's Italian Restaurant, *Cooksburg-Vowinckel Road, 1¼ mile north of Sawmill Theatre, Cook Forest; (814) 927–8516.* Open April through October for lunch and dinner. Children's menu. Near attractions.

Cook Forest Country Inn, *Cooksburg-Vowinckel Road; (814) 927–8925 or (800) 830–6133.* Home-style cooking, homemade rolls and pies.

Gateway Lodge Country Inn and Restaurant, *Route 36 in the heart of Cook Forest; (814) 744–8017 or (800) 843–6862.* Dine by kerosene light. Staff dressed Colonial-style. Breakfast and lunch daily. Dinner daily except for Monday.

Mama Doe's Restaurant, *Shiloh Ranch Resort, Route 36, Cook Forest; (814) 752–2361.* Fine dining and Italian cuisine. Breakfast, lunch, and dinner; daily specials, Sunday buffet. Also campground, cabins, and lodge.

Sawmill Restaurant, *Intersection of Routes 36 and 66 at the blinker light, Leeper; (814) 744–8578.* Soft ice cream, fresh-baked goods, home of the Sawdustburger. Open daily, year-round, 7:00 A.M. to midnight.

The Farmer's Inn, *2 miles north of Sigel on Route 949, near Clear Creek State Park; (814) 752–2942.* Restaurant, ice cream, bakery, gift shop, Amish furniture, horse-drawn wagon and pony rides, miniature golf, animal exhibits, petting zoo.

The Trails End, *Cooksburg-Vowinckel Road, near Cook Forest State Park; (814) 927–8400.* Steaks, seafood, sandwiches. Near theater and park attractions.

Vowinckel Hotel, *corner of Route 66 and Cooksburg-Vowinckel Road, 5 miles from Cook Forest; (814) 927–6610.* Homemade bread and pizza dough. Voted "Best Wings in Clarion County." Fireplace.

IN ERIE

Applebee's Restaurant, *7790 Peach Street; (814) 866–8210.*

Backstage Grill, *2025 Peach Street; (814) 452–1356.*

Bagel Basket, *3 East 18th Street; (814) 452–2435.*

Bob Evans Restaurant, *8041 Peach Street; (814) 864–5444.*

Caffe Royale, *25E 10th Street; (814) 455–2243.*

Calamari's Restaurant, *1317 State Street; (814) 459–4267.*

The Carriage House, *1535 West 26th Street; (814) 459–2330.*

China Garden Restaurant, *6801 Peach Street; (814) 868–2695.*

Chuck E Cheese, *7200 Peach Street, Summit Towne Center; (814) 864–3100.*

Connie's Ice Cream, *6032 Peach Street; (814) 866–1700.*

Hopper's Brewpub at Union Station, *123 West 14th Street; (814) 452–2787.*

Hoss's Steak & Sea House, *3302 West 26th Street; (814) 835–6836.*

Italian Oven, *2709 West 12th Street; (814) 835–6836.*

Julio's Family Restaurant & Pizzeria, *1117 Parade Street; (814) 455–6301.*

Old Country Buffet, *7200 Peach Street; (814) 866–5671.*

The Olive Garden, *5945 Peach Street; (814) 866–1105.*

Pio's Italian Restaurant & Pizzeria, *815 East Avenue; (814) 456–8866.*

Smuggler's Wharf, *3 State Street; (814) 459–4273.*

Where to Stay

IN THE WELLSBORO AREA

Comfort Inn Canyon Country. *300 Gateway Drive, Mansfield; (717) 662– 3000 or (800) 822–5470.* Conveniently located for events in Mansfield as well as touring nearby Pine Creek Gorge.

IN THE BRADFORD AREA

Howard Johnson Lodge and Restaurant. *100 Davis Street, South; (800) 344–4656.* Open year-round. A good base for Bradford and Allegheny Forest area explorations. Outdoor pool, special combination packages for the Knox, Kane, & Kinzua Railway excursions, skiing, and golf.

IN THE ALLEGHENY NATIONAL FOREST AREA

Kane View Motel. *Route 6 East, Kane; (814) 837–8600.* The Allegheny National Forest is in the backyard of this convenient motel.

IN WARREN

Super 8, *Warren, U.S. Routs 6 and 62N; (814) 723–8881.* Near major attractions and downtown. Continental breakfast.

Holiday Inn–Warren; *210 Ludlow Street, Warren; (814) 726–3000.* On-site restaurant, indoor pool, and a three-diamond rating from AAA make this a good choice for families exploring the national forest and other area attractions.

IN THE COOKSBURG AREA

Clarion River Lodge, *River Road in Cook Forest; (814) 744–8171 or (800) 648–6743.* Magnificent view of Clarion River. Guest rooms available. Open year-round.

IN PUNXSUTAWNEY

Pantall Hotel, *downtown; (814) 938–6600.* Beautifully restored Victorian hotel, restaurants onsite.

IN FRANKLIN

Inn at Franklin, *downtown; (814) 437–3031 or (800) 535–4052.* Free continental breakfast; restaurant, tavern, family plans.

IN OIL CITY AND TITUSVILLE

Holiday Inn–Oil City, *1 Seneca Street, Oil City; (814) 677–1221 or (800) HOLIDAY.* Kids stay 𝐅𝐫𝐞𝐞. Full-service restaurant, lounge, entertainment.

IN THE CONNAEUT LAKE AREA

Days Inn–Meadville, *just off exit 36A or I–79, Meadville; (814) 337–4264.* Minutes from Conneaut Lake. Family restaurant on site.

IN THE HERMITAGE AND SHARON AREAS

Radisson Hotel Sharon. *Route 18 and I–80, West Middlesex; (412) 528–2501 or (800) 333–3333.* On-site restaurant, indoor pool, hot tubs.

Holiday Inn of Sharon/Hermitage. *3200 South Hermitage Road, Route 18 North; (412) 981–1530 or (800) HOLIDAY.* Full-service hotel.

IN CLARION

Comfort Inn, *I–80 Exit 9, north on Route 66; (814) 226–5230.* Complimentary continental breakfast, outdoor pool.

Holiday Inn of Clarion, *Route 68 and I–80, exit 9; (814) 226–8850 or (800) 596–1313.* Free breakfast buffet. Tropical courtyard with indoor pool and saunas, restaurant, and lounge. Kids stay and eat 𝐅𝐫𝐞𝐞.

Super 8 Motel—Clarion, *I–80, exit 9; (814) 226–4550.* AAA-rated, first-floor, and nonsmoking rooms. Free continental breakfast and local calls, cable television, outdoor pool.

IN THE ERIE AREA

Erie has an impressive array of hotels and motels—with just about all the major chains represented. Most of the big-name places are equipped with indoor pools, definitely good news for families traveling in winter or when bad weather interrupts sight-seeing plans. Here are a few highlights:

Presque Isle Cottage Court. *320 Peninsula Drive; (814) 833–4956.* Located close to Waldermeer Water World and Presque Isle State Park.

Marriott Residence. *8061 Peach Street; (814) 864–2500; www.ncinter.net/ ~erieinns/.* This all-suite hotel has kitchens in the rooms, an indoor pool, and a breakfast buffet. (Website serves three other big hotels, so do some on-line comparison shopping!)

The Glass House Inn. *3202 West Twenty-sixth Street (Route 20); (814) 833–7751 or (800) 956–7222; www.velocity.net/~ghilel.* Family-friendly, family-run colonial-style inn with outdoor pool and lots of room to play.

For More Information

Allegheny National Forest Vacation Region, *P.O. Drawer G, Junction 219 and 770, Custer City, PA 16725; (814) 368–9370.* Call ahead or drop by for information about things to do and see and places to stay and eat in McKean County.

Crawford County Tourist Promotion Agency, *Box 786, Meadville, PA 16335; (800) 332–2338 or (814) 333–1258.* Titusville is actually just north of the border between Venango and Crawford counties. Call ahead for information about Crawford County.

Elk County Visitors Bureau, *P.O. Box 838, St. Marys, PA 15857; (814) 834–3723.* Call ahead for an information packet with things to do and see and places to stay in Elk County.

Erie Area of Chamber of Commerce. *Downtown office: Scenic Route 5, the Pennsylvania Seaway Trail. Mailing address:*

1006 State Street, Erie, PA 16501; (814) 454–7191; www.eriepa.com; e-mail: Erie-chamber@erie.net. Visit their extensive website, call ahead for information, or stop by one of several information centers along major routes for up-to-the-minute details on attractions, accommodations, and events in the Erie area. Some major festivals in the area include the Erie Summer Festival of the Arts (end of June) and We Love Erie Days (August). Both feature special events for children.

Galeton Chamber of Commerce, *P.O. Box 176, Galeton; (814) 435–2321.* For information on accommodations and the lowdown on what's happening in town, contact the chamber before your visit.

The Magic Forests Visitors Bureau, *c/o Brookville Office, RR 5, Brookville PA 15825; (800) 348–9393 or (814) 849–5197; www.magicforests.org.* Covering

Clarion, Clearfield, and Jefferson counties, this tourist organization can supply you with information about attractions, accommodations, and more.

Mercer County Convention and Visitors Bureau, *835 Perry Highway; Mercer, PA 16137; (800) 637–2370 or (412) 748–5315; www.merlink.org.* Your source for information on accommodations and attractions in Greenville, Sharon, Hermitage, Grove City, and all of Mercer County.

Northern Allegheny Vacation Region, *315 Second Avenue, Warren, PA 16365; (800) 624–7802 or (814) 726–1222; e-mail: tna@penn.com.* Tourist information for Forest and Warren counties.

Oil Heritage Region Tourist Promotion Agency, Inc., *National City Bank Building, Third Floor, 248 Seneca Street, Oil City, PA 16301; (800) 483–6264 or (814) 677–3152.* Call ahead for an information packet with brochures about attractions and accommodations in Venango County.

Potter County Recreation, Inc., *P.O. Box 245, Coudersport, PA 16915; (888) POTTER–2 or (814) 435–2290.* For more information on recreational opportunities in Potter County, give this tourist organization a call.

Tioga County Tourist Promotion Agency, *114 Main Street, Wellsboro; (800) 332–6718 or (717) 724–0634.* Call ahead or stop by for area information.

Wellsboro Chamber of Commerce, *Wellsboro; (717) 724–1926.* For more information about festivals, accommodations, and other attractions in Wellsboro, this is your source.

General Index

Activities Index

ARTS

Academy of Fine Arts, 27
African-American Museum, 11
Allentown Art Museum, 65
Andy Warhol Museum, 148
Artworks at Doneckers, 83
Banana Factory, 70
Barnes Foundation, 51
Bellefonte Arts and Crafts Fair, 227
BOTTLEWORKS, 128
Brandywine River Museum, 43
Carnegie Museum of Art, 153
Central Pennsylvania Festival of the
    Arts, 218
Cook Forest Sawmill Center for the
    Arts, 244
Erie Art Museum, 253
Hoyt Institute of Fine Arts, 164
James A. Michener Museum, 60
Kemerer Museum of Decorative
    Arts, 69
Mattress Factory, 149
Merrick Free Art Gallery, 165
Mum Puppet Theater, 13
Philadelphia Museum of Art, 21
Pittsburgh Center for the Arts, 156
Playhouse, 156
Rodin Museum, 20
Sight & Sound Theatres, 89
Society for Contemporary Crafts, 149
Whitaker Center for Science and the
    Arts, 99

CAMPING

Allegheny National Forest, 241
Cook Forest State Park, 244
Delaware Water Gap National
    Recreation Area, 174
Flying W Ranch, 243
Hills Creek State Park, 237

Knoebels Amusement Park and
    Campground, 212
Leonard Harrison State Park, 235
Little Pine State Park, 237
Lyman Run State Park, 238
Mauch Chunk Lake Park, 195
Ole Bull State Park, 238
Outer Limits, 247
Parker Dam State Park, 239
Pine Crest Cabins, 245
Promised Land State Park, 182
Pymatuning State Park, 251
Ricketts Glen State Park, 199
S. B. Elliot State Park, 239
Triple "W" Riding Stables, 184
Tuscarora State Forest, 216
Woodward Cave and
    Campground, 224
World's End State Park, 202
Yogi Bear's Jellystone Park, 121

FACTORY TOURS

Benzel's Pretzel Bakery, 133
Byer's Choice Ltd., 61
Callie's Candy Kitchen and Pretzey
    Factory, 180
Crayola Factory, 72
Daffin's Candies, 249
Drake Well Museum, 248
Eagle Iron Works and Curtin
    Village, 226
Gardners Candies, 134
Harley-Davidson, Inc., 95
Herr Foods, Inc., 90
Hershey's Chocolate World Visitors
    Center, 96
Holgate Toy Store and Museum, 241
Julius Sturgis Pretzel House, 83
Kreider Farms, 85
Malmark Inc. Bellcraftsmen, 61